Every Day With God

A Child's Daily Bible

Selections from the
International Children's Bible

Additional Text by Roy and Doris Nichols
Illustrations by Jim Padgett

WORD *Kids!*

WORD PUBLISHING
Dallas·London·Vancouver·Melbourne

EVERY DAY WITH GOD

Scripture quotations are from the International Children's Bible, New Century Version, copyright © 1983, 1986, 1988 by Word Publishing.

Illustrations © 1979-1983 Bible Discovery Aids; owners: Sweet Publishing, Fort Worth, TX, and Gospel Light, Regal Books, Ventura, CA.

Photographs used by permission of Jim Whitmer Photography and Bob Taylor Pictures.

Library of Congress Cataloging in Publication Data

Bible. English. New Century. Selections. 1990.
　　　Every day with God: a child's daily Bible / selections from the International children's Bible; additional text by Roy and Doris Nichols; illustrations by Jim Padgett.
　　　　p.　　cm.
　　　Summary: A devotional reader with an introduced Bible passage and a prayer for each day.
　　　ISBN 0-8499-0831-0.
　　　1. Children—Prayer-books and devotions—English. 2. Devotional calendars—Juvenile literature. [1. Prayer books and devotions. 2. Devotional calendars.]　　I. Nichols, Roy, 1929-　. II. Nichols, Doris. III. Padgett, Jim, ill. IV. Title.
BS390　　1990
220.2′208—dc20
　　　　　　　　　　　　　　　　　　　　　　　　　　　　　　　　　　　90-42711
　　　　　　　　　　　　　　　　　　　　　　　　　　　　　　　　　　　CIP
　　　　　　　　　　　　　　　　　　　　　　　　　　　　　　　　　　　AC

Printed in the United States of America.

012349 AGH 98765432

CONTENTS

God Creates Light and Land

Our story begins, not with
"once upon a time . . ." as
many stories do, but with
the words that belong to
this story alone: "In the
beginning, God . . . ."

1 In the beginning God created the sky and the earth. ²The earth was empty and had no form. Darkness covered the ocean, and God's Spirit was moving over the water.

³Then God said, "Let there be light!" And there was light. ⁴God saw that the light was good. So he divided the light from the darkness. ⁵God named the light "day" and the darkness "night." Evening passed, and morning came. This was the first day.

⁶Then God said, "Let there be something to divide the water in two!" ⁷So God made the air to divide the water in two. Some of the water was above the air, and some of the water was below it. ⁸God named the air "sky." Evening passed, and morning came. This was the second day.

⁹Then God said, "Let the water under the sky be gathered together so the dry land will appear." And it happened. ¹⁰God named the dry land "earth." He named the water that was gathered together "seas." God saw that this was good.

Today's Prayer

Dear God, thank you for all of the wonderful things you have made. Help me to see the good in everything you have put in this world. In Jesus' name, amen.

Memory Verse
"Surely you know. Surely you have heard. The Lord is the God who lives forever. He created all the world." Isaiah 40:28

God Creates Animals

Next God turned to the empty sky and land and continued the good work of his creation.

[11]Then God said, "Let the earth produce plants. Some plants will make grain for seeds. Others will make fruit with seeds in it. Every seed will produce more of its own kind of plant." And it happened. [13]Evening passed, and morning came. This was the third day.

[14]Then God said, "Let there be lights in the sky to separate day from night. These lights will be used for signs, seasons, days and years. [15]They will be in the sky to give light to the earth." And it happened.

[16]So God made the two large lights. He made the brighter light to rule the day. He made the smaller light to rule the night. He also made the stars.

[17]God put all these in the sky to shine on the earth. [18]They are to rule over the day and over the night. He put them there to separate the light from the darkness. God saw that all these things were good. [19]Evening passed, and morning came. This was the fourth day.

[20]Then God said, "Let the water be filled with living things. And let birds fly in the air above the earth." [23]Evening passed, and morning came. This was the fifth day.

[24]Then God said, "Let the earth be filled with animals. And let each produce more of its own kind. Let there be tame animals and small crawling animals and wild animals. And let each produce more of its kind." And it happened.

[25]So God made the wild animals, the tame animals and all the small crawling animals to produce more of their own kind. God saw that this was good.

Today's Prayer

I thank you, dear God, for the sun, the moon, the stars and all the plants and animals. Help me to take good care of your creation. I pray in Jesus' name, amen.

Memory Verse
"Surely you know. Surely you have heard. The Lord is the God who lives forever. He created all the world." Isaiah 40:28

God Creates People

In five days God filled the earth with plants, animals, birds and fish, but on the sixth day he created something very special. Then he rested.

²⁶Then God said, "Let us make human beings in our image and likeness. And let them rule over the fish in the sea and the birds in the sky. Let them rule over the tame animals, over all the earth and over all the small crawling animals on the earth."

²⁷So God created human beings in his image. In the image of God he created them. He created them male and female. ²⁸God blessed them and said, "Have many children and grow in number. Fill the earth and be its master. Rule over the fish in the sea and over the birds in the sky. Rule over every living thing that moves on the earth."

²⁹God said, "Look, I have given you all the plants that have grain for seeds. And I have given you all the trees whose fruits have seeds in them. They will be food for you. ³⁰I have given all the green plants to all the animals to eat. They will be food for every wild animal, every bird of the air and every small crawling animal." And it happened. ³¹God looked at everything he had made, and it was very good. Evening passed, and morning came. This was the sixth day.

2 So the sky, the earth and all that filled them were finished. ²By the seventh day God finished the work he had been doing. So on the seventh day he rested from all his work. ³God blessed the seventh day and made it a holy day. He made it holy because on that day he rested. He rested from all the work he had done in creating the world.

Today's Prayer

Dear God in heaven, thank you for all of the people on the earth. Help me to love other people as you love me. In the name of your son Jesus, amen.

Memory Verse
"Surely you know. Surely you have heard. The Lord is the God who lives forever. He created all the world." Isaiah 40:28

The Beginning of Adam

What great love and care God showed as he made Adam, the first man, and placed him in the garden he had made for him.

⁴This is the story of the creation of the sky and the earth. When the Lord God made the earth and the sky, ⁵there were no plants on the earth. Nothing was growing in the fields. The Lord God had not yet made it rain on the land. And there was no man to care for the ground. ⁶But a mist often rose from the earth and

watered all the ground.

⁷Then the Lord God took dust from the ground and formed man from it. The Lord breathed the breath of life into the man's nose. And the man became a living person. ⁸Then the Lord God planted a garden in the East, in a place called Eden. He put the man he had formed in that garden. ⁹The Lord God caused every beautiful tree and every tree that was good for food to grow out of the ground. In the middle of the garden, God put the tree that gives life. And he put there the tree that gives the knowledge of good and evil.

¹⁵The Lord God put the man in the garden of Eden to care for it and work it. ¹⁶The Lord God commanded him, "You may eat the fruit from any tree in the garden. ¹⁷But you must not eat the fruit from the tree which gives the knowledge of good and evil. If you ever eat fruit from that tree, you will die!"

Today's Prayer

Dear Lord, tnank you for making Adam with such care and love, and thank you for making me in such a special way. In Jesus' name, amen.

Memory Verse

"Surely you know. Surely you have heard. The Lord is the God who lives forever. He created all the world." Isaiah 40:28

The Beginning of Eve

God knew Adam would not be happy living alone, even with all the wonderful animals to enjoy. So God made a wife for him.

[18]Then the Lord God said, "It is not good for the man to be alone. I will make a helper who is right for him."

[19]From the ground God formed every wild animal and every bird in the sky. He brought them to the man so the man could name them. Whatever the man called each living thing, that became its name. [20]The man gave

names to all the tame animals, to the birds in the sky and to all the wild animals. But Adam did not find a helper that was right for him. [21]So the Lord God caused the man to sleep very deeply. While the man was asleep, God took one of the ribs from the man's body. Then God closed the man's skin at the place where he took the rib. [22]The Lord God used the rib from the man to make a woman. Then the Lord brought the woman to the man.

[23]And the man said,
"Now, this is someone whose
    bones came from my bones.
Her body came from my body.
I will call her 'woman,'
    because she was taken out of man."
[24]So a man will leave his father and mother and be united with his wife. And the two people will become one body. [25]The man and his wife were naked, but they were not ashamed.

Today's Prayer

Dear God in heaven, I am glad that you made Eve as well as Adam so he would not be alone. Please be with me when I am lonely and need your help. In the name of Jesus I pray, amen.

Memory Verse
"Surely you know. Surely you have heard. The Lord is the God who lives forever. He created all the world." Isaiah 40:28

The Snake's Trick

The snake tricked Eve by getting her to choose between something she wanted and something God had said she should not have.

3 Now the snake was the most clever of all the wild animals the Lord God had made. One day the snake spoke to the woman. He said, "Did God really say that you must not eat fruit from any tree in the garden?"

²The woman answered the snake, "We may eat fruit from the trees in the garden. ³But God told us, 'You must not eat fruit from the tree that is in the middle of the garden. You must not even touch it, or you will die.'"

⁴But the snake said to the woman, "You will not die. ⁵God knows that if you eat the fruit from that tree, you will learn about good and evil. Then you will be like God!"

⁶The woman saw that the tree was beautiful. She saw that its fruit was good to eat and that it would make her wise. So she took some of its fruit and ate it. She also gave some of the fruit to her husband, and he ate it.

⁷Then, it was as if the man's and the woman's eyes were opened. They realized they were naked. So they sewed fig leaves together and made something to cover themselves.

Today's Prayer

Thank you, dear God, for always planning good things for your people. Help me to listen to you instead of to people who want to take me away from you. In Jesus' name I pray, amen.

Memory Verse
"The Lord corrects those he loves, just as a father corrects the child that he likes."
Proverbs 3:12

God Punishes the Snake

Adam tried to blame Eve for his sin, and Eve tried to blame the snake. But God knew they had made their own choice. Then God placed a curse on the snake for his trickery.

⁸Then they heard the Lord God walking in the garden. This was during the cool part of the day. And the man and his wife hid from the Lord God among the trees in the garden. ⁹But the Lord God called to the man. The Lord said, "Where are you?"

¹⁰The man answered, "I heard you walking in the garden. I was afraid

because I was naked. So I hid."

¹¹God said to the man, "Who told you that you were naked? Did you eat fruit from that tree? I commanded you not to eat from that tree."

¹²The man said, "You gave this woman to me. She gave me fruit from the tree. So I ate it."

¹³Then the Lord God said to the woman, "What have you done?"

She answered, "The snake tricked me. So I ate the fruit."

¹⁴The Lord God said to the snake, "Because you did this,
    a curse will be put on you.
    You will be cursed more than
        any tame animal or wild
        animal.
You will crawl on your stomach,
    and you will eat dust all the days
        of your life.
¹⁵I will make you and the woman
    enemies to each other.
Your descendants and her
        descendants
    will be enemies.
Her child will crush your head.
    And you will bite his heel."

Today's Prayer

Dear God, I am glad that you are willing to listen when I pray. Help me to remember that I am responsible for what I do just as Adam and Eve were. In Jesus' name, amen.

Memory Verse

"The Lord corrects those he loves, just as a father corrects the child that he likes."
Proverbs 3:12

Adam and Eve Leave Eden

Adam and Eve had a wonderful place to live, but they chose to disobey God. Because of this choice, they had to pay a high price.

¹⁷Then God said to the man, "You listened to what your wife said. And you ate fruit from the tree that I commanded you not to eat from.
"So I will put a curse on the
   ground.
      You will have to work very hard
         for food.
In pain you will eat its food
   all the days of your life.
¹⁸The ground will produce thorns
      and weeds for you.
      And you will eat the plants of the
         field.
¹⁹You will sweat and work hard
      for your food.
      Later you will return to the ground.

This is because you were taken
   from the ground.
You are dust.
   And when you die, you will
      return to the dust."
[20]The man named his wife Eve. This
is because she is the mother of everyone who ever lived.

[21]The Lord God made clothes from
animal skins for the man and his wife.
And so the Lord dressed them. [22]Then
the Lord God said, "Look, the man
has become like one of us. He knows
good and evil. And now we must keep
him from eating some of the fruit
from the tree of life. If he does, he will
live forever." [23]So the Lord God forced
the man out of the garden of Eden. He
had to work the ground he was taken
from. [24]God forced the man out of the
garden. Then God put angels on the
east side of the garden. He also put a
sword of fire there. It flashed around
in every direction. This kept people
from getting to the tree of life.

Today's Prayer

Dear God, thank you for
taking care of me even
when I do not listen to you.
Forgive me when I make
bad choices and give me
strength to do better. In the
name of Jesus, amen.

Memory Verse
"The Lord corrects those he loves, just as a
father corrects the child that he likes."
Proverbs 3:12

Cain Kills Abel

Adam and Eve had two sons, named Cain and Abel, but they were very different from each other. Because Cain made a poor choice for an offering, God rejected it. Then Cain became jealous of his brother.

4 Adam had sexual relations with his wife Eve. She became pregnant and gave birth to Cain. Eve said, "With the Lord's help, I have given birth to a man." ²After that, Eve gave birth to Cain's brother Abel. Abel took care of sheep. Cain became a farmer.

³Later, Cain brought a gift to God. He brought some food from the ground. ⁴Abel brought the best parts of his best sheep. The Lord accepted Abel and his gift. ⁵But God did not accept Cain and his gift. Cain became very angry and looked unhappy.

⁶The Lord asked Cain, "Why are you angry? Why do you look so unhappy? ⁷If you do good, I will accept you. But if you do not do good, sin is ready to attack you. Sin wants you. But you must rule over it."

⁸Cain said to his brother Abel, "Let's go out into the field." So Cain and Abel went into the field. Then Cain attacked his brother Abel and killed him.

Today's Prayer

Dear God in heaven, I am so glad that you made us all different. Help me to be the best I can be. In Jesus' name, amen.

Memory Verse

"The Lord corrects those he loves, just as a father corrects the child that he likes."
Proverbs 3:12

God Punishes Cain

After Cain killed his brother Abel, God took away Cain's ability to grow good crops. He sent Cain away from his family. But the worst punishment of all was that God sent Cain away from him.

⁹Later, the Lord said to Cain, "Where is your brother Abel?"

Cain answered, "I don't know. Is it my job to take care of my brother?"

¹⁰Then the Lord said, "What have you done? Your brother's blood is on the ground. That blood is like a voice that tells me what happened. ¹¹And now you will be cursed in your work

with the ground. It is the same ground where your brother's blood fell. Your hands killed him. ¹²You will work the ground. But it will not grow good crops for you anymore. You will wander around on the earth."

¹³Then Cain said to the Lord, "This punishment is more than I can stand! ¹⁴Look! You have forced me to stop working the ground. And now I must hide from you. I will wander around on the earth. And anyone who meets me can kill me."

¹⁵Then the Lord said to Cain, "No! If anyone kills you, I will punish that person seven times more." Then the Lord put a mark on Cain. It was a warning to anyone who met him not to kill him.

¹⁶Then Cain went away from the Lord. Cain lived in the land of Nod, east of Eden.

Today's Prayer

Dear God, sometimes I get angry when others are better at something than I am. Help me never to be jealous of the things others are able to do. I pray in Jesus' name, amen.

Memory Verse

"The Lord corrects those he loves, just as a father corrects the child that he likes."
Proverbs 3:12

Noah Builds a Boat

People had become so evil that God decided to destroy them. Only Noah and his family were faithful to the Lord. Would God save them?

⁹This is the family history of Noah. Noah was a good man. He was the most innocent man of his time. He walked with God. ¹⁰Noah had three sons: Shem, Ham and Japheth.

¹¹People on earth did what God said was evil. Violence was everywhere. ¹²And God saw this evil. All people on the earth did only evil. ¹³So God said to Noah, "People have made the earth full of violence. So I will destroy all people from the earth. ¹⁴Build a boat of cypress wood for yourself. Make rooms in it and cover it inside and outside with tar. ¹⁵This is how big I want you to build the boat: 450 feet long, 75 feet wide and 45 feet high.

¹⁶Make an opening around the top of the boat. Make it 18 inches high from the edge of the roof down. Put a door in the side of the boat. Make an upper, middle and lower deck in it. ¹⁷I will bring a flood of water on the earth. I will destroy all living things that live under the sky. This includes everything that has the breath of life. Everything on the earth will die. ¹⁸But I will make an agreement with you. You, your sons, your wife and your sons' wives will all go into the boat. ¹⁹Also, you must bring into the boat two of every living thing, male and female. Keep them alive with you. ²⁰There will be two of every kind of bird, animal and crawling thing. They will come to you to be kept alive. ²¹Also gather some of every kind of food. Store it on the boat as food for you and the animals."

²²Noah did everything that God commanded him.

Today's Prayer

Dear God, it is hard to do what is right when others do wrong. Thank you for people like Noah who show me how to be faithful. Help me to be strong and follow your will. In Jesus' name, amen.

Memory Verse
"If you love me, you will do the things I command." John 14:15

The Flood Begins

Carefully, Noah built the boat and placed in it each thing God had told him. At last, the time had come.

7 Then the Lord said to Noah, "I have seen that you are the best man among the people of this time. So you and your family go into the boat. ²Take with you seven pairs, each male with its female, of every kind of clean animal. And take one pair, each male with its female, of every kind of unclean animal. ³Take seven pairs of all the birds of the sky, each male with its female. This will allow all these animals to continue living on the earth after the flood. ⁴Seven days from now I will send rain on the earth. It will rain 40 days and 40 nights. I will destroy from the earth every living thing that I made."

⁵Noah did everything that the Lord commanded him.

¹¹Noah was now 600 years old. The flood started on the seventeenth day of the second month of that year. That day the underground springs split open. And the clouds in the sky poured out rain. ¹²The rain fell on the earth for 40 days and 40 nights.

¹³On that same day Noah and his wife, his sons Shem, Ham and Japheth and their wives went into the boat. ¹⁴They had every kind of wild animal and tame animal. There was every kind of animal that crawls on the earth. Every kind of bird was there. ¹⁵They all came to Noah in the boat in groups of two. There was every creature that had the breath of life. ¹⁶One male and one female of every living thing came. It was just as God had commanded Noah. Then the Lord closed the door behind them.

Today's Prayer

Thank you, dear God, for protecting Noah and his family and all the animals. When I am lonely or afraid, help me to know you are always near to protect me. In Jesus' name, amen.

Memory Verse
"If you love me, you will do the things I command." John 14:15

The Flood Ends

For forty days and nights, it rained, and the floodwaters rose. Even the highest mountains were covered with more than twenty feet of water.

²¹All living things that moved on the earth died. This included all the birds, tame animals, wild animals and creatures that swarm on the earth. And all human beings died. ²²So everything on dry land died. This means everything that had the breath of life in its nose. ²³So God destroyed from the earth every living thing that

was on the land. This was every man, animal, crawling thing and bird of the sky. All that was left was Noah and what was with him in the boat. ²⁴And the waters continued to cover the earth for 150 days.

8 But God remembered Noah and all the wild animals and tame animals with him in the boat. God made a wind blow over the earth. And the water went down. ²The underground springs stopped flowing. And the clouds in the sky stopped pouring down rain. ³⁻⁴The water that covered the earth began to go down. After 150 days the water had gone down so much that the boat touched land again. It came to rest on one of the mountains of Ararat. This was on the seventeenth day of the seventh month. ⁵The water continued to go down. By the first day of the tenth month the tops of the mountains could be seen.

Today's Prayer

O Lord, my God, how great and powerful you are. Help me to understand that I can be safe and strong by obeying your word. Hear the prayer I pray in Jesus' name, amen.

Memory Verse
"If you love me, you will do the things I command." John 14:15

Noah Leaves the Boat

At last, after one hundred and fifty days, the boat came to rest on the top of a mountain. Then Noah and his family began to wonder when they could leave the boat.

⁶Forty days later Noah opened the window he had made in the boat. ⁷He sent out a raven. It flew here and there until the water had dried up from the earth. ⁸Then Noah sent out a dove. This was to find out if the water had dried up from the ground. ⁹The dove could not find a place to land because water still covered the earth.

So it came back to the boat. Noah reached out his hand and took the bird. And he brought it back into the boat.

[10]After seven days Noah again sent out the dove from the boat. [11]And that evening it came back to him with a fresh olive leaf in its mouth. Then Noah knew that the ground was almost dry. [12]Seven days later he sent the dove out again. But this time it did not come back.

[13]Noah was now 601 years old. It was the first day of the first month of that year. The water was dried up from the land. Noah removed the covering of the boat and saw that the land was dry. [14]By the twenty-seventh day of the second month the land was completely dry.

[15]Then God said to Noah, [16]"You and your wife, your sons and their wives should go out of the boat. [17]Bring every animal out of the boat with you—the birds, animals and everything that crawls on the earth. Let them have many young ones and let them grow in number."

Today's Prayer

Jehovah God in heaven, teach me to trust as Noah did. Help me to remember that even in a flood of trouble you are there to help. Thank you for your loving care. In Jesus' name, amen.

Memory Verse
"If you love me, you will do the things I command." John 14:15

God Sends a Rainbow

It was a time of new beginnings, a time of new agreements between Noah and God. God made Noah a promise and sealed it with a sign for everyone to see.

[8]Then God said to Noah and his sons, [9]"Now I am making my agreement with you and your people who will live after you. [10]And I also make it with every living thing that is with you. It is with the birds, the tame animals and the wild animals. It is with all that came out of the boat with you. I make my agreement with every

living thing on earth. [11]I make this agreement with you: I will never again destroy all living things by floodwaters. A flood will never again destroy the earth."

[12]And God said, "I am making an agreement between me and you and every living creature that is with you. It will continue from now on. This is the sign: [13]I am putting my rainbow in the clouds. It is the sign of the agreement between me and the earth. [14]When I bring clouds over the earth, a rainbow appears in the clouds. [15]Then I will remember my agreement. It is between me and you and every living thing. Floodwaters will never again destroy all life on the earth. [16]When the rainbow appears in the clouds, I will see it. Then I will remember the agreement that continues forever. It is between me and every living thing on the earth."

[17]So God said to Noah, "That rainbow is a sign. It is the sign of the agreement that I made with all living things on earth."

Today's Prayer

Great God in heaven, thank you for promising to protect and care for me. Help me to see your promises of love each time I see a rainbow. This prayer I offer in Jesus' name, amen.

Memory Verse
"If you love me, you will do the things I command." John 14:15

The Tower of Babel

After the great flood, Noah's sons had children, and their children had children, until finally the earth was full of people again. These descendants of Noah's sons became new nations, and they were very proud.

11 At this time the whole world spoke one language. Everyone used the same words. ²As people moved from the East, they found a plain in the land of Babylonia. They settled there to live.

³They said to each other, "Let's make bricks and bake them to make them hard." So they used bricks

instead of stones, and tar instead of mortar. ⁴Then they said to each other, "Let's build for ourselves a city and a tower. And let's make the top of the tower reach high into the sky. We will become famous. If we do this, we will not be scattered over all the earth."

⁵The Lord came down to see the city and the tower that the people had built. ⁶The Lord said, "Now, these people are united. They all speak the same language. This is only the beginning of what they will do. They will be able to do anything they want. ⁷Come, let us go down and confuse their language. Then they will not be able to understand each other."

⁸So the Lord scattered them from there over all the earth. And they stopped building the city. ⁹That is where the Lord confused the language of the whole world. So the place is called Babel. So the Lord caused them to spread out from there over all the whole world.

Today's Prayer

Dear Lord, help me to know your will and to obey it. Forgive me when I am proud. In Jesus' name I ask you to lead me, amen.

Memory Verse
"We know that in everything God works for the good of those who love him." Romans 8:28

God Calls Abram

Abram, a descendant of Noah, lived with all his family in the city of Haran, but God had other plans for Abram.

12 Then the Lord said to Abram, "Leave your country, your relatives and your father's family. Go to the land I will show you.
²I will make you a great nation,
  and I will bless you.
I will make you famous.
  And you will be a blessing to
    others.
³I will bless those who bless you.
  I will place a curse on those who
    harm you.
And all the people on earth
  will be blessed through you."
⁴So Abram left Haran as the Lord had told him. And Lot went with him. At this time Abram was 75 years old.

⁵Abram took his wife Sarai, his nephew Lot and everything they owned. They took all the servants they had gotten in Haran. They set out from Haran, planning to go to the land of Canaan. In time they arrived there.

⁶Abram traveled through that land. He went as far as the great tree of Moreh at Shechem. The Canaanites were living in the land at that time. ⁷The Lord appeared to Abram. The Lord said, "I will give this land to your descendants." So Abram built an altar there to the Lord, who had appeared to him. ⁸Then Abram traveled from Shechem to the mountain east of Bethel. And he set up his tent there. Bethel was to the west, and Ai was to the east. There Abram built another altar to the Lord and worshiped him. ⁹After this, he traveled on toward southern Canaan.

Today's Prayer

Dear God, I don't always know what I should do. Help me to open my mind and heart so I can know your will. Thank you for Jesus who teaches me how to live. In his name I pray, amen.

Memory Verse
"We know that in everything God works for the good of those who love him." Romans 8:28

Abram Lets Lot Choose

Because Abram followed God's plan for his life, God blessed him and his family. But soon the blessing became a problem for Abram and his nephew, Lot.

²Abram was very rich in cattle, silver and gold.

³He left southern Canaan and went back to Bethel. He went where he had camped before, between Bethel and Ai. ⁴It was the place where Abram had built an altar before. So he worshiped the Lord there.

⁵During this time Lot was traveling with Abram. Lot also had many sheep, cattle and tents. ⁶Abram and Lot had so many animals that the land could not support both of them together. ⁷Abram's herders and Lot's herders began to argue. The Canaanites and the Perizzites were living in the land at this time.

⁸So Abram said to Lot, "There should be no arguing between you and me. Your herders and mine should not argue either. We are brothers. ⁹We should separate. The whole land is there in front of you. If you go to the left, I will go to the right. If you go to the right, I will go to the left."

¹⁰Lot looked all around and saw the whole Jordan Valley. He saw that there was much water there. It was like the Lord's garden, like the land of Egypt in the direction of Zoar. (This was before the Lord destroyed Sodom and Gomorrah.) ¹¹So Lot chose to move east and live in the Jordan Valley. In this way Abram and Lot separated. ¹²Abram lived in the land of Canaan. But Lot lived among the cities in the Jordan Valley. He moved very near to Sodom.

Today's Prayer

O Lord my Lord, be with me when I have to make choices in my life. Help me to make good choices and not selfish ones. I pray in Jesus' name, amen.

Memory Verse
"We know that in everything God works for the good of those who love him." Romans 8:28

Isaac Is Born

All her life Sarah had hoped and longed for a son. But she was over ninety years old and Abraham was one hundred. How could God keep his promise to give them a son when they were so old?

17 When Abram was 99 years old, the Lord appeared to him. The Lord said, "I am God All-Powerful. Obey me and do what is right. ²I will make an agreement between us. I will make you the ancestor of many people."

³Then Abram bowed facedown on the ground. God said to him, ⁴"I am making my agreement with you: I will make you the father of many nations. ⁵I am changing your name from Abram to Abraham. This is because I am making you a father of many nations."

¹⁵God said to Abraham, "I will change the name of Sarai, your wife.

Her new name will be Sarah. [16]I will bless her. I will give her a son, and you will be the father. She will be the mother of many nations. Kings of nations will come from her."

21 The Lord cared for Sarah as he had said. He did for her what he had promised. [2]Sarah became pregnant. And she gave birth to a son for Abraham in his old age. Everything happened at the time God had said it would. [3]Abraham named his son Isaac. Sarah gave birth to this son of Abraham. [4]Abraham circumcised Isaac when he was eight days old as God had commanded.

[5]Abraham was 100 years old when his son Isaac was born. [6]And Sarah said, "God has made me laugh. Everyone who hears about this will laugh with me. [7]No one thought that I would be able to have Abraham's child. But I have given Abraham a son while he is old."

Today's Prayer

Dear heavenly Father, help me to trust you more, to believe your word, and to know that you keep your promises. Thank you for Jesus and his love. In his name I pray, amen.

Memory Verse
"We know that in everything God works for the good of those who love him." Romans 8:28

God Tests Abraham

Abraham loved his son Isaac very much. Then God asked Abraham to offer him as a sacrifice! Abraham trusted God, so he prepared to offer the sacrifice, just as God had commanded.

[6]Abraham took the wood for the sacrifice and gave it to his son to carry. Abraham took the knife and the fire. So Abraham and his son went on together.

[7]Isaac said to his father Abraham, "Father!"

Abraham answered, "Yes, my son."

Isaac said, "We have the fire and

the wood. But where is the lamb we will burn as a sacrifice?"

⁸Abraham answered, "God will give us the lamb for the sacrifice, my son."

So Abraham and his son went on together. ⁹They came to the place God had told him about. There, Abraham built an altar. He laid the wood on it. Then he tied up his son Isaac. And he laid Isaac on the wood on the altar. ¹⁰Then Abraham took his knife and was about to kill his son.

¹¹But the angel of the Lord called to him from heaven. The angel said, "Abraham! Abraham!"

Abraham answered, "Yes."

¹²The angel said, "Don't kill your son or hurt him in any way. Now I can see that you respect God. I see that you have not kept your son, your only son, from me."

¹³Then Abraham looked up and saw a male sheep. Its horns were caught in a bush. So Abraham went and took the sheep and killed it. He offered it as a whole burnt offering to God. Abraham's son was saved.

Today's Prayer

Dear God, sometimes it is hard for me to keep my promises. Thank you for always keeping your promises to love me and to watch over me. In Jesus' name, amen.

Memory Verse
"We know that in everything God works for the good of those who love him." Romans 8:28

Esau's Birthright

Isaac and Rebekah, his wife, had twin sons, named Jacob and Esau. One day Jacob forced Esau to give up his special rights as the firstborn son.

²⁴And when the time came, Rebekah gave birth to twins. ²⁵The first baby was born red. His skin was like a hairy robe. So he was named Esau. ²⁶When the second baby was born, he was holding on to Esau's heel. So that baby was named Jacob. Isaac was 60 years old when they were born.

²⁷When the boys grew up, Esau

became a skilled hunter. He loved to be out in the fields. But Jacob was a quiet man. He stayed among the tents. [28]Isaac loved Esau. Esau hunted the wild animals that Isaac enjoyed eating. But Rebekah loved Jacob.

[29]One day Jacob was boiling a pot of vegetable soup. Esau came in from hunting in the fields. He was weak from hunger. [30]So Esau said to Jacob, "Let me eat some of that red soup. I am weak with hunger." (That is why people call him Edom.)

[31]But Jacob said, "You must sell me your rights as the firstborn son."

[32]Esau said, "I am almost dead from hunger. If I die, all of my father's wealth will not help me."

[33]But Jacob said, "First, promise me that you will give it to me," So Esau made a promise to Jacob. In this way he sold his part of their father's wealth to Jacob. [34]Then Jacob gave Esau bread and vegetable soup. Esau ate and drank and then left. So Esau showed how little he cared about his rights as the firstborn son.

Today's Prayer

Dear Lord, it's hard to wait for something in the future when it means I have to give up something I want now. Help me learn to make wise choices. In Jesus' name, amen.

Memory Verse

"It is good and pleasant when God's people live together in peace!" Psalm 133:1

Isaac Redigs Wells

Isaac was a peaceful man who wanted to get along with his neighbors. But getting along with the Philistines and their king, Abimelech, wasn't easy.

[13]Isaac became rich. He gathered more wealth until he became a very rich man. [14]He had many slaves and many flocks and herds. The Philistines envied him. [15]So they stopped up all the wells the servants of Isaac's father Abraham had dug. (They had dug them when Abraham was alive.) The Philistines filled those wells with

dirt. [16]And Abimelech said to Isaac, "Leave our country. You have become much more powerful than we are."

[17]So Isaac left that place. He camped in the Valley of Gerar and lived there. [18]Long before this time Abraham had dug many wells. After Abraham died, the Philistines filled them with dirt. So Isaac dug those wells again. He gave them the same names his father had given them. [19]Isaac's servants dug a well in the valley. From it a spring of water flowed. [20]But the men who herded sheep in Gerar argued with Isaac's servants. They said, "This water is ours." So Isaac named that well Argue because they argued with him. [21]Then Isaac's servants dug another well. The people also argued about it. So Isaac named that well Fight. [22]Isaac moved from there and dug another well. No one argued about this one. So he named that well Room Enough. Isaac said, "Now the Lord has made room for us. We will be successful in this land."

Today's Prayer

Dear God, thank you for the example of Isaac, who was patient with his bad neighbors. Help me to be patient with others and to be a good neighbor. In Jesus' name I pray, amen.

Memory Verse
"It is good and pleasant when God's people live together in peace!" Psalm 133:1

Jacob Tricks Isaac

Isaac was old and almost blind. Before he died, he wanted to bless his older son Esau. But Rebekah and Jacob had a plan to trick Isaac into giving the blessing to Jacob instead.

[14]Jacob went out and got two goats and brought them to his mother. Then she cooked them in the special way Isaac enjoyed. [15]She took the best clothes of her older son Esau that were in the house. She put them on the younger son Jacob. [16]She took the skins of the goats. And she put them on Jacob's hands and neck. [17]Then

she gave Jacob the tasty food and the bread she had made.

[18]Jacob went in to his father and said, "Father."

And his father said, "Yes, my son. Who are you?"

[19]Jacob said to him, "I am Esau, your first son. I have done what you told me. Now sit up and eat some meat of the animal I hunted for you. Then bless me."

[20]But Isaac asked his son, "How did you find and kill the animal so quickly?"

Jacob answered, "Because the Lord your God led me to find it."

[21]Then Isaac said to Jacob, "Come near so I can touch you, my son. If I can touch you, I will know if you are really my son Esau."

[22]So Jacob came near to Isaac his father. Isaac touched him and said, "Your voice sounds like Jacob's voice. But your hands are hairy like the hands of Esau." [23]Isaac did not know it was Jacob, because his hands were hairy like Esau's hands. So Isaac blessed Jacob.

Today's Prayer

Loving God, please help me not to want things that belong to someone else. Instead, help me to share with my family, my friends and those in need. In Jesus' name I pray, amen.

Memory Verse

"It is good and pleasant when God's people live together in peace!" Psalm 133:1

A Ladder to Heaven

After receiving Isaac's blessing, Jacob was sent on a long journey to Haran, the home of his mother's family. One night he had a dream about the Lord of heaven.

¹⁰Jacob left Beersheba and set out for Haran. ¹¹He came to a place and spent the night there because the sun had set. He found a stone there and laid his head on it to go to sleep. ¹²Jacob dreamed that there was a ladder resting on the earth and reaching up into heaven. And he saw angels of God going up and coming down the ladder. ¹³And then Jacob saw the Lord standing above the ladder. The Lord said, "I am the Lord, the God of Abraham, your grandfather. And I am the God of Isaac. I will give you and your descendants the land on which you are now sleeping. ¹⁴Your descendants will be as many as the dust of the earth. They will spread west and east, north and south. All the families of the earth will be blessed through you and your descendants. ¹⁵I am with you, and I will protect you everywhere you go. And I will bring you back to this land. I will not leave you until I have done what I have promised you."

¹⁶Then Jacob woke from his sleep. He said, "Surely the Lord is in this place. But I did not know it."

Today's Prayer

Dear Lord of heaven and earth, I am thankful that you never run out of blessings. Help me to be unselfish and to share with people who don't know you. In Jesus' name, amen.

Memory Verse
"It is good and pleasant when God's people live together in peace!" Psalm 133:1

Jacob Wrestles with God

God chose Jacob to be a special servant. One night God appeared to Jacob in the form of a man. They had a contest, and Jacob's name was changed.

[22]During the night Jacob rose and crossed the Jabbok River at the crossing. [23]He sent his family and everything he had across the river. [24]But Jacob stayed behind alone. And a man came and wrestled with him until the sun came up. [25]The man saw that he could not defeat Jacob. So he struck Jacob's hip and put it out of

joint. ²⁶Then the man said to Jacob, "Let me go. The sun is coming up."

But Jacob said, "I will let you go if you will bless me."

²⁷The man said to him, "What is your name?"

And he answered, "Jacob."

²⁸Then the man said, "Your name will no longer be Jacob. Your name will now be Israel, because you have wrestled with God and with men. And you have won."

²⁹Then Jacob asked him, "Please tell me your name."

But the man said, "Why do you ask my name?" Then he blessed Jacob there.

³⁰So Jacob named that place Peniel. He said, "I have seen God face to face. But my life was saved." ³¹Then the sun rose as he was leaving that place. Jacob was limping because of his leg. ³²So even today the people of Israel do not eat the muscle that is on the hip joint of animals. This is because Jacob was touched there.

Today's Prayer

Dear God thank you for being with me wherever I go. Help me to be faithful to you so that I will always be a winner just as Jacob was. In the name of your son Jesus, amen.

Memory Verse

"It is good and pleasant when God's people live together in peace!" Psalm 133:1

Joseph's Dreams

Jacob, whom God renamed Israel, had twelve sons. They would become the fathers of the twelve tribes of Israel. Of all of the sons, Jacob loved Joseph best.

Joseph was a young man, 17 years old. He and his brothers cared for the flocks. His brothers were the sons of Bilhah and Zilpah, his father's wives. Joseph gave his father bad reports about his brothers. ³Joseph was born when his father Israel, also called Jacob, was old. So Israel loved Joseph more than his other sons. He made Joseph a special robe with long sleeves. ⁴Joseph's brothers saw that their father loved Joseph more than he loved them. So they hated their brother and could not speak to him politely.

⁵One time Joseph had a dream. When he told his brothers about it,

they hated him even more. ⁶Joseph said, "Listen to the dream I had. ⁷We were in the field tying bundles of wheat together. My bundle stood up, and your bundles of wheat gathered around mine. Your bundles bowed down to mine."

⁸His brothers said, "Do you really think you will be king over us? Do you truly think you will rule over us?" His brothers hated him even more now. They hated him because of his dreams and what he had said.

⁹Then Joseph had another dream. He told his brothers about it also. He said, "Listen, I had another dream. I saw the sun, moon and 11 stars bowing down to me."

¹⁰Joseph also told his father about this dream. But his father scolded him, saying, "What kind of dream is this? Do you really believe that your mother, your brothers and I will bow down to you?" ¹¹Joseph's brothers were jealous of him. But his father thought about what all these things could mean.

Today's Prayer

Dear Lord, thank you for helping me when others are unkind to me. Help me not to think I am better or more important than other people. In Jesus' name, amen.

Memory Verse
"You can trust God. He will not let you be tempted more than you can stand."
1 Corinthians 10:13

Joseph's Brothers' Plan

Joseph's brothers were herding sheep in another part of the country. Jacob sent Joseph to check on them, but Joseph couldn't find them.

When Joseph came to Shechem, [15]a man found him wandering in the field. He asked Joseph, "What are you looking for?"

[16]Joseph answered, "I am looking for my brothers. Can you tell me where they are herding the sheep?"

[17]The man said, "They have already gone. I heard them say they were

going to Dothan." So Joseph went to look for his brothers and found them in Dothan.

[18]Joseph's brothers saw him coming from far away. Before he reached them, they made a plan to kill him. [19]They said to each other, "Here comes that dreamer. [20]Let's kill him and throw his body into one of the wells. We can tell our father that a wild animal killed him. Then we will see what will become of his dreams."

[21]But Reuben heard their plan and saved Joseph. He said, "Let's not kill him. [22]Don't spill any blood. Throw him into this well here in the desert. But don't hurt him!" Reuben planned to save Joseph later and send him back to his father. [23]So when Joseph came to his brothers, they pulled off his robe with long sleeves. [24]Then they threw him into the well. It was empty. There was no water in it.

Today's Prayer

Dear God, your plans are wonderful. Even when I am afraid, I know you won't forget to protect me from danger. Help me to trust you, just as Joseph did. In the name of Christ I pray, amen.

Memory Verse
"You can trust God. He will not let you be tempted more than you can stand."
1 Corinthians 10:13

Joseph Is Sold as a Slave

Jealousy can cause people to do terrible things. Joseph's brothers were so jealous they had decided to kill him, but then they had another idea.

^{25}While Joseph was in the well, the brothers sat down to eat. When they looked up, they saw a group of Ishmaelites. They were traveling from Gilead to Egypt. Their camels were carrying spices, balm and myrrh. ^{26}Then Judah said to his brothers, "What will we gain if we kill our brother and hide his death? ^{27}Let's sell him to these Ishmaelites. Then we will not be guilty of killing our own brother. After all, he is our brother, our own flesh and blood." And the other brothers agreed. ^{28}So when the Midianite traders came by, the brothers took Joseph out of the well. They sold him to the Ishmaelites for eight ounces of silver. And the Ishmaelites took him to Egypt.

²⁹Reuben was not with his brothers when they sold Joseph to the Ishmaelites. When Reuben came back to the well, Joseph was not there. Reuben tore his clothes to show he was sad. ³⁰Then he went back to his brothers and said, "The boy is not there! What will I do?" ³¹The brothers killed a goat and dipped Joseph's long-sleeved robe in its blood. ³²Then they brought the robe to their father. They said, "We found this robe. Look it over carefully. See if it is your son's robe."

³³Jacob looked it over and said, "It is my son's robe! Some savage animal has eaten him. My son Joseph has been torn to pieces!" ³⁴Then Jacob tore his clothes and put on rough cloth to show that he was sad. He continued to be sad about his son for a long time.

Today's Prayer

Wonderful God, thank you for giving us so much. Help me not to be jealous of others who have more than I do, because everything good comes from you. In Christ's name, amen.

Memory Verse

"You can trust God. He will not let you be tempted more than you can stand."
1 Corinthians 10:13

Joseph Rules Egypt

In spite of his brothers, Joseph was blessed by God. He was sent to explain the king of Egypt's dreams of seven good years and seven bad years.

²⁹"You will have seven years of good crops and plenty to eat in all the land of Egypt. ³⁰But after those seven years, there will come seven years of hunger. All the food that grew in the land of Egypt will be forgotten. The time of hunger will eat up the land."

³⁹So the king said to Joseph, "God has shown you all this. There is no

one as wise and understanding as you are. ⁴⁰I will put you in charge of my palace. All the people will obey your orders. Only I will be greater than you."

⁴⁶Joseph was 30 years old when he began serving the king of Egypt. And he left the king's court and traveled through all the land of Egypt. ⁴⁷During the seven good years, the crops in the land grew well. ⁴⁸And Joseph gathered all the food which was produced in Egypt during those seven years of good crops. He stored the food in cities. In every city he stored grain that had been grown in the fields around that city. ⁴⁹Joseph stored much grain, as much as the sand of the seashore. He stored so much grain that he could not measure it.

⁵³The seven years of good crops came to an end in the land of Egypt. ⁵⁴Then the seven years of hunger began, just as Joseph had said. In all the lands people had nothing to eat. But in Egypt there was food.

Today's Prayer

Dear Lord, I am so thankful that you never forget me just as you did not forget Joseph. Help me to remember that I cannot do anything without your help. In Jesus' name, amen.

Memory Verse
"You can trust God. He will not let you be tempted more than you can stand."
1 Corinthians 10:13

Joseph Forgives His Brothers

Joseph's brothers had to go to Egypt to buy grain because there was no food in Canaan. They were frightened when they discovered that the Egyptian ruler was the brother they had sold into slavery!

45 Joseph could not control himself in front of his servants any longer. He cried out, "Have everyone leave me." When only the brothers were left with Joseph, he told them who he was. ²Joseph cried so loudly that the Egyptians heard him. And the people in the king's palace heard about it. ³He said to his brothers, "I am Joseph. Is my father still alive?" But the brothers could not answer him, because they were very afraid of him.

⁴So Joseph said to them, "Come close to me." So the brothers came close to him. And he said to them, "I am your brother Joseph. You sold me

as a slave to go to Egypt. [5]Now don't be worried. Don't be angry with yourselves because you sold me here. God sent me here ahead of you to save people's lives. [6]No food has grown on the land for two years now. And there will be five more years without planting or harvest. [7]So God sent me here ahead of you. This was to make sure you have some descendants left on earth. And it was to keep you alive in an amazing way. [8]So it was not you who sent me here, but God. God has made me the highest officer of the king of Egypt. I am in charge of his palace. I am the master of all the land of Egypt.

[9]"So leave quickly and go to my father. Tell him, 'Your son Joseph says: God has made me master over all Egypt. Come down to me quickly.' "

Today's Prayer

Dear God, thank you for forgiving me when I hurt others. Let me have a forgiving heart, and let me learn to love those who are not always lovable. I ask this in Jesus' name, amen.

Memory Verse

"You can trust God. He will not let you be tempted more than you can stand."
1 Corinthians 10:13

The Israelites Become Slaves

Many years went by. Even the great-grandchildren of Joseph grew old. At last, the people of Egypt didn't remember who Joseph was.

⁸Then a new king began to rule Egypt. He did not know who Joseph was. ⁹This king said to his people, "Look! The people of Israel are too many! And they are too strong for us to handle! ¹⁰We must make plans against them. If we don't, the number of their people will grow even more. Then if there is a war, they might join

our enemies. Then they could fight us and escape from the country!"

[11]So the Egyptians made life hard for the people of Israel. They put slave masters over the Israelites. The slave masters forced the Israelites to build the cities Pithom and Rameses for the king. These cities were supply centers in which the Egyptians stored things. [12]The Egyptians forced the Israelites to work even harder. But this made the Israelites grow in number and spread more. So the Egyptians became more afraid of them. [13]They forced the Israelites to work even harder. [14]The Egyptians made life hard for the Israelites. They forced the Israelites to work very hard making bricks and mortar. They also forced them to do all kinds of hard work in the fields. The Egyptians were not merciful to them in all their hard work.

Today's Prayer

Dear Lord in heaven, when troubles come and nothing I do seems to make things right, help me to know you understand and care. Help me to find the strength I need. In Jesus' name, amen.

Memory Verse

"God is our protection and our strength. He always helps in times of trouble." Psalm 46:1

Moses Is Born

To keep the Hebrews or Israelites from growing in numbers, the king of Egypt ordered the nurses to kill all the Hebrew baby boys at birth. So, some Hebrew mothers tried to hide their babies.

2 There was a man from the family of Levi. He married a woman who was also from the family of Levi. ²She became pregnant and gave birth to a son. She saw how wonderful the baby was, and she hid him for three months. ³But after three months, she was not able to hide the baby any longer. So she got a basket and covered it with tar so that it would float. She put the baby in the basket. Then she put the basket among the tall grass at the edge of the Nile River. ⁴The baby's sister stood a short distance away. She wanted to see what would happen to him.

⁵Then the daughter of the king of

Egypt came to the river. She was going to take a bath. Her servant girls were walking beside the river. She saw the basket in the tall grass. So she sent her slave girl to get it. ⁶The king's daughter opened the basket and saw the baby boy. He was crying, and she felt sorry for him. She said, "This is one of the Hebrew babies."

⁷Then the baby's sister asked the king's daughter, "Would you like me to find a Hebrew woman to nurse the baby for you?"

⁸The king's daughter said, "Yes, please." So the girl went and got the baby's own mother.

⁹The king's daughter said to the woman, "Take this baby and nurse him for me. I will pay you." So the woman took her baby and nursed him. ¹⁰After the child had grown older, the woman took him to the king's daughter. She adopted the baby as her own son. The king's daughter named him Moses, because she had pulled him out of the water.

Today's Prayer

Dear God, you give me courage. Help me to become the kind of person you want me to be — someone who is kind and loving and helpful to those in need. In the name of the Savior I pray, amen.

Memory Verse
"God is our protection and our strength. He always helps in times of trouble." Psalm 46:1

Moses Takes a Wife

One day, after Moses had become a young man, he saw an Egyptian mistreating a Hebrew slave. Moses became angry and killed the Egyptian.

¹⁵When the king heard about what Moses had done, he tried to kill Moses. But Moses ran away from the king and went to live in the land of Midian. There he sat down near a well.

¹⁶There was a priest in Midian who had seven daughters. His daughters went to that well to get water for their father's sheep. They were trying to fill

the water troughs for their father's sheep. [17]But some shepherds came and chased the girls away. Then Moses defended the girls and watered their sheep.

[18]Then they went back to their father, Reuel, also called Jethro. He asked them, "Why have you come home early today?"

[19]The girls answered, "The shepherds chased us away. But an Egyptian defended us. He got water for us and watered our sheep."

[20]He asked his daughters, "Where is this man? Why did you leave him? Invite him to eat with us."

[21]Moses agreed to stay with Jethro. And he gave his daughter Zipporah to Moses to be his wife. [22]Zipporah gave birth to a son, and Moses named him Gershom. Moses named him this because Moses was a stranger in a land that was not his own.

Today's Prayer

Father of us all, many things in life don't seem fair. Help me not to become angry or bitter when I see these things. Teach me always to trust you. I pray in Jesus' name, amen.

Memory Verse
"God is our protection and our strength. He always helps in times of trouble." Psalm 46:1

The Burning Bush

Moses lived in Midian for forty years, but God had not forgotten him or the troubles of the Israelite slaves in Egypt. God began to work his plan.

3 One day Moses was taking care of Jethro's sheep. Jethro was the priest of Midian and also Moses' father-in-law. Moses led the sheep to the west side of the desert. He came to Sinai, the mountain of God. ²There the angel of the Lord appeared to Moses in flames of fire coming out of a bush. Moses saw that the bush was

on fire, but it was not burning up. ³So Moses said, "I will go closer to this strange thing. How can a bush continue burning without burning up?"

⁴The Lord saw Moses was coming to look at the bush. So God called to him from the bush, "Moses, Moses!"

And Moses said, "Here I am."

⁵Then God said, "Do not come any closer. Take off your sandals. You are standing on holy ground. ⁶I am the God of your ancestors. I am the God of Abraham, the God of Isaac and the God of Jacob." Moses covered his face because he was afraid to look at God.

⁷The Lord said, "I have seen the troubles my people have suffered in Egypt. And I have heard their cries when the Egyptian slave masters hurt them. I am concerned about their pain. ¹⁰So now I am sending you to the king of Egypt. Go! Bring my people, the Israelites, out of Egypt!"

Today's Prayer

My Lord, just as you sent Moses to free Israel and lead them to a better land, you have sent Jesus to set me free from sin and lead me to a better place. Thank you for loving me that much. In Jesus' name, amen.

Memory Verse
"God is our protection and our strength. He always helps in times of trouble." Psalm 46:1

Proof for Moses

When Moses heard God's plan, he was sure he couldn't do what God was asking. God told him, "I will be with you." Then God showed Moses the proof of his great power.

4 Then Moses answered, "What if the people of Israel do not believe me or listen to me? What if they say, 'The Lord did not appear to you'?"

²The Lord said to him, "What is that in your hand?"

Moses answered, "It is my walking stick."

³The Lord said, "Throw it on the ground."

So Moses threw it on the ground. And it became a snake. Moses ran from the snake. ⁴But the Lord said to him, "Reach out and grab the snake by its tail." So Moses reached out and took hold of the snake. When he did this, it again became a stick in his

hand. [5]The Lord said, "When this happens, the Israelites will believe that the Lord appeared to you. I am the God of their ancestors. I am the God of Abraham, the God of Isaac and the God of Jacob."

[6]Then the Lord said to Moses, "Put your hand inside your coat." So Moses put his hand inside his coat. When he took his hand out, it was white with a harmful skin disease.

[7]Then the Lord said, "Now put your hand inside your coat again." So Moses put his hand inside his coat again. When he took it out, his hand was healthy again. It was like the rest of his skin.

[8]Then the Lord said, "The people may not believe you or be convinced by the first miracle. They may believe you when you show them this second miracle. [9]After these two miracles they still may not believe or listen to you. Then take some water from the Nile River. Pour it on the dry ground. The water will become blood when it touches the ground."

Today's Prayer

Mighty God, how great is your power. Your promise to always be with me gives me strength. Help me to find the courage to do your will. In Jesus' name, amen.

Memory Verse
"God is our protection and our strength. He always helps in times of trouble." Psalm 46:1

Moses Argues with God

"I'm not a good speaker," was Moses' last excuse for not going to Egypt as God told him. God solved this problem in a special way.

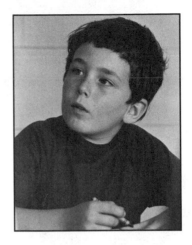

[10]Moses said to the Lord, "But Lord, I am not a skilled speaker. I have never been able to speak well. And now, even after talking to you, I am not a good speaker. I speak slowly and can't find the best words."

[11]Then the Lord said to him, "Who made man's mouth? And who makes him deaf or not able to speak? Or who gives a man sight or makes him blind? It is I, the Lord. [12]Now go! I will help you speak. I will tell you what to say."

[13]But Moses said, "Please, Lord, send someone else."

[14]The Lord became angry with Moses. He said, "Your brother Aaron, from the family of Levi, is a skilled speaker. He is already coming to meet you. And he will be happy when he sees you. [15]I will tell you what to say. Then you will tell Aaron. I will help both of you know what to say and do. [16]And Aaron will speak to the people for you. You will tell him what God says. And he will speak for you. [17]Take your walking stick with you. Use it to do the miracles."

Today's Prayer

God in heaven, forgive me when I make excuses for not doing what you want. Help me find strength in Jesus to live and grow as I should each day. In Jesus' name, amen.

Memory Verse
"I can do all things through Christ because he gives me strength." Philippians 4:13

The King of Egypt

At last, with Aaron to speak for him, Moses sets out for Egypt to tell the Israelites the exciting news about God's plan for their freedom.

²⁹So Moses and Aaron gathered all the older leaders of the Israelites. ³⁰Aaron told them everything that the Lord had told Moses. Then Moses did the miracles for all the people to see. ³¹So the Israelites believed. They heard that the Lord was concerned about them and had seen their troubles. Then they bowed down and worshiped him.

5 After Moses and Aaron talked to the people, they went to the king of Egypt. They said, "This is what the Lord, the God of Israel, says: 'Let my people go so they may hold a feast for me in the desert.' "

²But the king of Egypt said, "Who is

the Lord? Why should I obey him and let Israel go? I do not know the Lord. And I will not let Israel go."

³Then Aaron and Moses said, "The God of the Hebrews has talked with us. Now let us travel three days into the desert. There we will offer sacrifices to the Lord our God. If we don't do this, he may kill us with a disease or in war."

⁴But the king said to them, "Moses and Aaron, why are you taking the people away from their work? Go back to your hard work! ⁵There are very many Hebrews. And now you want them to quit their hard work!"

⁶That same day the king gave a command to the slave masters and foremen. ⁷He said, "Don't give the people straw to make bricks as you used to do. Let them gather their own straw."

Today's Prayer

Holy Lord, I am thankful for your love. Help me, like Moses and Aaron, to find the courage to take the good news of your love to others. In Jesus' name, amen.

Memory Verse
"I can do all things through Christ because he gives me strength." Philippians 4:13

The First Plague

God warned Moses and Aaron that the king would be stubborn. He even refused to believe their miracles. So the Lord brought the first of ten terrible disasters on Egypt.

[14]Then the Lord said to Moses, "The king is being stubborn. He refuses to let the people go. [15]In the morning the king will go out to the Nile River. Go meet him by the edge of the river. Take with you the walking stick that became a snake. [16]Tell him this: The Lord, the God of the Hebrews, sent me to you. He said, 'Let my people go worship me in the desert.' Until now you have not listened. [17]This is what the Lord says: 'This is how you will know that I am the Lord. I will strike the water of the Nile River with this stick in my hand. And the water will change into blood. [18]Then the fish in the Nile will die, and the river will

begin to stink. And the Egyptians will not be able to drink the water from the Nile.' "

[19]The Lord said to Moses, "Tell Aaron to stretch the walking stick in his hand over the rivers, canals, ponds and pools in Egypt. The water will become blood everywhere in Egypt. There even will be blood in the wooden buckets and stone jars."

[20]So Moses and Aaron did just as the Lord had commanded. Aaron raised his walking stick and struck the water in the Nile River. He did this in front of the king and his officers. So all the water in the Nile changed into blood. [21]The fish in the Nile died, and the river began to stink. So the Egyptians could not drink water from it. Blood was everywhere in the land of Egypt.

[22]Using their tricks, their magicians of Egypt did the same thing. So the king was stubborn and refused to listen to Moses and Aaron. This happened just as the Lord had said.

Today's Prayer

Dear God, sometimes I am like the king of Egypt long ago. I see your power all around me and still I don't do what you have said. Forgive me when I am stubborn. This I ask in Jesus' name, amen.

Memory Verse
"I can do all things through Christ because he gives me strength." Philippians 4:13

The Darkness

Even after God sent frogs, gnats, flies, disease, boils, hail and locust, the king still wouldn't let God's people go. But God was not yet through with him.

[21]Then the Lord told Moses, "Raise your hand toward the sky, and darkness will cover the land of Egypt. It will be so dark you will be able to feel it." [22]So Moses raised his hand toward the sky. Then total darkness was everywhere in Egypt for three days. [23]No one could see anyone else. And no one could go anywhere for three

days. But the Israelites had light where they lived.

²⁴Again the king of Egypt called for Moses. He said, "All of you may go and worship the Lord. You may take your women and children with you. But you must leave your sheep and cattle here."

²⁵Moses said, "You must let us have animals to use as sacrifices and burnt offerings. We have to offer them to the Lord our God. ²⁶So we must take our animals with us. Not a hoof will be left behind. We have to use some of the animals to worship the Lord our God. We do not yet know exactly what we will need to worship the Lord. We will know when we get there."

²⁷But the Lord made the king stubborn again. So he refused to let them go. ²⁸Then he told Moses, "Get out of here! Don't come here again! The next time you see me, you will die."

²⁹Then Moses told the king, "I'll do what you say. I will not come to see you again."

Today's Prayer

O God my Father, help me make today the best that it can be. Help me feel your presence as you guide me through each hour of my life. In Jesus' name I pray, amen.

Memory Verse

"I can do all things through Christ because he gives me strength." Philippians 4:13

Death of the Firstborn

The Lord told Moses and Aaron about the terrible and final disaster he was about to bring upon Egypt. But he also told them how to protect the Israelites from it.

²¹Then Moses called all the older leaders of Israel together. He told them, "Get the animals for your families. Kill the animals for the Passover. ²²Take a branch of the hyssop plant and dip it into the bowl filled with blood. Wipe the blood on the sides and tops of the doorframes. No one may leave his house until morning.

²³The Lord will go through Egypt to kill the Egyptians. He will see the blood on the sides and tops of the doorframes. Then the Lord will pass over that house. He will not let the one who brings death come into your houses and kill you.

²⁴"You must keep this command. This law is for you and your descendants from now on." ²⁸They did just as the Lord commanded Moses and Aaron.

²⁹At midnight the Lord killed all the firstborn sons in the land of Egypt. The firstborn of the king, who sat on the throne, died. Even the firstborn of the prisoner in jail died. Also all the firstborn farm animals died. ³⁰The king, his officers and all the Egyptians got up during the night. Someone had died in every house. So there was loud crying everywhere in Egypt.

Today's Prayer

Holy Lord, as you protected Israel from the terrible plagues, protect me from the things that would harm me. I thank you for this day and each good thing you have given me. In Jesus' name, amen.

Memory Verse
"I can do all things through Christ because he gives me strength." Philippians 4:13

Israelites Leave Egypt

Finally, the king of Egypt understood he couldn't fight against the power of the Lord, so the Egyptians urged the Israelites to leave.

³¹During the night the king called for Moses and Aaron. He said to them, "Get up and leave my people. You and your people may do as you have asked. Go and worship the Lord."

³⁵The people of Israel did what Moses told them to do. They asked their Egyptian neighbors for things made of silver and gold and for clothing. ³⁶The Lord caused the Egyptians to think well of the Israelites. So the Israelites took rich gifts from the Egyptians.

³⁷The Israelites traveled from Rameses to Succoth. There were about 600,000 men walking. This does not include the women and children.

⁴⁰The people of Israel had lived in Egypt for 430 years.

⁵⁰So all the Israelites did just as the Lord had commanded Moses and Aaron. ⁵¹Then on that same day, the Lord led the Israelites out of Egypt. The people left by divisions.

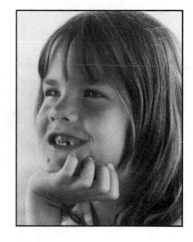

Today's Prayer

Dear God, your power is greater than I can imagine. Thank you for letting me ask for your power when I need to be strong. In Jesus' name, amen.

Memory Verse

"Give all your worries to him <God>, because he cares for you." 1 Peter 5:7

The Egyptians Follow

Thousands of Israelites with all their possessions moved out of Egypt guided by the Lord. Meanwhile, the king and his officers began to think about what they had done.

²¹The Lord showed them the way. During the day he went ahead of them in a pillar of cloud. And during the night the Lord was in a pillar of fire to give them light. They could travel during the day or night.

⁵The king of Egypt was told that the people of Israel had already left. Then he and his officers changed their minds about them. They said, "What have we done? We have let the people of Israel leave. We have lost our slaves!" ⁶So the king prepared his war chariot and took his army with him.

¹⁰The Israelites saw the king and his army coming after them. They were very frightened and cried to the Lord for help.

[15]Then the Lord said to Moses, "Why are you crying out to me? Command the people of Israel to start moving. [16]Raise your walking stick and hold it over the sea. The sea will split. Then the people can cross the sea on dry land."

[21]Moses held his hand over the sea. All that night the Lord drove back the sea with a strong east wind. And so he made the sea become dry ground. The water was split. [22]And the Israelites went through the sea on dry land. A wall of water was on both sides.

[23]Then all the king's horses, chariots and chariot drivers followed them into the sea.

[26]Then the Lord told Moses, "Hold your hand over the sea. Then the water will come back over the Egyptians, their chariots and chariot drivers." [27]So Moses raised his hand over the sea. And at dawn the water became deep again. The Egyptians were trying to run from it. But the Lord swept them away into the sea.

Today's Prayer

Dear Lord, our God, thank you for your loving concern for me when I need to be protected. Help me know that you will be with me when dangers make me afraid. I pray in Jesus' name, amen.

Memory Verse
"Give all your worries to him <God>, because he cares for you." 1 Peter 5:7

Waters of Marah

After escaping the Egyptians, the Israelites traveled in the desert for three days without water. But then God showed his power again.

²²Moses led the people of Israel away from the Red Sea. The people went into the Desert of Shur. They traveled for three days in the desert but found no water. ²³Then they came to Marah, where there was water. But they could not drink it because it was too bitter. That is why the place was named Marah. ²⁴The people

grumbled to Moses. They asked, "What will we drink?"

²⁵Moses cried out to the Lord. So the Lord showed him a tree. Moses threw the tree into the water. And the water became good to drink.

There the Lord gave the people a rule and a law to live by. There he also tested their loyalty to him. ²⁶He said, "You must obey the Lord, your God. You must do what the Lord said is right. You must obey all his laws and keep his rules. If you do these things, I will not give you any of the sicknesses I gave the Egyptians. I am the Lord. I am the Lord who heals you."

²⁷Then the people traveled to Elim. At Elim there were 12 springs of water and 70 palm trees. So the people camped there near the water.

Today's Prayer

Our God in heaven, you can solve any problem I may face. Do not let me ever forget to thank you for everything you do for me. In the name of your son Jesus, amen.

Memory Verse
"Give all your worries to him <God>, because he cares for you." 1 Peter 5:7

Quail and Manna

The Lord delivered the Israelites from the Egyptians at the Red Sea, and he gave them water to drink at Marah. Yet they still didn't trust that he would take care of them.

²Then the whole Israelite community grumbled to Moses and Aaron in the desert. ³The Israelites said to them, "It would have been better if the Lord had killed us in the land of Egypt. There we had meat to eat. We had all the food we wanted. But you have brought us into this desert. You will starve us to death here."

⁴Then the Lord said to Moses, "I will cause food to fall like rain from the sky. This food will be for all of you. Every day the people must go out and gather what they need for that day. I will do this to see if the people will do what I teach them. ⁵On the sixth day of each week, they are to gather twice as much as they

gather on other days. Then they are to prepare it."

⁶So Moses and Aaron said to all the Israelites: "This evening you will know that the Lord is the one who brought you out of Egypt. ⁷Tomorrow morning you will see the greatness of the Lord. He has heard you grumble against him. We are nothing. You are not grumbling against us, but against the Lord." ⁸And Moses said, "Each evening the Lord will give you meat to eat. And every morning he will give you all the bread you want."

¹³That evening, quail came and covered the camp. And in the morning dew lay around the camp. ¹⁴When the dew was gone, thin flakes like frost were on the desert ground. ¹⁵When the Israelites saw it, they asked each other, "What is that?" They asked this question because they did not know what it was.

Today's Prayer

Dear God, I know you are able to supply everything your people need. Help me to remember that you watch over me always and that you listen no matter what I ask. In Jesus' name, amen.

Memory Verse
"Give all your worries to him <God>, because he cares for you." 1 Peter 5:7

Water from the Rock

The Lord had provided all the food the Israelites needed. This food would be given to them until their journey ended at the land God had promised them. But what about water?

17The whole Israelite community left the Desert of Sin. They traveled from place to place as the Lord commanded. They camped at Rephidim. But there was no water there for the people to drink. ²So they quarreled with Moses. They said, "Give us water to drink."

But Moses said to them, "Why do

you quarrel with me? Why are you testing the Lord?"

³But the people were very thirsty for water. So they grumbled against Moses. They said, "Why did you bring us out of Egypt? Was it to kill us, our children and our farm animals with thirst?"

⁴So Moses cried to the Lord, "What can I do with these people? They are almost ready to kill me with stones."

⁵The Lord said to Moses, "Go ahead of the people of Israel. And take some of the older leaders of Israel with you. Carry with you the walking stick that you used to strike the Nile River. Now go! ⁶I will stand in front of you on a rock at Mount Sinai. Hit that rock with the stick, and water will come out of it. Then the people can drink." Moses did these things as the older leaders of Israel watched. ⁷Moses named that place Massah because the Israelites tested the Lord. They asked, "Is the Lord with us or not?" He also named it Meribah because they quarreled.

Today's Prayer

Dear Lord, thank you for food and water and everything I need for good health. Many times I forget to thank you for the things that are always here when I want them. I pray in Jesus' name, amen.

Memory Verse
"Give all your worries to him <God>, because he cares for you." 1 Peter 5:7

Battle with the Amalekites

The Israelites had to follow the orders of their leaders to make their way through the harsh desert land. This was especially important when they were attacked by enemies.

⁸At Rephidim the Amalekites came and fought the Israelites. ⁹So Moses said to Joshua, "Choose some men and go and fight the Amalekites. Tomorrow I will stand on the top of the hill. I will hold the stick God gave me to carry."

¹⁰Joshua obeyed Moses and went to fight the Amalekites. At the same time Moses, Aaron and Hur went to the top of the hill. ¹¹As long as Moses held his hands up, the Israelites would win the fight. But when Moses put his hands down, the Amalekites would win. ¹²Later, Moses' arms became tired. So the men put a large rock under Moses, and he sat on it. Then Aaron and Hur held up Moses' hands. Aaron was on one side of Moses, and Hur was on the other side. They held his hands up like this until the sun went down. ¹³So Joshua defeated the Amalekites in this battle.

¹⁴Then the Lord said to Moses, "Write about this battle in a book so people will remember. And be sure to tell Joshua. Tell him because I will completely destroy the Amalekites from the earth."

¹⁵Then Moses built an altar. He named it The Lord is my Banner.

Today's Prayer

Almighty God, thank you for life. Thank you for sending Jesus to show me how to live with others. Teach me to know your word and to obey it.
In the name of Christ I pray, amen.

Memory Verse
"Honor your father and your mother. Then you will live a long time in the land." Exodus 20:12

The Ten Commandments

God called Moses to the top of Mt. Sinai, and the people were ordered to wait below. From Mt. Sinai, God gave these rules to His people.

20 Then God spoke all these words: ²"I am the Lord your God. I brought you out of the land of Egypt where you were slaves.

³"You must not have any other gods except me.

⁴"You must not make for yourselves any idols. Don't make something that looks like anything in the

sky above or on the earth below or in the water below the land.

⁷"You must not use the name of the Lord your God thoughtlessly. The Lord will punish anyone who is guilty and misuses his name.

⁸"Remember to keep the Sabbath as a holy day.

¹²"Honor your father and your mother. Then you will live a long time in the land. The Lord your God is going to give you this land.

¹³"You must not murder anyone.

¹⁴"You must not be guilty of adultery.

¹⁵"You must not steal.

¹⁶"You must not tell lies about your neighbor in court.

¹⁷"You must not want to take your neighbor's house. You must not want his wife or his men or women slaves. You must not want his ox or his donkey. You must not want to take anything that belongs to your neighbor."

Today's Prayer

I am thankful, God in heaven, for your commandments which tell me how to live. When I break your laws, forgive me and help me to become all I can be. In Jesus' name, amen.

Memory Verse

"Honor your father and your mother. Then you will live a long time in the land." Exodus 20:12

The Golden Calf

Moses stayed on Mt. Sinai for forty days and forty nights while he met with God and received God's laws written on stone tablets. He was gone so long the people thought that God and Moses had forgotten them.

32 The people saw that a long time had passed. And Moses had not come down from the mountain. So they gathered around Aaron. They said to him, "Moses led us out of Egypt. But we don't know what has happened to him. So make us gods who will lead us."

²Aaron said to the people, "Take off the gold earrings that your wives, sons and daughters are wearing. Bring them to me." ³So all the people took their gold earrings and brought them to Aaron. ⁴Aaron took the gold from the people. Then he melted it and made a statue of a calf. He finished it with a tool. Then the

people said, "Israel! These are your gods who brought you out of the land of Egypt!"

⁷And the Lord said to Moses, "Go down from this mountain. Your people, the people you brought out of the land of Egypt, have done a terrible sin. ⁸They have quickly turned away from the things I commanded them to do. They have made for themselves a calf of melted gold. They have worshiped that calf and offered sacrifices to it. The people have said, 'Israel, these are your gods who brought you out of Egypt.'"

⁹The Lord said to Moses, "I have seen these people. I know that they are very stubborn people. ¹⁰So now do not stop me. I am so angry with them that I am going to destroy them. Then I will make you and your descendants a great nation."

¹¹But Moses begged the Lord his God. Moses said, "Lord, don't let your anger destroy your people. You brought these people out of Egypt with your great power and strength."

¹⁴So the Lord changed his mind. He did not destroy the people as he had said he might.

Today's Prayer

O Lord, there is no other god but you. I praise you for your power and your patience. Hear my prayer in Jesus' name, amen.

Memory Verse

"Honor your father and your mother. Then you will live a long time in the land." Exodus 20:12

The New Tablets

When Moses came down from the mountain, he found the people worshiping the golden calf. He was so angry, he threw down the stone tablets on which God had written his law and broke them.

34 The Lord said to Moses, "Cut two more stone tablets like the first two. I will write the same words on them that were on the first two stones which you broke. ²Be ready tomorrow morning. Then come up on Mount Sinai. Stand before me there on the top of the mountain. ³No one may come with you. No one should even be seen any place on the mountain. Not even the sheep or cattle may eat grass near that mountain."

⁴So Moses cut two stone tablets like the first ones. Then early the next morning he went up Mount Sinai. He did this just as the Lord had commanded him. Moses carried the two

stone tablets with him. ⁵Then the Lord came down in the cloud and stood there with Moses. And the Lord called out his name, the Lord.

⁶The Lord passed in front of Moses and said, "I am the Lord. The Lord is a God who shows mercy and is kind. The Lord doesn't become angry quickly. The Lord has great love and faithfulness. ⁷The Lord is kind to thousands of people. The Lord forgives people for wrong and sin and turning against him. But the Lord does not forget to punish guilty people. The Lord will punish not only the guilty people. He will also punish their children, their grandchildren, their great-grandchildren and their great-great-grandchildren."

⁸Then Moses quickly bowed to the ground and worshiped.

Today's Prayer

Jehovah, long ago you wrote your commands on tablets of stone. Now write your commands in my mind and heart so that I will never forget them. In Jesus' name I pray, amen.

Memory Verse
"Honor your father and your mother. Then you will live a long time in the land." Exodus 20:12

"Teach Me Your Laws"

Many years later, the writer of the Psalms told of his love for God's laws and their importance to the people.

97How I love your teachings!
  I think about them all day long.
98Your commands make me wiser
      than my enemies
    because they are mine forever.
99I am wiser than all my teachers
    because I think about your rules.
100I have more understanding than
      the older leaders
    because I follow your orders.
101I have avoided every evil way
    so I could obey your word.
102I haven't stopped obeying your laws
    because you yourself are my
      teacher.
103Your promises are so sweet to me.
    They are like honey to my mouth!
104Your orders give me understanding.
    So I hate lying ways.

105Your word is like a lamp for my feet
    and a light for my way.
106I will do what I have promised
    and obey your fair laws.

Today's Prayer

God in heaven, teach me
to love your laws as David
did. Help me to understand
your word and to use it to
measure everything I do. In
Jesus' name I pray, amen.

Memory Verse
"Honor your father and your mother. Then you
will live a long time in the land." Exodus 20:12

The Spies

The young nation of Israel needed a land of its own, and God planned to give them the land of Canaan. But first, with God's help, they had to capture the land.

13 The Lord said to Moses, [2]"Send men to explore the land of Canaan. I will give that land to the Israelites. Send one leader from each tribe."

[17]Moses sent them to explore Canaan. He said, "Go through southern Canaan and then into the mountains. [18]See what the land looks like. Are the people who live there strong or weak? Are there a few or many? [19]What kind of land do they live in? Is it good or bad? What about the towns they live in—do they have walls, or are they open like camps? [20]What about the soil? Is it fertile or poor? Are there trees there? Try to bring back some of the fruit from that land."

(It was the season for the first grapes.)
²¹So they went up and explored the land. They went from the Desert of Zin all the way to Rehob by Lebo Hamath.

²⁵After 40 days of exploring the land, the men returned to the camp. ²⁷They told Moses, "We went to the land where you sent us. It is a land where much food grows! Here is some of its fruit. ²⁸But the people who live there are strong. Their cities are walled and large. We even saw some Anakites there."

³⁰Then Caleb told the people near Moses to be quiet. Caleb said, "We should go up and take the land for ourselves. We can do it."

³¹But the men who had gone with him said, "We can't attack those people. They are stronger than we are." ³²And those men gave the Israelites a bad report about the land they explored.

Today's Prayer

Dear God, sometimes I have to do things that seem too hard for me. Help me know that your power can make me strong. Thank you for helping me live each day. In the name of Jesus I pray, amen.

Memory Verse
"The Lord says, 'I will make you wise. I will show you where to go. I will guide you and watch over you.'" Psalm 32:8

Joshua and Caleb's Report

Ten of the spies gave bad reports about the land they had explored, and this frightened the Israelites. But two of the men told a different story.

14 That night all the people in the camp began crying loudly. ²All the Israelites complained against Moses and Aaron. All the people said to them, "We should have died in Egypt. Or we should have died in the desert. ³Why is the Lord bringing us to this land? We will be killed with swords. Our wives and children will be taken away. We would be better off going back to Egypt." ⁴They said to each other, "Let's get a leader and go back to Egypt."

⁵Then Moses and Aaron bowed facedown in front of all the Israelites gathered there. ⁶Joshua son of Nun and Caleb son of Jephunneh were among those who had explored the land. They tore their clothes. ⁷They said to all of the Israelites, "The land we went to explore is very good. ⁸If the Lord is pleased with us, he will lead us into that land. He will give us that land where much food grows. ⁹Don't turn against the Lord! Don't be afraid of the people in that land! We will chew them up. They have no protection, but we have the Lord. So don't be afraid of them."

Today's Prayer

Dear Lord, thank you for helping me do things that seem very hard to do. Give me the courage to always say the things that are right and good. In Christ I pray, amen.

Memory Verse
"The Lord says, 'I will make you wise. I will show you where to go. I will guide you and watch over you.'" Psalm 32:8

Wandering in the Desert

The people of Israel forgot about God's power and didn't listen to the good report Joshua and Caleb gave. So the Israelites had to wander in the desert for forty years.

²⁶The Lord said to Moses and Aaron, ²⁷"How long will these evil people complain about me? I have heard these Israelites' grumbling and complaining. ²⁸So tell them, 'This is what the Lord says. I heard what you said. As surely as I live, I will do those things to you. ²⁹You will die in this desert. Every one of you who is 20 years old or older and who was counted with the people will die. You complained against me, the Lord. ³⁰Not one of you will enter and live in the land I promised to you. Only Caleb son of Jephunneh and Joshua son of Nun will go in. ³¹You said that your children would be taken away.

But I will bring them into the land. They will enjoy what you refused. ³²As for you, you will die in this desert. ³³Your children will be shepherds here for 40 years. They will suffer because you were not loyal. They will suffer until you lie dead in the desert. ³⁴For 40 years you will suffer for your sins. That is a year for each of the 40 days you explored the land. You will know me as your enemy.' ³⁵I, the Lord, have spoken. I will certainly do these things to all these evil people. They have come together against me. So they will all die here in this desert."

³⁶The men Moses had sent to explore the land had returned. They had spread complaints among all the Israelites. They had given a bad report about the land. ³⁷They were responsible for the bad report. So the Lord killed them with a terrible sickness. ³⁸Only two of the men did not die. They were Joshua son of Nun and Caleb son of Jephunneh.

Today's Prayer

Holy Lord, thank you for being patient. Sometimes the things I want to do are not the things you want. Keep me from selfish thoughts. In Jesus' name, amen.

Memory Verse
"The Lord says, 'I will make you wise. I will show you where to go. I will guide you and watch over you.'" Psalm 32:8

Joshua Takes Over

Moses had served God long and faithfully, but now he was old. Israel needed a strong and courageous leader to take them into the promised land. However, Moses had some important last words for the people.

31 Then Moses went and spoke these words to all the Israelites: ²"I am now 120 years old. I cannot lead you anymore. The Lord told me I would not cross the Jordan River. ³The Lord your God will lead you across himself. He will destroy those nations for you. You will take over their land. Joshua will also lead you

across. This is what the Lord has said. ⁴The Lord will do to these nations what he did to Sihon and Og. They were the kings of the Amorites. He destroyed them and their land. ⁵The Lord will give those nations to you. Do to them everything I told you. ⁶Be strong and brave. Don't be afraid of them. Don't be frightened. The Lord your God will go with you. He will not leave you or forget you."

⁷Then Moses called Joshua and spoke to him in front of the people. Moses said, "Be strong and brave. Lead these people into the land the Lord promised to give their ancestors. Help the people take it as their own. ⁸The Lord himself will go before you. He will be with you. He will not leave you or forget you. Don't be afraid. Don't worry."

Today's Prayer

My God in heaven, help me to be brave and willing to serve you all my life as Joshua was. Be my friend as you were a friend to him. I pray in Jesus' name, amen.

Memory Verse
"The Lord says, 'I will make you wise. I will show you where to go. I will guide you and watch over you.'" Psalm 32:8

The Death of Moses

At last Moses' work was done. Before he died, God let him look over into the promised land to see Israel's future homeland.

34 Then Moses climbed up Mount Nebo. He went from the plains of Moab to the top of Mount Pisgah. It is across from Jericho. From there the Lord showed him all the land. He could see from Gilead to Dan.

⁴Then the Lord said to Moses, "This is the land I promised to Abraham, Isaac and Jacob. I said to them, 'I will give this land to your descendants.' I have let you look at it, Moses. But you will not cross over there."

⁵Then Moses, the servant of the Lord, died there in Moab. It was as the Lord had said. ⁶The Lord buried Moses in Moab in the valley opposite Beth Peor. But even today no one

knows where his grave is. ⁷Moses was 120 years old when he died. His eyes were not weak. And he was still strong. ⁸The Israelites cried for Moses for 30 days. They stayed in the plains of Moab until the time of sadness was over.

⁹Joshua son of Nun was then filled with wisdom. Moses had put his hands on Joshua. So the Israelites listened to Joshua. And they did what the Lord had commanded Moses.

¹⁰There has never been another prophet like Moses. The Lord knew Moses face to face. ¹¹The Lord sent Moses to do signs and miracles in Egypt. He did them to the king, to all his officers and to the whole land of Egypt. ¹²Moses had great power. He did wonderful things for all the Israelites to see.

Today's Prayer

Thank you, God, for giving Israel a home long ago and for making a home in heaven for me. Thank you for sending Jesus to lead me to that home. Help me always to follow him. I pray in his name, amen.

Memory Verse

"The Lord says, 'I will make you wise. I will show you where to go. I will guide you and watch over you.'" Psalm 32:8

Spies in Canaan

As Joshua prepared to capture Canaan, he sent two spies into Jericho. There they went to the house of a woman named Rahab.

²Someone told the king of Jericho, "Some men from Israel have come here tonight. They are spying out the land."

³So the king of Jericho sent this message to Rahab: "Bring out the men who came to you and entered your house. They have come to spy out our whole land."

⁴Now the woman had hidden the two men. She said, "They did come here. But I didn't know where they came from. ⁵In the evening, when it was time to close the city gate, they left. I don't know where they went. Go quickly. Maybe you can catch them." ⁶(But the woman had taken the men

up to the roof. She had hidden them there under stalks of flax. She had spread the flax out there to dry.) ⁷So the king's men went out looking for the spies from Israel. They went to the places where people cross the Jordan River. The city gate was closed just after the king's men left the city.

⁸The spies were ready to sleep for the night. So Rahab went to the roof and talked to them. ⁹She said, "I know the Lord has given this land to your people. You frighten us very much. Everyone living in this land is terribly afraid of you.' ¹³Promise me you will allow my family to live. Save my father, mother, brothers, sisters and all of their families from death."

¹⁴The men agreed. They said, "We will trade our lives for your lives. Don't tell anyone what we are doing. When the Lord gives us our land, we will be kind to you. You may trust us."

Today's Prayer

Thank you, God, for my family. Be with us and guide us and protect us from harm. This I pray in Jesus' name, amen.

Memory Verse
"Remember that I commanded you to be strong and brave. So don't be afraid. The Lord your God will be with you everywhere you go." Joshua 1:9

The Spies Escape

With Rahab's help, the spies escaped from the king's men and made their way back to Joshua with their report.

[15]The house Rahab lived in was built on the city wall. So she used a rope to let the men down through a window. [16]She said to them, "Go into the hills. The king's men will not find you there. Hide there for three days. After the king's men return, you may go on your way."

[17]The men said to her, "You must do as we say. If not, we cannot be responsible for keeping our promise. [18]You are using a red rope to help us escape. When we return to this land, you must tie it in the window through which you let us down. Bring your father, mother, brothers and all your family into your house. [19]We can keep

everyone safe who stays in this house. If anyone in your house is hurt, we will be responsible. If anyone goes out of your house and is killed, it is his own fault. We cannot be responsible for him. [20]But you must not tell anyone about this agreement. If you do, we are free from it."

[21]Rahab answered, "I agree to this." So she sent them away, and they left. Then she tied the red rope in the window.

[22]The men left and went into the hills. There they stayed for three days. The king's men looked for them all along the road. But after three days, the king's men returned to the city without finding them. [23]Then the two men started back to Joshua. They left the hills and crossed the river. They went to Joshua son of Nun and told him everything that had happened to them. [24]They said to Joshua, "The Lord surely has given us all of the land. All the people in that land are terribly afraid of us."

Today's Prayer

My Lord, teach me kindness and show me ways to help others who are in need. Thank you for the many ways you help me live each day. In Jesus' name, amen.

Memory Verse
"Remember that I commanded you to be strong and brave. So don't be afraid. The Lord your God will be with you everywhere you go." Joshua 1:9

Entering Canaan

After hearing the spies' report, Joshua was ready to lead Israel into Canaan. As they came to the edge of the Jordan River, once again God showed his great power in an unusual way.

⁷Then the Lord said to Joshua, "Today I will begin to make you a great man to all the Israelites. So the people will know I am with you just as I was with Moses. ⁸The priests will carry the Box of the Agreement. Tell them this: 'Go to the edge of the Jordan River and stand in the water.' "

¹⁴So the priests carried the Box of

the Agreement. And the people left the place where they had camped. Then they started across the Jordan River. [15]During harvest the Jordan is flooded. So the river was at its fullest. The priests who were carrying the Holy Box came to the edge of the river. And they stepped into the water. [16]Just at that moment, the water stopped flowing. It stood up in a heap a great distance away at Adam. This is a town near Zarethan. The water flowing down to the Sea of Arabah (the Dead Sea) was completely cut off. So the people crossed the river near Jericho. [17]The ground there became dry. The priests carried the Box of the Agreement with the Lord to the middle of the river and stopped. They waited there while all the people of Israel walked across. They crossed the Jordan River on dry land.

Today's Prayer

Almighty God, help me to have faith in you as Joshua did. I pray that, like Joshua, I may always trust your word and obey your commands. In the name of Jesus my Savior I pray, amen.

Memory Verse
"Remember that I commanded you to be strong and brave. So don't be afraid. The Lord your God will be with you everywhere you go." Joshua 1:9

The March on Jericho

God brought Israel safely across the Jordan River, but before them stood the great walled city of Jericho. God had a strange battle plan for capturing the city.

6Now the people of Jericho were afraid because the Israelites were near. So they closed the city gates and guarded them. No one went into the city. And no one came out.

²Then the Lord spoke to Joshua. He said, "Look, I have given you Jericho, its king and all its fighting men. ³March around the city with your army one time every day. Do this for six days. ⁴Have seven priests carry trumpets made from horns of male sheep. Tell them to march in front of the Holy Box. On the seventh day march around the city seven times. On that day tell the priests to blow the trumpets as they march. ⁵They

will make one long blast on the trumpets. When you hear that sound, have all the people give a loud shout. Then the walls of the city will fall. And the people will go straight into the city."

⁶So Joshua son of Nun called the priests together. He said to them, "Carry the Box of the Agreement with the Lord. Tell seven priests to carry trumpets and march in front of it." ⁷Then Joshua ordered the people, "Now go! March around the city. The soldiers with weapons should march in front of the Box of the Agreement with the Lord."

⁸So Joshua finished speaking to the people. Then the seven priests began marching before the Lord. They carried the seven trumpets and blew them as they marched. The priests carrying the Box of the Agreement with the Lord followed them. ⁹The soldiers with weapons marched in front of the priests. And armed men walked behind the Holy Box. They were blowing their trumpets.

Today's Prayer

Jehovah God, when I am faced with problems that seem too large, give me the faith to trust in you. Help me to follow your directions as Joshua did. In Jesus' name, amen.

Memory Verse
"Remember that I commanded you to be strong and brave. So don't be afraid. The Lord your God will be with you everywhere you go." Joshua 1:9

Jericho Falls

For six days the people of Israel marched around the city once each day, just as God had told them to do. What will happen on the seventh day?

¹⁵On the seventh day they got up at dawn. They marched around the city seven times. They marched just as they had on the days before. But on that day they marched around the city seven times. ¹⁶The seventh time around the priests blew their trumpets. Then Joshua gave the command: "Now, shout! The Lord has given you this city! ¹⁷The city and everything in it are to be destroyed as an offering to the Lord. Only Rahab the prostitute and everyone in her house should remain alive. They must not be killed. This is because Rahab hid the two spies we sent out. ¹⁸Don't take any of the things that are

to be destroyed as an offering to the Lord. If you take them and bring them into our camp, then you yourselves will be destroyed. You will also bring trouble to all of Israel. [19]All the silver and gold and things made from bronze and iron belong to the Lord. They must be saved for him."

[20]When the priests blew the trumpets, the people shouted. At the sound of the trumpets and the people's shout, the walls fell. And everyone ran straight into the city. So the Israelites defeated that city.

[25]Joshua saved Rahab the prostitute, her family and all who were with her. He let them live. This was because Rahab had helped the men he had sent to spy out Jericho. Rahab still lives among the Israelites today.

[27]So the Lord was with Joshua. And Joshua became famous through all the land.

Today's Prayer

Dear Lord, I am glad you are such a powerful God. I know you can do anything. Bless me, I pray in Jesus' name, amen.

Memory Verse
"Remember that I commanded you to be strong and brave. So don't be afraid. The Lord your God will be with you everywhere you go." Joshua 1:9

Achan Disobeys God

Mighty Jericho had fallen. The weak city of Ai was the next target, but this time Israel's army was defeated and chased from the town! Joshua knew he needed God's help to find why.

[10]The Lord said to Joshua, "Stand up! Why are you down on your face? [11]The Israelites have sinned. They have broken the agreement I commanded them to obey. They took some of the things I commanded them to destroy. They have stolen from me. They have lied. They have taken those things for themselves. [12]That is why the Israelites cannot face their enemies."

[17]So all the family groups of Judah stood before the Lord. The Lord then chose the family group of Zerah. And all the families of Zerah stood before the Lord. Then the family of Zimri was chosen. [18]And Joshua told all the

men in that family to come before the Lord. The Lord chose Achan son of Carmi.

¹⁹Then Joshua said to Achan, "My son, you should tell the truth. Confess to the Lord, the God of Israel. Tell me what you did. Don't try to hide anything from me."

²⁰Achan answered, "It is true! I have sinned against the Lord, the God of Israel. This is what I did: ²¹Among the things I saw was a beautiful coat from Babylonia. And I saw about five pounds of silver and more than one and one-quarter pounds of gold. I wanted these things very much for myself. So I took them. You will find them buried in the ground under my tent. The silver is under the coat."

²⁵Joshua said, "I don't know why you caused so much trouble for us. But now the Lord will bring trouble to you." Then all the people threw stones at Achan until he died.

Today's Prayer

Dear God in heaven, thank you for everything you have given me. Sometimes I want more than I need. Help me accept what I am given and not take anything that I should not have. In Jesus' name, amen.

Memory Verse
"Remember the Lord in everything you do. And he will give you success." Proverbs 3:6

Ai Is Captured

After Achan was punished for his sin, God gave Israel a second chance to take the city of Ai.

[11]All of the soldiers who were with Joshua marched to Ai. They stopped in front of the city and made camp north of Ai. There was a valley between them and the city. [12]Then Joshua chose about 5,000 men. He set them in ambush in the area west of the city between Bethel and Ai. [13]So the people took their positions. The main camp was north of the city. The other men were hiding to the west. That night Joshua went down into the valley.

[14]Now the king of Ai saw the army of Israel. So he and his people got up early the next morning and hurried out to fight them. They went out to a

place east of the city. The king did not know soldiers were waiting in ambush behind the city. [15]Joshua and all the men of Israel let the army of Ai push them back. Then they ran east toward the desert. [17]All the men of Ai and Bethel chased the army of Israel. The city was left open. Not a man stayed to protect it.

[18]Then the Lord said to Joshua, "Hold your spear toward Ai. I will give you that city." So Joshua held his spear toward the city of Ai. [19]The men of Israel who were in ambush saw this. They quickly came out of their hiding place and hurried toward the city. They entered the city and took control of it. Then they quickly set it on fire.

[20]When the men of Ai looked back, they saw smoke rising from their city. At the same time the men of Israel stopped running. They turned against the men of Ai. The men of Ai could not escape in any direction.

Today's Prayer

Dear loving God, thank you for being willing to give us another chance as you did the Israelites. When I am wrong, forgive me. Change my heart and help me try again. In the name of Jesus I pray, amen.

Memory Verse
"Remember the Lord in everything you do. And he will give you success." Proverbs 3:6

The Gibeonites' Trick

When all of the kings in the area heard about Joshua's defeat of Jericho and Ai, they decided to join forces against Israel. However, the people of Gibeon decided to take care of themselves.

[3]The people of Gibeon heard how Joshua had defeated Jericho and Ai. [4]So they decided to trick the Israelites. They gathered old leather wine bags that were cracked and mended. They put them on the backs of their donkeys. They also put old sacks on their donkeys. [5]The men put old san-

dals on their feet and wore old clothes. They took some dry, moldy bread. [6]Then they went to Joshua in the camp near Gilgal.

[12]"Look at our bread. When we left home it was warm and fresh. But now it is dry and moldy. [13]Look at our leather winebags. When we left home they were new and filled with wine. Now they are cracked and old. Look at our clothes and sandals. The long journey has almost destroyed them."

[14]The men of Israel tasted the bread. But they did not ask the Lord what to do. [15]So Joshua agreed to make peace with the Gibeonites. He agreed to let them live. The leaders of the Israelites made a promise to keep the agreement.

[16]Three days later the Israelites learned that the Gibeonites lived nearby.

[26]So Joshua saved their lives. He did not allow the Israelites to kill them.

Today's Prayer

Dear Lord, thank you for the strength you give to people who serve you. In any trouble I want to be on your side, not with those who turn away from you. I pray in Jesus' name, amen.

Memory Verse

"Remember the Lord in everything you do. And he will give you success." Proverbs 3:6

The Sun Stands Still!

Fierce Amorite kings attacked the Gibeonites because of their peace agreement with Israel. When Joshua heard of the attack, he and his army came to rescue them.

⁷So Joshua marched out of Gilgal with his whole army. His best fighting men were with him. ⁸The Lord said to Joshua, "Don't be afraid of those armies. I will allow you to defeat them. None of them will be able to defeat you."

⁹Joshua and his army marched all night to Gibeon. So Joshua surprised them when he attacked. ¹¹They chased the enemy down the road from Beth Horon to Azekah. While they were chasing them, the Lord threw large hailstones on them from the sky. Many of the enemy were killed by the hailstones. More men were killed by the hailstones than the

Israelites killed with their swords.

¹²That day the Lord allowed the Israelites to defeat the Amorites. And that day Joshua stood before all the people of Israel and said to the Lord:

"Sun, stand still over Gibeon.

Moon, stand still over the Valley of Aijalon."

¹³So the sun stood still.

And the moon stopped

until the people defeated

their enemies.

These words are written in the Book of Jashar.

The sun stopped in the middle of the sky. It waited to go down for a full day. ¹⁴That has never happened at any time before that day or since. That was the day the Lord listened to a man. Truly the Lord was fighting for Israel!

Today's Prayer

Thank you, dear Lord, for showing us your great power. Help me always to be a person who can be counted on to follow where you lead. In the name of Christ Jesus, amen.

Memory Verse
"Remember the Lord in everything you do. And he will give you success." Proverbs 3:6

Joshua's Farewell

Joshua was now an old man who had served the Lord well. He knew he would soon die, so he called Israel together to make an agreement for them to serve God.

¹⁴Then Joshua spoke to the people. He said, "Now you have heard the Lord's words. So you must respect the Lord and serve him fully and sincerely. Throw away the false gods that your people worshiped. That happened on the other side of the Euphrates River and in Egypt. Now you must serve the Lord. ¹⁵But maybe you don't want to serve the Lord. You must choose for yourselves today. You must decide whom you will serve. You may serve the gods that your people worshiped when they lived on the other side of the Euphrates River. Or you may serve the gods of the Amorites who lived in this

land. As for me and my family, we will serve the Lord."

[16]Then the people answered, "No! We will never stop following the Lord. We will never serve other gods! [17]We know it was the Lord our God who brought our people out of Egypt. We were slaves in that land. But the Lord did great things for us there. He brought us out. He protected us while we traveled through other lands. [18]Then he helped us defeat the people living in these lands. He helped us defeat the Amorites who lived here. So we will continue to serve the Lord because he is our God."

[24]Then the people said to Joshua, "We will serve the Lord our God. We will obey him."

[28]Then Joshua told the people to go back to their homes. And everyone went back to his own land.

[29]After that, Joshua son of Nun died. He was 110 years old.

Today's Prayer

Dear God thank you for faithful men like Joshua. I want to be like him and say I will always serve you. Give me the heart and will to put service to you first in my life. In Jesus' name, amen.

Memory Verse
"Remember the Lord in everything you do. And he will give you success." Proverbs 3:6

Deborah Leads Israel

When the people forgot God, he allowed their enemies to capture them. When they turned back to him, he sent judges to rescue them. One of these judges was a woman named Deborah.

⁴There was a prophetess named Deborah. She was the wife of Lappi- doth. She was judge of Israel at that time. ⁵Deborah would sit under the Palm Tree of Deborah. This was be- tween the cities of Ramah and Bethel, in the mountains of Ephraim. And the people of Israel would come to her to settle their arguments.

⁶Deborah sent a message to a man named Barak. He was the son of Abi- noam. Barak lived in the city of Ke- desh, which is in the area of Naphtali. Deborah said to Barak, "The Lord, the God of Israel, commands you: 'Go and gather 10,000 men of Naphtali and Zebulun. Lead them to Mount

Tabor. ⁷I will make Sisera, the commander of Jabin's army, come to you. Sisera, his chariots and his army will meet you at the Kishon River. I will help you to defeat Sisera there.' "

⁸Then Barak said to Deborah, "I will go if you will go with me. But if you will not go with me, I won't go."

⁹"Of course I will go with you," Deborah answered. "But you will not get credit for the victory. The Lord will let a woman defeat Sisera." So Deborah went with Barak to Kedesh.

¹⁴Then Deborah said to Barak, "Get up! Today is the day the Lord will help you defeat Sisera. You know the Lord has already cleared the way for you." So Barak led 10,000 men down from Mount Tabor. ¹⁵He and his men attacked Sisera and his men. During the battle the Lord confused Sisera and his army and chariots. So Barak and his men used their swords to defeat Sisera's army. But Sisera left his chariot and ran away on foot.

Today's Prayer

Dear God, our father, be with our leaders so that they can guide us as they should. Help me to obey those you have chosen to lead me. In Jesus' name, amen.

Memory Verse
"I look up to the hills. But where does my help come from? My help comes from the Lord. He made heaven and earth." Psalm 121:1,2

Gideon Chooses an Army

After the time of Deborah, the fierce and cruel Midianites captured Israel and destroyed their crops and animals. God chose Gideon to rescue them. Gideon chose a great army, but God had other, surprising plans.

²Then the Lord said to Gideon, "You have too many men to defeat the Midianites. I don't want the Israelites to brag that they saved themselves. ³So now, announce to the people, 'Anyone who is afraid may leave Mount Gilead. He may go back home.' " And 22,000 men went back home. But 10,000 remained.

⁴Then the Lord said to Gideon, "There are still too many men. Take the men down to the water, and I will test them for you there. If I say, 'This man will go with you,' he will go. But if I say, 'That one will not go with you,' he will not go."

⁵So Gideon led the men down to the

water. There the Lord said to him, "Separate them. Those who drink water by lapping it up like a dog will be in one group. Those who bend down to drink will be in the other group." ⁶There were 300 men who used their hands to bring water to their mouths. They lapped it as a dog does. All the rest got down on their knees to drink.

⁷Then the Lord said to Gideon, "I will save you, using the 300 men who lapped the water. And I will allow you to defeat Midian. Let all the other men go to their homes." ⁸So Gideon sent the rest of Israel to their homes. But he kept 300 men. He took the jars and the trumpets of those who went home.

Now the camp of Midian was in the valley below Gideon. ⁹That night the Lord spoke to Gideon. He said, "Get up. Go down and attack the camp of the Midianites. I will allow you to defeat them."

Today's Prayer

Dear Lord, even leaders need to have you in charge. Help me to be a good follower when I need to be. Teach me to be a leader also so that I can bring others to you. In the name of Jesus, amen.

Memory Verse
"I look up to the hills. But where does my help come from? My help comes from the Lord. He made heaven and earth." Psalm 121:1,2

Gideon Defeats Midian

God sent Gideon and his servant into the Midianite camp to hear what they were saying. When Gideon came to the camp, he heard two Midianites discussing a strange dream, a dream that God would let Gideon win the battle.

[15]When Gideon heard about the dream and what it meant, he worshiped God. Then Gideon went back to the camp of Israel. He called out to them, "Get up! The Lord has defeated the army of Midian for you!" [16]Then Gideon divided the 300 men into three groups. He gave each man a trumpet and an empty jar. A burning torch was inside each jar.

[17]Gideon told the men, "Watch me and do what I do. When I get to the edge of the camp, do what I do. [18]Surround the enemy camp. I and everyone with me will blow our trumpets. When we blow our trumpets, you blow your trumpets, too. Then

shout, 'For the Lord and for Gideon!' "

[19]So Gideon and the 100 men with him came to the edge of the enemy camp. They came just after the enemy had changed guards. It was during the middle watch of the night. Then Gideon and his men blew their trumpets and smashed their jars. [20]All three groups of Gideon's men blew their trumpets and smashed their jars. They held the torches in their left hands and the trumpets in their right hands. Then they shouted, "A sword for the Lord and for Gideon!" [21]Each of Gideon's men stayed in his place around the camp. But inside the camp, the men of Midian began shouting and running away.

[22]When Gideon's 300 men blew their trumpets, the Lord caused all the men of Midian to fight each other with their swords! The enemy army ran away to the city of Beth Shittah.

Today's Prayer

Almighty God, thank you for hearing me when I ask for your help. Make me a good listener so I may hear your word and win victories in your name. Through Jesus I pray, amen.

Memory Verse
"I look up to the hills. But where does my help come from? My help comes from the Lord. He made heaven and earth." Psalm 121:1,2

Delilah Betrays Samson

Samson was a man of great strength who had killed many Philistines, Israel's enemies. A woman named Delilah had tried three times to find the secret of Samson's strength so she could sell the secret to his enemies. But each time Samson had fooled her.

¹⁵Then Delilah said to him, "How can you say, 'I love you,' when you don't even trust me? This is the third time you have made me look foolish. You haven't told me the secret of your great strength." ¹⁶She kept bothering Samson about his secret day after day. He became so tired of it he felt he was going to die!

¹⁷So he told her everything. He said, "I have never had my hair cut. I have been set apart to God as a Nazirite since I was born. If someone shaved my head, then I would lose my strength. I would become as weak as any other man."

¹⁸Delilah saw that he had told her

everything sincerely. So she sent a message to the kings of the Philistines. She said, "Come back one more time. He has told me everything." So the kings of the Philistines came back to Delilah. They brought the silver they had promised to give her. [19]Delilah got Samson to go to sleep. He was lying in her lap. Then she called in a man to shave off the seven braids of Samson's hair. In this way she began to make him weak. And Samson's strength left him.

[20]Then she called out to him, "Samson, the Philistines are about to capture you!"

He woke up and thought, "I'll get loose as I did before and shake myself free." But he did not know that the Lord had left him.

[21]Then the Philistines captured Samson. They tore out his eyes. And they took him down to Gaza. They put bronze chains on him. They put him in prison and made him grind grain.

Today's Prayer

Dear God, thank you for loving me when I am strong but also when I am weak. Help me not to think I am so strong that I can take care of everything by myself. In Jesus' name, amen.

Memory Verse
"I look up to the hills. But where does my help come from? My help comes from the Lord. He made heaven and earth." Psalm 121:1,2

Samson Dies

Though Samson was blind, in prison, and working like an animal, he had not given up. His hair began to grow again.

²³The kings of the Philistines gathered to celebrate. They were going to offer a great sacrifice to their god Dagon. They said, "Our god has given us Samson our enemy."

²⁵The people were having a good time at the celebration. They said "Bring Samson out to perform for us." So they brought Samson from the

prison. He performed for them. They made him stand between the pillars of the temple of Dagon. [26]A servant was holding his hand. Samson said to him, "Let me feel the pillars that hold up the temple. I want to lean against them." [27]Now the temple was full of men and women. All the kings of the Philistines were there. There were about 3,000 men and women on the roof. They watched Samson perform. [28]Then Samson prayed to the Lord. He said, "Lord God, remember me. God, please give me strength one more time. Let me pay these Philistines back for putting out my two eyes!" [29]Then Samson held the two center pillars of the temple. These two pillars supported the whole temple. He braced himself between the two pillars. His right hand was on one, and his left hand was on the other. [30]Samson said, "Let me die with these Philistines!" Then he pushed as hard as he could. And the temple fell on the kings and all the people in it. So Samson killed more of the Philistines when he died than when he was alive.

Today's Prayer

Dear Lord, when days are their darkest, you bring light. I need you to make me strong and to light the roads I travel. Guide me through Jesus your son, the light of the world, amen.

Memory Verse
"I look up to the hills. But where does my help come from? My help comes from the Lord. He made heaven and earth." Psalm 121:1,2

Ruth and Naomi

Ruth and her mother-in-law Naomi moved to Israel after both their husbands died. In order to get food, Ruth gathered the grain that was left behind by the field workers of a rich man named Boaz. One day Boaz spoke to Ruth.

¹⁰Then Ruth bowed low with her face to the ground. She said to Boaz, "I am a stranger. Why have you been so kind to notice me?"

¹¹Boaz answered her, "I know about all the help you have given to Naomi, your mother-in-law. You helped her even after your husband died. You left your father and mother and your own country. You came to this nation where you did not know anyone. ¹²The Lord will reward you for all you have done. You will be paid in full by the Lord, the God of Israel. You have come to him as a little bird finds shelter under the wings of its mother."

¹⁷So Ruth gathered grain in the field

until evening. Then she separated the grain from the chaff. There was about one-half bushel of barley.

[19]Naomi asked her, "Where did you gather all this grain today? Where did you work? Blessed be the man who noticed you!"

Ruth told her about whose field she had worked in. She said, "The man I worked with today is named Boaz."

[20]Naomi told her daughter-in-law, "The Lord bless him! The Lord still continues to be kind to all people—the living and the dead!" Then Naomi told Ruth, "Boaz is one of our close relatives, one who will take care of us."

[23]So Ruth continued working closely with the women servants of Boaz. She gathered grain until the barley harvest was finished. She also worked there through the end of the wheat harvest. And Ruth continued to live with Naomi, her mother-in-law.

Today's Prayer

Thank you, Lord, for being my friend. I can always depend on you. Teach me to be loyal to you and my friends as Ruth was loyal to Naomi. I pray in the name of Jesus, my best friend, amen.

Memory Verse
"You must decide whom you will serve. As for me and my family, we will serve the Lord."
Joshua 24:15

Ruth Marries Boaz

Boaz fell in love with Ruth and decided to marry her. He called together the village leaders to tell them he was going to take care of Ruth and Naomi and protect their property. Many years later Ruth's grandson would become a famous king.

⁹Then Boaz spoke to the older leaders and to all the people. He said, "You are witnesses today of what I am buying from Naomi. I am buying everything that belonged to Elimelech and Kilion and Mahlon. ¹⁰I am also taking Ruth as my wife. She is the Moabite who was the wife of Mahlon. I am doing this so her dead husband's property will stay with his family. This way, his name will not be separated from his family and his land. You are witnesses this day."

¹¹So all the people and older leaders who were at the city gate said, "We are witnesses. This woman will be coming into your home. We hope

the Lord will make her like Rachel and Leah. They had many children. So the people of Israel grew in number. May you become powerful in the district of Ephrathah. May you become famous in Bethlehem!"

¹³So Boaz took Ruth and married her. The Lord let her become pregnant, and she gave birth to a son. ¹⁴The women told Naomi, "Praise the Lord who gave you this grandson. And may he become famous in Israel. ¹⁵He will give you new life. And he will take care of you in your old age. This happened because of your daughter-in-law. She loves you. And she is better for you than seven sons. She has given birth to your grandson."

¹⁶Naomi took the boy, held him in her arms and cared for him. ¹⁷The neighbors gave the boy his name. These women said, "This boy was born for Naomi." The neighbors named him Obed. Obed was Jesse's father. And Jesse was the father of David.

Today's Prayer

Give me strength, dear God, to do what is right and to protect the rights of those who need my help. Help me to be kind as Boaz was kind to Ruth and Naomi. In the name of Jesus, amen.

Memory Verse
"You must decide whom you will serve. As for me and my family, we will serve the Lord."
Joshua 24:15

Samuel Is Born

Hannah wanted a son more than anything else in the world, but she couldn't have children. She and her husband Elkanah traveled to Shiloh to pray at the Lord's Holy Tent, asking God for a son.

[9]Once, after they had eaten their meal in Shiloh, Hannah got up. Now Eli the priest was sitting on a chair near the entrance to the Lord's Holy Tent. [10]Hannah was very sad. She cried much and prayed to the Lord. [11]She made a promise. She said, "Lord of heaven's armies, see how bad I feel. Remember me! Don't forget me.

If you will give me a son, I will give him back to you all his life. And no one will ever use a razor to cut his hair."

²⁰So Hannah became pregnant, and in time she gave birth to a son. She named him Samuel. She said, "His name is Samuel because I asked the Lord for him."

²⁴When Samuel was old enough to eat, Hannah took him to the Tent of the Lord at Shiloh. She also took a three-year-old bull, one-half bushel of flour and a leather bag filled with wine. ²⁵They killed the bull for the sacrifice. Then Hannah brought Samuel to Eli. ²⁶She said to Eli, "As surely as you live, my master, I am the same woman who stood near you praying to the Lord. ²⁷I prayed for this child. The Lord answered my prayer and gave him to me. ²⁸Now I give him back to the Lord. He will belong to the Lord all his life." And he worshiped the Lord there.

Today's Prayer

My heavenly father, thank you for listening to my prayers. I know you hear me when I pray as you heard Hannah long ago. I know you give us good gifts. Help me trust you each day. In Jesus' name, amen.

Memory Verse
"You must decide whom you will serve. As for me and my family, we will serve the Lord."
Joshua 24:15

God Talks to Samuel

The boy Samuel served the Lord under Eli the priest. One night, as Samuel was sleeping, God spoke to him and told him what he planned to do in Israel. So Samuel became a prophet of the Lord.

[4]Then the Lord called Samuel. Samuel answered, "I am here!" [5]He ran to Eli and said, "I am here. You called me."

But Eli said, "I didn't call you. Go back to bed." So Samuel went back to bed.

[6]The Lord called again, "Samuel!"

Samuel again went to Eli and said, "I am here. You called me."

Again Eli said, "I didn't call you. Go back to bed."

[7]Samuel did not yet know the Lord. The Lord had not spoken directly to him yet.

[8]The Lord called Samuel for the third time. Samuel got up and went

to Eli. He said, "I am here. You called me."

Then Eli realized the Lord was calling the boy. 9So he told Samuel, "Go to bed. If he calls you again, say, 'Speak, Lord. I am your servant, and I am listening.' " So Samuel went and lay down in bed.

10The Lord came and stood there. He called as he had before. He said, "Samuel, Samuel!"

Samuel said, "Speak, Lord. I am your servant, and I am listening."

11The Lord said to Samuel, "See, I am going to do something in Israel. It will shock those who hear about it."

19The Lord was with Samuel as he grew up. He did not let any of Samuel's messages fail to come true. 20Then all Israel, from Dan to Beersheba, knew Samuel was a prophet of the Lord.

Today's Prayer

How great you are, O God. Show me how to serve you and obey your will. Help me to be ready to listen to you and to serve you faithfully. This I ask in the name of Jesus, amen.

Memory Verse
"You must decide whom you will serve. As for me and my family, we will serve the Lord."
Joshua 24:15

God Chooses Saul

The people of Israel wanted a king to rule them, as the other nations had. So God chose a young man from the tribe of Benjamin. But when Samuel called the people together to show them their new king, he couldn't be found!

[17]Samuel called all the people of Israel to meet with the Lord at Mizpah. [18]He said, "This is what the Lord, the God of Israel, says: 'I led Israel out of Egypt. I saved you from Egypt's control. And I saved you from other kingdoms that were troubling you.' [19]But now you have rejected your God. He saves you from all your troubles and problems. But you said, 'No! We want a king to rule over us.' Now come, stand before the Lord in your tribes and family groups."

[20]Samuel brought all the tribes of Israel near. And the tribe of Benjamin was chosen. [21]Samuel had them pass by in family groups, and Matri's

family was chosen. Then he had each man of Matri's family pass by. And Saul son of Kish was chosen. But when they looked for Saul, they could not find him. ²²Then they asked the Lord, "Has Saul come here yet?"

The Lord said, "Yes. He's hiding behind the baggage."

²³So they ran and brought him out. When Saul stood among the people, he was a head taller than anyone else. ²⁴Then Samuel said to the people, "See the man the Lord has chosen. There is no one like him among all the people."

Then the people shouted, "Long live the king!"

²⁵Samuel explained the rights and duties of the king. He wrote the rules in a book and put the book before the Lord. Then he told the people to go to their homes.

Today's Prayer

Holy Lord, how you love your people. You have given us Jesus to be king over our lives. Help me to serve him as a loyal subject and a friend. It is in his name I pray, amen.

Memory Verse
"You must decide whom you will serve. As for me and my family, we will serve the Lord."
Joshua 24:15

Goliath Challenges Israel

Mighty King Saul was leading Israel's army against the Philistines, their longtime enemies.

17 The Philistines gathered their armies for war. They met at Socoh in Judah. Their camp was at Ephes Dammim between Socoh and Azekah. ²Saul and the Israelites gathered in the Valley of Elah. And they camped there. They took their positions to fight the Philistines. ³The Philistines controlled one hill. The Israelites controlled another. The valley was between them.

⁴The Philistines had a champion fighter named Goliath. He was from Gath. He was about nine feet four inches tall. He came out of the Philistine camp. ⁵He had a bronze helmet on his head. And he wore a coat of

scale armor. It was made of bronze and weighed about 125 pounds. ⁶He wore bronze protectors on his legs. And he had a small spear of bronze tied on his back. ⁷The wooden part of his larger spear was like a weaver's rod. And its blade weighed about 15 pounds. The officer who carried his shield walked in front of him.

⁸Goliath stood and shouted to the Israelite soldiers, "Why have you taken positions for battle? I am a Philistine, and you are Saul's servants! Choose a man and send him to fight me. ⁹If he can fight and kill me, we will become your servants. But if I defeat and kill him, you will become our servants." ¹⁰Then he said, "Today I stand and dare the army of Israel! Send one of your men to fight me!" ¹¹When Saul and the Israelites heard the Philistine's words, they were very afraid.

¹⁶The Philistine Goliath came out every morning and evening. He stood before the Israelite army. This continued for 40 days.

Today's Prayer

Dear God, sometimes problems come in giant sizes that are too large for me alone. Teach me not to fear them but to trust in your power. Thank you for loving me. In Jesus' name, amen.

Memory Verse
"Trust the Lord with all your heart. Don't depend on your own understanding. Remember the Lord in everything you do. And he will give you success."
Proverbs 3:5,6

David Goes to Saul

David was a young shepherd, who had brought food for his brothers in Saul's army. When he heard Goliath's challenge, David decided to do something about it.

³²David said to Saul, "Don't let any one be discouraged. I, your servant, will go and fight this Philistine!"

³³Saul answered, "You can't go out against this Philistine and fight him. You're only a boy. Goliath has been a warrior since he was a young man."

³⁴But David said to Saul, "I, your servant, have been keeping my father's sheep. When a lion or bear came and took a sheep from the flock, ³⁵I would chase·it. I would attack it and save the sheep from its mouth. When it attacked me, I caught it by its fur. I would hit it and kill it. ³⁶I, your servant, have killed both a lion and a bear! Goliath, the Philistine who is

not circumcised, will be like the lion or bear I killed. He will die because he has stood against the armies of the living God. [37]The Lord saved me from a lion and a bear. He will also save me from this Philistine."

Saul said to David, "Go, and may the Lord be with you." [38]Saul put his own clothes on David. He put a bronze helmet on David's head and armor on his body. [39]David put on Saul's sword and tried to walk around. But he was not used to all the armor Saul had put on him.

He said to Saul, "I can't go in this. I'm not used to it." Then David took it all off. [40]He took his stick in his hand. And he chose five smooth stones from a stream. He put them in his pouch and held his sling in his hand. Then he went to meet Goliath.

Today's Prayer

Almighty God, help me to be strong and to trust you. When people around me don't respect you, it is sometimes hard to stand alone. Teach me always to honor your name. I pray in Jesus' name, amen.

Memory Verse
"Trust the Lord with all your heart. Don't depend on your own understanding. Remember the Lord in everything you do. And he will give you success." Proverbs 3:5,6

David Fights Goliath

David had gone to fight Goliath with only a sling and five smooth stones to protect himself, but he had God on his side.

⁴²Goliath looked at David. He saw that David was only a boy, tanned and handsome. He looked down at David with disgust. ⁴³He said, "Do you think I am a dog, that you come at me with a stick?" He used his gods' names to curse David. ⁴⁴He said to David, "Come here. I'll feed your body to the birds of the air and the wild animals!"

⁴⁵But David said to him, "You come to me using a sword, a large spear and a small spear. But I come to you in the name of the Lord of heaven's armies. He's the God of the armies of Israel! You have spoken out against him. ⁴⁶Today the Lord will give you to me. I'll kill you, and I'll cut off your

head. Today I'll feed the bodies of the Philistine soldiers to the birds of the air and the wild animals. Then all the world will know there is a God in Israel! ⁴⁷Everyone gathered here will know the Lord does not need swords or spears to save people. The battle belongs to him! And he will help us defeat all of you."

⁴⁸As Goliath came near to attack him, David ran quickly to meet him. ⁴⁹He took a stone from his pouch. He put it into his sling and slung it. The stone hit the Philistine on his forehead and sank into it. Goliath fell facedown on the ground.

⁵⁰So David defeated the Philistine with only a sling and a stone! He hit him and killed him. He did not even have a sword in his hand. ⁵¹David ran and stood beside the Philistine. He took Goliath's sword out of its holder and killed him. Then he cut off Goliath's head.

When the Philistines saw that their champion was dead, they turned and ran.

Today's Prayer

Loving God, when problems come, I sometimes feel alone and outnumbered. Help me understand that you are always with me and will give me strength. This I pray in Jesus' name, amen.

Memory Verse
"Trust the Lord with all your heart. Don't depend on your own understanding. Remember the Lord in everything you do. And he will give you success."
Proverbs 3:5,6

David and Jonathan

As David became more popular, King Saul became jealous and afraid of him. Saul tried to kill David, but Saul's son, Jonathan, was a good and true friend to David. He arranged to signal David if the king were still angry.

[32]Jonathan asked his father, "Why should David be killed? What wrong has he done?" [33]Then Saul threw his spear at Jonathan, trying to kill him. So Jonathan knew that his father really wanted to kill David. [34]Jonathan was very angry and left the table. That second day of the month he refused to eat. He was upset about what his father wanted to do to David.

[35]The next morning Jonathan went out to the field. He went to meet David as they had agreed. He had a young boy with him. [36]Jonathan said to the boy, "Run and find the arrows I shoot." When he ran, Jonathan shot an arrow beyond him. [37]The boy ran

to the place where Jonathan's arrow fell. But Jonathan called, "The arrow is beyond you!" ³⁸Then he shouted, "Hurry! Go quickly! Don't stop!" The boy picked up the arrow and brought it back to his master. ⁴⁰Then Jonathan gave his weapons to the boy. He told him, "Go back to town."

⁴¹When the boy left, David came out from the south side of the rock. He bowed facedown on the ground before Jonathan. He did this three times. Then David and Jonathan kissed each other. They cried together, but David cried the most.

⁴²Jonathan said to David, "Go in peace. We have promised by the Lord that we will be friends. We said, 'The Lord will be a witness between you and me, and between our descendants forever.'" Then David left, and Jonathan went back to town.

Today's Prayer

Dear Lord, give me friends like Jonathan, and when they are not with me, remind me that Jesus is always my friend and I am never alone. In his name I pray, amen.

Memory Verse

"Trust the Lord with all your heart. Don't depend on your own understanding. Remember the Lord in everything you do. And he will give you success."
Proverbs 3:5,6

Saul Chases David

Saul continued to try to kill David, but David still honored Saul as king. To prove his loyalty, David slipped into Saul's camp and took the king's spear and water jug, but didn't harm the king.

¹³David crossed over to the other side of the hill. He stood on top of the mountain far from Saul's camp. David's and Saul's camps were far apart. ¹⁴David shouted to the army and to Abner son of Ner, "Answer me, Abner!"

Abner answered, "Who is calling for the king? Who are you?"

¹⁵David said, "You're the greatest man in Israel. Isn't that true? Then why didn't you guard your master the king? Someone came into your camp to kill your master the king! ¹⁶What you have done is not good. As surely as the Lord lives, you and your men should die. You haven't guarded your master, the Lord's appointed king.

Look! Where are the king's spear and water jug that were near his head?"

[17]Saul knew David's voice. He said, "Is that your voice, David my son?"

David answered, "Yes, it is, my master and king." [18]David also said, "Why are you chasing me, my master? What wrong have I done? What evil am I guilty of? [19]My master and king, listen to me. If the Lord caused you to be angry with me, let him accept an offering. But if men caused you to be angry with me, let the Lord curse them! They have made me leave the land the Lord gave me. They have told me, 'Go and serve other gods.' [20]Now don't let me die far away from the Lord's presence. The king of Israel has come out looking for a flea! You're like a man hunting a partridge bird in the mountains!"

[21]Then Saul said, "I have sinned. Come back, David my son. Today you respected my life. So I will not try to hurt you. I have acted foolishly. I have made a big mistake."

Today's Prayer

God in heaven, when people are unkind or treat me badly, help me to return good for evil, as David did. Teach me to forgive them as you forgive me. In Jesus' name I pray, amen.

Memory Verse
"Trust the Lord with all your heart. Don't depend on your own understanding. Remember the Lord in everything you do. And he will give you success."
Proverbs 3:5,6

David Becomes King

After Saul died, David became king of all Israel. David loved and trusted God, so God helped Israel and made it a powerful kingdom.

[4]David was 30 years old when he became king. He ruled 40 years. [5]He was king over Judah in Hebron for 7 years and 6 months. And he was king over all Israel and Judah in Jerusalem for 33 years.

[6]The king and his men went to Jerusalem to attack the Jebusites who lived there. The Jebusites said to David, "You can't come into our city. Even our people who are blind and crippled can stop you." They said this because they thought David could not enter their city. [7]But David did take the city of Jerusalem with its strong walls. It became the City of David.

⁸That day David said to his men, "To defeat the Jebusites you must go through the water tunnel. Then you can reach those 'crippled' and 'blind' enemies. This is why people say, 'The blind and the crippled cannot enter the palace.' "

⁹So David lived in the city with its strong walls. He called it the City of David. David built more buildings around it. He began where the land was filled in on the east side of the city. He also built more buildings inside the city. ¹⁰He became stronger and stronger, because the Lord of heaven's armies was with him.

¹¹Hiram king of the city of Tyre sent messengers to David. He also sent cedar logs, carpenters and men to cut stone. They built a palace for David. ¹²Then David knew the Lord really had made him king of Israel. And he knew the Lord had made his kingdom very important. This was because the Lord loved his people, the Israelites.

Today's Prayer

Dear God in heaven, thank you for loving your people so much. I know that loving you and trusting you will give me strength. Please forgive me when I have done wrong. I pray in Jesus' name, amen.

Memory Verse
"Only the Lord gives wisdom. Knowledge and understanding come from him." Proverbs 2:6

Solomon's Wisdom

Solomon loved God, as his father David had. One night God came to Solomon in a dream with an amazing gift.

⁵While he was at Gibeon, the Lord came to him in a dream during the night. God said, "Ask for anything you want. I will give it to you."

⁶Solomon answered, "You were very kind to your servant, my father David. He obeyed you. He was honest and lived right. And you showed great kindness to him when you allowed his son to be king after him. ⁷Lord my God, you have allowed me to be king in my father's place. But I am like a little child. I do not have the wisdom I need to do what I must do. ⁸I, your servant, am here among your chosen people. There are too many of them to count. ⁹So I ask that you give me

wisdom. Then I can rule the people in the right way. Then I will know the difference between right and wrong. Without wisdom, it is impossible to rule this great people of yours."

[10]The Lord was pleased that Solomon had asked him for this. [11]So God said to him, "You did not ask for a long life. And you did not ask for riches for yourself. You did not ask for the death of your enemies. Since you asked for wisdom to make the right decisions, [12]I will give you what you asked. I will give you wisdom and understanding. Your wisdom will be greater than anyone has had in the past. And there will never be anyone in the future like you. [13]Also, I will give you what you did not ask for. You will have riches and honor. During your life no other king will be as great as you. [14]I ask you to follow me and obey my laws and commands. Do this as your father David did. If you do, I will also give you a long life."

Today's Prayer

O Lord, thank you for being able to talk to you through prayer. I ask for wisdom to make decisions that will always please you. In the name of Christ Jesus I pray, amen.

Memory Verse
"Only the Lord gives wisdom. Knowledge and understanding come from him." Proverbs 2:6

A Wise Decision

God blessed Solomon with great wisdom, and he used his wisdom to settle arguments between the people. One day when two women came before him, he gave a strange answer.

[17]One of the women said, "My master, this woman and I live in the same house. I gave birth to a baby while she was there with me. [18]Three days later this woman also gave birth to a baby. No one else was in the house with us. There were only the two of us. [19]One night this woman rolled over on her baby, and it died. [20]So during the night she took my son from my bed while I was asleep. She carried him to her bed. Then she put the dead baby in my bed. [21]The next morning I got up to feed my baby. But I saw that he was dead! Then I looked at him more closely. I saw that he was not my son."

²²But the other woman said, "No! The living baby is my son. The dead baby is yours!"

²³Then King Solomon said, "Each of you says the living baby is your own. And each of you says the dead baby belongs to the other woman."

²⁴Then King Solomon sent his servants to get a sword. When they brought it to him, ²⁵he said, "Cut the living baby into two pieces. Give each woman half of the baby."

²⁶The real mother of the living child was full of love for her son. She said to the king, "Please, my master, don't kill him! Give the baby to her!"

But the other woman said, "Neither of us will have him. Cut him into two pieces!"

²⁷Then King Solomon said, "Give the baby to the first woman. Don't kill him. She is the real mother."

²⁸When the people of Israel heard about King Solomon's decision, they respected him very much. They saw he had wisdom from God to make the right decisions.

Today's Prayer

Dear loving God, thank you for helping me make good decisions. Give me the wisdom to be fair and not be selfish. In Jesus' name, amen.

Memory Verse

"Only the Lord gives wisdom. Knowledge and understanding come from him." Proverbs 2:6

The Queen of Sheba

The Lord blessed Solomon as he had promised, and Solomon became rich. He built a beautiful temple for the Lord and a palace for the king. Soon Solomon's fame spread throughout the world.

10Now the queen of Sheba heard about Solomon's fame. So she came to test him with hard questions. ²She traveled to Jerusalem with a very large group of servants. There were many camels carrying spices, jewels and much gold. She came to Solomon and talked with him about all that she had in mind. ³Solomon answered all her questions. Nothing was too hard for him to explain to her. ⁴The queen of Sheba learned that Solomon was very wise. She saw the palace he had built. ⁵She saw his many officers and the food on his table. She saw the palace servants and their good clothes. She was shown the servants who served him at feasts. And she was shown the whole burnt offerings he made in the Temple of the Lord. All these things amazed her.

⁶So she said to King Solomon, "I heard in my own country about your achievements and wisdom. And all of it is true. ⁷I could not believe it then. But now I have come and seen it with my own eyes. I was not told even half of it! Your wisdom and wealth are much greater than I had heard. ⁸Your men and officers are very lucky! In always serving you, they are able to hear your wisdom! ⁹Praise the Lord your God! He was pleased to make you king of Israel. The Lord has constant love for Israel. So he made you king to keep justice and to rule fairly."

¹⁰Then the queen of Sheba gave the king about 9,000 pounds of gold. She also gave him many spices and jewels. No one since that time has brought more spices into Israel than the queen of Sheba gave King Solomon.

Today's Prayer

Dear God, thank you for the wonders of the world around us. Thank you for the beautiful things we see each day—the sky, the stars, the flowers. Help me remember that I am beautiful to you. In Jesus' name, amen.

Memory Verse

"Only the Lord gives wisdom. Knowledge and understanding come from him." Proverbs 2:6

Wise Words

The people of Israel respected Solomon's wisdom. He wrote many wise sayings which were collected with other teachings to form the book of Proverbs.

2 My child, believe what I say.
And remember what I command you.
[2] Listen to wisdom.
Try with all your heart to gain understanding.
[3] Cry out for wisdom.
Beg for understanding.

⁴Search for it as you would for
            silver.
      Hunt for it like hidden treasure.
⁵Then you will understand what it
            means to respect the Lord.
      Then you will begin to know
            God.
⁶Only the Lord gives wisdom.
      Knowledge and understanding
            come from him.
⁷He stores up wisdom for those who
            are honest.
      Like a shield he protects those
            who are innocent.
⁸He guards those who are fair to
            others.
      He protects those who are loyal
            to him.
⁹Then you will understand what is
            honest and fair and right.
      You will understand what is
            good to do.
¹⁰You will have wisdom in your
            heart.
      And knowledge will be pleasing
            to you.

Today's Prayer

Dear Lord, thank you for the
wise words you have given
us in the Bible to teach us
what is right and good. Help
me to understand your
words so that I may teach
others about you. In Jesus'
name, amen.

Memory Verse
"Only the Lord gives wisdom. Knowledge and
understanding come from him." Proverbs 2:6

Elijah Stops the Rain

After Solomon's death, evil kings ruled the land, and it was divided into two kingdoms, Israel and Judah. God sent his prophet Elijah to warn Ahab, the most wicked king of Israel.

[29]So Ahab son of Omri became king of Israel. This was during Asa's thirty-eighth year as king of Judah. Ahab ruled Israel in the town of Samaria for 22 years. [30]Ahab did many things that the Lord said were wrong. He did more evil than any of the kings before him.

[32]He built a temple in Samaria for worshiping Baal. And he put an altar

there for Baal. [33]Ahab also made an idol for worshiping Asherah. He did more things to make the Lord, the God of Israel, angry than all the other kings before him.

17 Now Elijah was a prophet from the town of Tishbe in Gilead. Elijah said to King Ahab, "I serve the Lord, the God of Israel. As surely as the Lord lives, I tell you the truth. No rain or dew will fall during the next few years unless I command it." [2]Then the Lord spoke his word to Elijah: [3]"Leave this place. Go east and hide near Kerith Ravine. It is east of the Jordan River. [4]You may drink from the brook. And I have commanded ravens to bring you food there." [5]So Elijah did what the Lord told him to do. He went to Kerith Ravine, east of the Jordan, and lived there. [6]The birds brought Elijah bread and meat every morning and every evening. And he drank water from the brook.

Today's Prayer

Dear God in heaven, thank you for the sun, the rain, and all of the things that make my days pleasant. Help me to make the days pleasant for those around me. In Jesus' name, amen.

Memory Verse

"Pray with all kinds of prayers, and ask for everything you need. Never give up. Always pray for all God's people." Ephesians 6:18

Elijah Helps a Widow

The land had gone so long without rain that the brook dried up from which Elijah got water to drink. Then the Lord sent Elijah to Zarephath to help a poor widow and her son.

[7]After a while the brook dried up because there was no rain. [8]Then the Lord spoke his word to Elijah, [9]"Go to Zarephath in Sidon. Live there. I have commanded a widow there to take care of you."

[10]So Elijah went to Zarephath. When he reached the town gate, he saw a widow there. She was gathering wood for a fire. Elijah asked her, "Would you bring me a little water in a cup? I would like to have a drink." [11]As she was going to get his water, Elijah said, "Please bring me a piece of bread, too."

[12]The woman answered, "As surely as the Lord your God lives, I tell you

the truth. I have no bread. I have only a handful of flour in a jar. And I have only a little olive oil in a jug. I came here to gather some wood. I will take it home and cook our last meal. My son and I will eat it and then die from hunger."

¹³Elijah said to her, "Don't worry. Go home and cook your food as you have said. But first make a small loaf of bread from the flour you have. Bring it to me. Then cook something for yourself and your son. ¹⁴The Lord, the God of Israel, says, 'That jar of flour will never become empty. The jug will always have oil in it. This will continue until the day the Lord sends rain to the land.' "

¹⁵So the woman went home. And she did what Elijah told her to do. So Elijah, the woman and her son had enough food every day.

Today's Prayer

Kind and loving God, thank you for providing for our needs. Whether I have plenty or just a little, help me always to share what you have given me. This I pray in Jesus' name, amen.

Memory Verse

"Pray with all kinds of prayers, and ask for everything you need. Never give up. Always pray for all God's people." Ephesians 6:18

Prophets of Baal

Elijah challenged the prophets of Baal. He told them to prepare a sacrifice on an altar and ask their god to set it on fire. He would do the same. Then they would see whose god was real.

²⁷At noon Elijah began to make fun of them. He said, "Pray louder! If Baal really is a god, maybe he is thinking. Or maybe he is busy or traveling! Maybe he is sleeping so you will have to wake him!"

²⁹The afternoon passed, and the prophets continued to act wildly. They continued until it was time for the evening sacrifice. But no voice was heard. Baal did not answer. No one paid attention.

³⁰Then Elijah said to all the people, "Now come to me." So they gathered around him. Elijah rebuilt the altar of the Lord because it had been torn down.

³²Elijah used these stones to rebuild the altar in honor of the Lord. Then he dug a small ditch around it. It was big enough to hold about 13 quarts of seed. ³³Elijah put the wood on the altar. He cut the bull into pieces and laid them on the wood. Then he said, "Fill four jars with water. Put the water on the meat and on the wood."

³⁴Then Elijah said, "Do it again." And they did it again.

Then he said, "Do it a third time." And they did it the third time. ³⁵So the water ran off of the altar and filled the ditch.

³⁶It was time for the evening sacrifice. So the prophet Elijah went near the altar. He prayed, "Lord, you are the God of Abraham, Isaac and Israel. I ask you now to prove that you are the God of Israel."

³⁸Then fire from the Lord came down. It burned the sacrifice, the wood, the stones and the ground around the altar. It also dried up the water in the ditch. ³⁹When all the people saw this, they fell down to the ground. They cried, "The Lord is God! The Lord is God!"

Today's Prayer

Mighty God, I am so thankful that I can always depend on you. Give me more confidence to defend you when others try to make me doubt your power. In Jesus' name I pray, amen.

Memory Verse

"Pray with all kinds of prayers, and ask for everything you need. Never give up. Always pray for all God's people." Ephesians 6:18

Horses of Fire

As Elijah grew old, God chose Elisha to be the prophet's helper. When it was time for Elijah to die, God took him to heaven in an extraordinary way.

⁷Fifty men from a group of the prophets came. They stood far from where Elijah and Elisha were by the Jordan. ⁸Elijah took off his coat. Then he rolled it up and hit the water. The water divided to the right and to the left. Then Elijah and Elisha crossed over on dry ground.

⁹After they had crossed over, Elijah said to Elisha, "What can I do for you before I am taken from you?"

Elisha said, "Leave me a double share of your spirit."

¹⁰Elijah said, "You have asked a hard thing. But if you see me when I am taken from you, it will be yours. If you don't, it won't happen."

¹¹Elijah and Elisha were still walking and talking. Then a chariot and horses of fire appeared. The chariot and horses of fire separated Elijah from Elisha. Then Elijah went up to heaven in a whirlwind. ¹²Elisha saw it and shouted, "My father! My father! The chariots of Israel and their horsemen!" Elisha did not see him any more. Elisha grabbed his own clothes and tore them to show how sad he was.

¹³He picked up Elijah's coat that had fallen from him. Then Elisha returned and stood on the bank of the Jordan. ¹⁴Elisha hit the water with Elijah's coat. He said, "Where is the Lord, the God of Elijah?" When he hit the water, it divided to the right and to the left. Then Elisha crossed over.

¹⁵A group of the prophets at Jericho were watching. They said, "Elisha now has the spirit Elijah had." They came to meet him. And they bowed down to the ground before him.

Today's Prayer

Heavenly father, thank you for all of the people who help me in so many ways. Give me a willing heart to help my family, my friends, and those in need. In the name of Jesus I pray, amen.

Memory Verse

"Pray with all kinds of prayers, and ask for everything you need. Never give up. Always pray for all God's people." Ephesians 6:18

A Room for Elisha

Even though Elisha was a great prophet, he was always concerned with the needs of ordinary people. When a woman from the city of Shunem showed him great kindness, Elisha showed his thankfulness in a very special way.

[8]One day Elisha went to Shunem. An important woman lived there. She begged Elisha to stay and eat. So every time Elisha passed by, he stopped there to eat. [9]The woman said to her husband, "I know that Elisha is a holy man of God. He passes by our house all the time. [10]Let's make a small room on the roof. Let's put a bed in the room for Elisha. And we can put a table, a chair and a lampstand there. Then when he comes by, he can stay there."

[11]One day Elisha came to the woman's house. He went to his room and rested. [12]He said to his servant

Gehazi, "Call the Shunammite."

When the servant called her, she stood in front of him. [13]Elisha told his servant, "Now say to her, 'You have gone to all this trouble for us. What can I do for you? Do you want me to speak to the king or the commander of the army for you?' "

The woman answered, "I live among my own people."

[14]Elisha said, "But what can we do for her?"

Gehazi answered, "She has no son, and her husband is old."

[15]Then Elisha said, "Call her." So he called her, and she stood in the doorway. [16]Then Elisha said, "About this time next year, you will hold a son in your arms."

The woman said, "No, master, man of God. Don't lie to me!"

[17]But the woman became pregnant. And she gave birth to a son at that time the next year as Elisha had told her.

Today's Prayer

Dear Lord in heaven, thank you for caring about the needs of everyone. When someone shows me kindness, help me find ways to show kindness in return. In Jesus' name, amen.

Memory Verse
"Pray with all kinds of prayers, and ask for everything you need. Never give up. Always pray for all God's people." Ephesians 6:18

A Boy Lives Again

While Elisha was at Mt. Carmel, he looked up and saw his old friend, the Shunammite woman, hurrying toward him. He sent his servant Gehazi to find out what was wrong. The woman's son had died, and she had come to Elisha for help.

²⁷Then she came to Elisha at the hill. She caught hold of his feet. Gehazi came near to pull her away. But Elisha said to him, "Let her alone. She's very upset, and the Lord has not told me about it. He has hidden it from me."

²⁸She said, "Master, I didn't tell you I wanted a son. I told you, 'Don't fool me.'"

²⁹Then Elisha said to Gehazi, "Get ready. Take my walking stick in your hand and go quickly. If you meet anyone, don't greet him. If anyone greets you, don't answer him. Lay my walking stick on the face of the boy."

³⁰But the child's mother said, "As

surely as the Lord lives and as you live, I won't leave you!" So he got up and followed her.

³¹Gehazi went on ahead. He laid the walking stick on the child's face. But the child did not talk or move. Then Gehazi went back to meet Elisha. He told Elisha, "The child has not awakened."

³²Elisha came into the house. There was the child, lying dead on his bed. ³³When Elisha entered the room, he shut the door. Only he and the child were in the room. Then Elisha prayed to the Lord. ³⁴He went to the bed and lay on the child. He put his mouth on the child's mouth. He put his eyes on the child's eyes and his hands on the child's hands. He stretched himself out on top of the child. Then the child's skin became warm. ³⁵Elisha turned away and walked around the room. Then he went back and put himself on the child again. Then the child sneezed seven times and opened his eyes.

Today's Prayer

Dear God in heaven, thank you for my friends. Help me to be a good and loving friend who helps those in trouble. In Jesus' name, amen.

Memory Verse

"Remember your Creator while you are young."
Ecclesiastes 12:1

Naaman Asks for Help

Naaman was a great man. He was the mighty and brave commander of the army of the king of Aram. But he had a terrible skin disease. Only a young Israelite slave girl knew how to help him.

²The Arameans had gone out to steal from the Israelites. And they had taken a little girl as a captive from Israel. This little girl served Naaman's wife. ³She said to her mistress, "I wish that my master would meet the prophet who lives in Samaria. He would heal Naaman of his disease."

⁴Naaman went to the king. He told him what the girl from Israel had said. ⁵The king of Aram said, "Go now. And I will send a letter to the king of Israel." So Naaman left and took about 750 pounds of silver. He also took about 150 pounds of gold and ten changes of clothes with him. ⁶He brought the letter to the king of

Israel. It read, "I am sending my servant Naaman to you. I'm sending him so you can heal him of his skin disease."

⁷The king of Israel read the letter. Then he tore his clothes to show how upset he was. He said, "I'm not God! I can't kill and make alive again! Why does this man send someone with a harmful skin disease for me to heal? You can see that the king of Aram is trying to start trouble with me!"

⁸Elisha, the man of God, heard that the king of Israel had torn his clothes. So he sent a message to the king. It said, "Why have you become so upset that you tore your clothes? Let Naaman come to me. Then he will know there is a prophet in Israel!" ⁹So Naaman went with his horses and chariots to Elisha's house. And he stood outside the door.

¹⁰Elisha sent a messenger to Naaman. The messenger said, "Go and wash in the Jordan River seven times. Then your skin will be healed, and you will be clean."

Today's Prayer

Dear Lord, my God, thank you for allowing me to serve you. Help me to remember that in serving others I am also serving you. In Christ's name, amen.

Memory Verse
"Remember your Creator while you are young."
Ecclesiastes 12:1

Naaman Is Healed

Elisha had sent word to Naaman that if he would wash in the Jordan River seven times his skin would be healed. However, Naaman thought that was too simple.

[11]Naaman became angry and left. He said, "I thought Elisha would surely come out and stand before me. I thought he would call on the name of the Lord his God. I thought he would wave his hand over the place and heal the disease! [12]Abana and Pharpar, the rivers of Damascus, are better than all the waters of Israel! Why can't I wash in them and become clean?" So Naaman went away very angry.

[13]But Naaman's servants came near and talked to him. They said, "My father, if the prophet had told you to do some great thing, wouldn't you have done it? Doesn't it make more

sense just to do it? After all, he only told you, 'Wash, and you will be clean.' " ¹⁴So Naaman went down and dipped in the Jordan seven times. He did just as Elisha had said. Then Naaman's skin became new again. It was like the skin of a little boy. And Naaman was clean!

¹⁵Naaman and all his group came back to Elisha. He stood before Elisha and said, "Look. I now know there is no God in all the earth except in Israel! Now please accept a gift from me."

¹⁶But Elisha said, "I serve the Lord. As surely as the Lord lives, I won't accept anything." Naaman urged him to take the gift, but he refused.

¹⁷Then Naaman said, "If you won't take the gift, then please give me some dirt. Give me as much as two of my mules can carry. From now on I'll not offer any burnt offering or sacrifice to any other gods. I'll only offer sacrifices to the Lord."

Today's Prayer

Almighty God, thank you for being patient with me. Keep me from being proud and wanting to do things my way. Your ways are always best. I pray in the name of Jesus, amen.

Memory Verse
"Remember your Creator while you are young."
Ecclesiastes 12:1

Joash Repairs the Temple

When Joash became king, the beautiful Temple Solomon had built for the Lord was very old and needed repairs. Joash decided it was time to make the Temple like new again.

24 Joash was seven years old when he became king. And he ruled 40 years in Jerusalem.

⁴Later, Joash decided to repair the Temple of the Lord. ⁵He called the priests and the Levites together. He said to them, "Go to the towns of Judah. Gather the money all the Israelites have to pay every year. Use it to repair the Temple of your God. Do this now." But the Levites did not hurry.

⁶So King Joash called Jehoiada the leading priest. Joash said to him, "Why haven't you made the Levites bring in the tax money from Judah and Jerusalem? Moses the Lord's

servant and the people of Israel used that money for the Holy Tent."

⁸King Joash commanded that a box for contributions be made. It was to be put outside, at the gate of the Temple of the Lord. ⁹Then the Levites made an announcement in Judah and Jerusalem. They told the people to bring the tax money to the Lord. Moses the servant of God had made the Israelites give it while they were in the desert. ¹⁰All the officers and people were happy to give their money. They put it in the box until the box was full. ¹¹Then the Levites would take the box to the king's officers. They would see that it was full of money. Then the king's royal assistant and the leading priest's officer would come and take out the money. Then they would take the box back to its place. They did this often and gathered much money.

¹³The people worked hard. And the work to repair the Temple went well. They rebuilt the Temple of God to be as it was before. And they made it stronger.

Today's Prayer

Dear God, thank you for loving me as much when I am young as you will when I am older and wiser. Help me be like Joash and serve you now. In Jesus' name, amen.

Memory Verse

"Remember your Creator while you are young."
Ecclesiastes 12:1

God Heals Hezekiah

Before Hezekiah became king, there had been many evil kings. But Hezekiah was a good man, and God listened to his prayers. God gave Hezekiah a strange sign to prove he had answered Hezekiah's prayer.

20At that time Hezekiah became very sick. He was almost dead. The prophet Isaiah son of Amoz went to see him. Isaiah told him, "This is what the Lord says: You are going to die. So you should give your last orders to everyone. You will not get well."

²Hezekiah turned toward the wall and prayed to the Lord. He said, ³"Lord, please remember that I have always obeyed you. I have given myself completely to you. I have done what you said was right." And Hezekiah cried loudly.

⁴Before Isaiah had left the middle courtyard, the Lord spoke his word

to Isaiah: ⁵"Go back and tell Hezekiah, the leader of my people: 'This is what the Lord, the God of your ancestor David, says: I have heard your prayer. And I have seen your tears. So I will heal you. Three days from now you will go up to the Temple of the Lord. ⁶I will add 15 years to your life. I will save you and this city from the king of Assyria. And I will protect the city for myself and for my servant David.'"

⁸Hezekiah asked Isaiah, "What will be the sign that the Lord will heal me? What is the sign that I will go up to the Temple of the Lord on the third day?"

⁹Isaiah said, "The Lord will do what he says. This is the sign from the Lord to show you: Do you want the shadow to go forward ten steps? Or do you want it to go back ten steps?"

¹⁰Hezekiah answered, "It's easy for the shadow to go forward ten steps. Instead, let it go back ten steps."

¹¹Then Isaiah the prophet called to the Lord. And the Lord brought the shadow back ten steps. It went back up the stairway of Ahaz that it had gone down.

Today's Prayer

My dear Lord, thank you for watching over me when I am sick. Help me to take care of my body so that I may be strong in service to you. In the name of Jesus my Savior, amen.

Memory Verse
"Remember your Creator while you are young."
Ecclesiastes 12:1

The Captives Return

After King Nebuchadnezzar captured Jerusalem, he took most of the people back to Babylon where they were slaves for seventy years. Then God chose Cyrus, King of Persia, to capture Babylon and free the people. He sent an announcement throughout the kingdom.

²This is what Cyrus king of Persia says: "The Lord, the God of heaven, has given all the kingdoms of the earth to me. And he has appointed me to build a Temple for him at Jerusalem in Judah. ³Now all of you who are God's people are free to go to Jerusalem. May your God be with you. And you may build the Temple of the Lord. He is the God of Israel, who is in Jerusalem. ⁴Those who stay behind should support anyone who wants to go. Give them silver and gold, supplies and cattle. And give them special gifts for the Temple of God in Jerusalem."

⁵Then the family leaders of Judah

and Benjamin got ready to go to Jerusalem. So did the priests and the Levites. They were going to Jerusalem to build the Temple of the Lord. God made all these people want to go. ⁶All their neighbors helped them. They gave them things made of silver and gold, along with supplies, cattle and valuable gifts. And they gave them the special gifts for the Temple. ⁷Also, King Cyrus brought out the bowls and pans that belonged in the Temple of the Lord. Nebuchadnezzar had taken them from Jerusalem. And he had put them in the temple of his own god. ⁸Cyrus king of Persia had Mithredath the treasurer get them out. So he made a list of the things for Sheshbazzar the prince of Judah.

¹¹There was a total of 5,400 pieces of gold and silver. Sheshbazzar brought all these things along when the captives went from Babylon to Jerusalem.

Today's Prayer

Kind and loving God, thank you for giving me hope when I am tired and discouraged. Bless me with a mind and heart that will never give up. In the name of your son Jesus, amen.

Memory Verse

"We have troubles all around us, but we are not defeated. We do not know what to do, but we do not give up." 2 Corinthians 4:8

Rebuilding the Temple

When the captives returned, they found their homeland in ruins and the Temple of God destroyed, so they began to rebuild. Their enemies tried to stop them, but Darius, the new king of Persia, wrote them a letter of warning.

[7]"Do not bother or interrupt the work on that Temple of God. Let the governor of the Jews and the older Jewish leaders rebuild this Temple. Let them build it where it was before.

[11]"Also, I give this order: If any one changes this order, a wooden beam is to be pulled from his house. Drive one end of the beam through his

body. And because he did this crime, make his house a pile of ruins. [12]God has chosen Jerusalem as the place he is to be worshiped. May he defeat any king or person who tries to change this order. May God destroy anyone who tries to destroy this Temple.

"I, Darius, have given this order. Let it be obeyed quickly and carefully."

[14]So the older Jewish leaders continued to build. And they were successful because of the preaching of Haggai the prophet and Zechariah son of Iddo. They finished building the Temple as the God of Israel had said. It was also done to obey the kings Cyrus, Darius and Artaxerxes of Persia. [15]The Temple was finished on the third day of the month Adar. It was the sixth year that Darius was king.

[16]Then the people of Israel celebrated. They gave the Temple to God to honor him. Everybody was happy: the priests, the Levites and the rest of the Jews who had returned from captivity.

Today's Prayer

Almighty God, thank you for being with me when I have to do something that seems impossible. Protect me from those who would try to stop me from doing my best for you. I pray in Christ Jesus, amen.

Memory Verse
"We have troubles all around us, but we are not defeated. We do not know what to do, but we do not give up." 2 Corinthians 4:8

Nehemiah's Request

Nehemiah was one of God's people who had stayed behind to serve the King of Persia. When Nehemiah heard that Jerusalem was in ruins, he became very sad and prayed to God for help.

2 It was the month of Nisan. It was in the twentieth year King Artaxerxes was king. He wanted some wine. So I took some and gave it to the king. I had not been sad in his presence before. ²So the king said, "Why does your face look sad? You are not sick. Your heart must be sad."

Then I was very afraid. ³I said to the king, "May the king live forever! My face is sad because the city where my ancestors are buried lies in ruins. And its gates have been destroyed by fire."

⁴Then the king said to me, "What do you want?"

First I prayed to the God of heaven.

⁵Then I answered the king, "Send me to the city in Judah where my ancestors are buried. I will rebuild it. Do this if you are willing and if I have pleased you."

⁶The queen was sitting next to the king. He asked me, "How long will your trip take? When will you get back?" It pleased the king to send me. So I set a time.

⁷I also said to him, "If you are willing, give me letters for the governors west of the Euphrates River. Tell them to let me pass safely through their lands on my way to Judah. ⁸And may I have a letter for Asaph? He is the keeper of the king's forest. Tell him to give me timber. I will need it to make boards for the gates of the palace. It is by the Temple. The wood is also for the city wall and the house I will live in." So the king gave me the letters. This was because God was showing kindness to me. ⁹So I went to the governors west of the Euphrates River. I gave them the king's letters. The king had also sent army officers and soldiers on horses with me.

Today's Prayer

Thank you, dear God, for understanding me when I am sad. Comfort me and help me to overcome my troubles so that I may work joyfully for you. This is my prayer in Christ Jesus, amen.

Memory Verse
"We have troubles all around us, but we are not defeated. We do not know what to do, but we do not give up." 2 Corinthians 4:8

Jerusalem's New Walls

When Nehemiah arrived in Jerusalem, he made a tour of the city to find out how badly it was damaged. Then he talked to the Jewish leaders.

¹¹I went to Jerusalem and stayed there three days. ¹²Then at night I started out with a few men. I had not told anyone what God had caused me to do for Jerusalem. There were no animals with me except the one I was riding.

¹³It was night. I went out through the Valley Gate. I rode toward the Dragon Well and the Trash Gate. I was inspecting the walls of Jerusalem. They had been broken down. And the gates had been destroyed by fire. ¹⁶The officers did not know where I had gone or what I was doing. I had not yet said anything to the Jews, the priests, the important men or the

officers. I had not said anything to any of the others who would do the work.

¹⁷Then I said to them, "You can see the trouble we have here. Jerusalem is a pile of ruins. And its gates have been burned. Come, let's rebuild the wall of Jerusalem. Then we won't be full of shame any longer." ¹⁸I also told them how God had been kind to me. And I told them what the king had said to me.

Then they answered, "Let's start rebuilding." So they began to work hard.

¹⁹But Sanballat the Horonite, Tobiah the Ammonite leader and Geshem the Arab heard about it. They made fun of us and laughed at us. They said, "What are you doing? Are you turning against the king?"

²⁰But I answered them, "The God of heaven will give us success. We are God's servants. We will start rebuilding. But you have no share in Jerusalem. You have no claim or past right to it."

Today's Prayer

Almighty God, help me to see what I can do to make my home better. I want to be like Nehemiah and to know that you will give me success when I do what is right. Hear my prayer in Jesus' name, amen.

Memory Verse
"We have troubles all around us, but we are not defeated. We do not know what to do, but we do not give up." 2 Corinthians 4:8

Ezra Reads the Teachings

After the Temple and the city walls were rebuilt, the people settled in their own towns and homes. Then they all came together to hear Ezra, the teacher, read from the Book of the Teachings of Moses.

8All the people of Israel gathered together in the square by the Water Gate. They asked Ezra the teacher to bring out the Book of the Teachings of Moses. These are the Teachings the Lord had given to Israel.

³Ezra read the Teachings out loud. He read from early morning until noon. He was facing the square by the Water Gate. He read to the men, women and everyone who could listen and understand. All the people listened carefully to the Book of the Teachings.

⁵Ezra opened the book. All the people could see him because he was above them. As he opened it, all the

people stood up. ⁶Ezra praised the Lord, the great God. And all the people held up their hands and said, "Amen! Amen!" Then they bowed down and worshiped the Lord with their faces to the ground.

⁸They read the Book of the Teachings of God. They read so the people could understand. And they explained what it meant. Then the people understood what was being read.

⁹Then Nehemiah the governor and Ezra the priest and teacher spoke up. And the Levites who were teaching spoke up. They said to all the people, "This is a holy day to the Lord your God. Don't be sad or cry." All the people had been crying as they listened to the words of the Teachings.

¹⁰Nehemiah said, "Go and enjoy good food and sweet drinks. Send some to people who have none. Today is a holy day to the Lord. Don't be sad. The joy of the Lord will make you strong."

Today's Prayer

Dear God, thank you for making it possible for me to read and hear your teachings. Help me to make your word part of my life to give me strength every day. In Jesus' name, amen.

Memory Verse
"We have troubles all around us, but we are not defeated. We do not know what to do, but we do not give up." 2 Corinthians 4:8

Haman's Evil Plan

Xerxes, King of Persia, chose a Jewish girl named Esther to be his queen. Haman, an officer of the king, hated the Jews. So he thought of an evil plan.

[8]Then Haman said to King Xerxes, "There is a certain group of people in all the areas of your kingdom. They are scattered among the other people. They keep themselves separate. Their customs are different from those of all the other people. And they do not obey the king's laws. It is not right for you to allow them to continue living in your kingdom. [9]If it pleases the king, let an order be given to destroy those people. Then I will pay 375 tons of silver to those who do the king's business. They will put it into the royal treasury."

[10]So the king took his signet ring off and gave it to Haman. Haman son of

Hammedatha, the Agagite, was the enemy of the Jews. [11]Then the king said to Haman, "The money and the people are yours. Do with them as you please."

[12]On the thirteenth day of the first month, the royal secretaries were called. They wrote out all of Haman's orders. They wrote to the king's governors and to the captains of the soldiers in each area. And they wrote to the important men of each group of people. The orders were written to each area in its own form of writing. And they were written to each group of people in their own language. They were written in the name of King Xerxes and sealed with his signet ring. [13]Letters were sent by messengers to all the king's empire. They stated the king's order to destroy, kill and completely wipe out all the Jews. That meant young and old, women and little children, too. The order said to kill all the Jews on a single day. That was to be the thirteenth day of the twelfth month, which was Adar. And it said to take all the things that belonged to the Jews.

Esther Risks Her Life

Esther heard from her servants that her cousin Mordecai was crying loudly in front of the king's gate. So she sent her servant Hathach to find out the reason.

⁷Then Mordecai told Hathach everything that had happened to him. And he told Hathach about the amount of money Haman had promised to pay into the king's treasury for the killing of the Jews. ⁸Mordecai also gave him a copy of the order to kill the Jews, which had been given in Susa. He wanted Hathach to show it to Esther and to tell her about it. And Mordecai told him to order Esther to go into the king's presence. He wanted her to beg for mercy and to plead with him for her people.

⁹Hathach went back and reported to Esther everything Mordecai had said. ¹⁰Then Esther told Hathach to say to Mordecai, ¹¹"All the royal offi-

cers and people of the royal areas know this: No man or woman may go to the king in the inner courtyard without being called. There is only one law about this. Anyone who enters must be put to death. But if the king holds out his gold scepter, that person may live. And I have not been called to go to the king for 30 days."

¹²And Esther's message was given to Mordecai. ¹³Then Mordecai gave orders to say to Esther: "Just because you live in the king's palace, don't think that out of all the Jews you alone will escape. ¹⁴You might keep quiet at this time. Then someone else will help and save the Jews. But you and your father's family will all die. And who knows, you may have been chosen queen for just such a time as this."

¹⁵Then Esther sent this answer to Mordecai: ¹⁶"Go and get all the Jews in Susa together. For my sake, give up eating. Do not eat or drink for three days, night and day. I and my servant girls will also give up eating. Then I will go to the king, even though it is against the law. And if I die, I die."

Today's Prayer

Our loving Father, I want to be brave as Esther was. Guide me to find friends who serve you too so that we can help each other. In Jesus' name, amen.

Memory Verse
"The Lord is kind and shows mercy. He does not become angry quickly but is full of love."
Psalm 145:8

Esther Helps Her People

While Mordecai followed the queen's orders, Esther prepared a special feast for the king and Haman. The king was so pleased with Esther that he promised to give her anything she wanted.

³Then Queen Esther answered, "My king, I hope you are pleased with me. If it pleases you, let me live. This is what I ask. And let my people live, too. This is what I want. ⁴I ask this because my people and I have been sold to be destroyed. We are to be killed and completely wiped out. If we had been sold as male and female slaves, I would have kept quiet. That would not be enough of a problem to bother the king."

⁵Then King Xerxes asked Queen Esther, "Who is he? Where is he? Who has done such a thing?"

⁶Esther said, "A man who is against us! Our enemy is this wicked Haman!"

Then Haman was filled with terror before the king and queen. [7]The king was very angry. He got up, left his wine and went out into the palace garden. But Haman stayed inside to beg Queen Esther to save his life. He could see that the king had already decided to kill him.

[8]The king came back from the palace garden to the banquet hall. And he saw Haman falling on the couch where Esther was lying. The king said, "Will he even attack the queen while I am in the house?"

As soon as the king said that, servants came in and covered Haman's face. [9]Harbona was one of the eunuchs there serving the king. He said, "Look, a platform for hanging people stands near Haman's house. It is 75 feet high. This is the one Haman had prepared for Mordecai, who gave the warning that saved the king."

The king said, "Hang Haman on it!" [10]So they hanged Haman on the platform he had prepared for Mordecai. Then the king was not so angry anymore.

Today's Prayer

Dear Lord, when problems come, I know you will help me just as you did Queen Esther. Give me a loving heart and a willing mind to accept your answers to my prayers. In the name of Christ, amen.

Memory Verse
"The Lord is kind and shows mercy. He does not become angry quickly but is full of love."
Psalm 145:8

God Talks to Job

Job was truly a good man, but to test him Satan took away his wealth, his family, and his health. Job's friends told him to turn against God, but Job didn't. In the end, God comforted him and blessed him even more than he had before.

42 Then Job answered the Lord:
²"I know that you can do all things.
No plan of yours can be ruined.
³You asked, 'Who is this that made my purpose unclear by saying things that are not true?'
Surely I talked about things I did not understand.
I spoke of things too wonderful for me to know.
⁵My ears had heard of you before.
But now my eyes have seen you."
¹⁰After Job had prayed for his friends, God gave him success again. God gave Job twice as much as he had owned before. ¹¹Job's brothers

and sisters came to his house. Everyone who had known him before came to his house. They all ate with him there. They comforted Job and spoke kindly to him. They made him feel better about the trouble the Lord had brought on him. And each one gave Job a piece of silver and a gold ring.

[12]The Lord blessed the last part of Job's life even more than the first part. Job had 14,000 sheep and 6,000 camels. He had 1,000 pairs of oxen and 1,000 female donkeys. [13]Job also had seven sons and three daughters. [15]There were no other women in all the land as beautiful as Job's daughters. And their father Job gave them land to own along with their brothers.

[16]After this, Job lived 140 years. He lived to see his children, grandchildren, great-grandchildren and great-great-grandchildren.

Today's Prayer

Dear God in heaven, even when bad things happen in my life, you are always beside me. Thank you. Help me never to blame you for my problems, but to pray for your help. In Jesus' name, amen.

Memory Verse

"The Lord is kind and shows mercy. He does not become angry quickly but is full of love."
Psalm 145:8

Advice to Young People

The writer of Ecclesiastes, the Teacher, was a wise person who had studied life. He gives good advice and wisdom to people of all ages, but especially to young people.

⁵You don't know where the wind will blow.
  And you don't know how a baby grows in its mother's body.
In the same way, God certainly made all things.
  But you can't understand what he is doing.
⁶Begin planting early in the morning.
  and don't stop working until evening.
This is because you don't know which things you do will succeed.
  It is even possible that everything you do will succeed.
⁷It is good to be alive

to enjoy the light of day.
[8]A person ought to enjoy every day of
his life.
This is true no matter how long he
lives.
But he should also remember this:
You will be dead much longer
than you live.
After you are dead, you accom-
plish nothing.
[9]Young people, enjoy yourselves
while you are young.
Be happy while you are young.
Do whatever your heart desires.
Do whatever you want to do.
But remember that God will judge
you
for everything you do.
[10]So avoid sorrow and sadness.
Forget about all the bad things
that happen to you.
This is because the joys of youth
pass quickly away.

12 Remember your Creator while
you are young.

Today's Prayer

Dear loving God, thank you
for teaching me how to live.
Let me learn from your
faithful servants who are
older and wiser than I am so
that I may become a better
person. I pray in Christ Jesus,
amen.

Memory Verse

"The Lord is kind and shows mercy. He does not
become angry quickly but is full of love."
Psalm 145:8

Be Happy

The Book of Psalms is very old and yet very modern, because it is a book about human feelings. Many of the psalms tell about joy and happiness for those who follow the Lord.

1 Happy is the person who doesn't
listen to the wicked.
He doesn't go where sinners go.
He doesn't do what bad people do.
²He loves the Lord's teachings.
He thinks about the teachings day
and night.
³He is strong, like a tree planted by a
river.
It produces fruit in season.
Its leaves don't die.
Everything he does will succeed.

⁴But wicked people are not like that.
They are like useless chaff
that the wind blows away.
⁵So the wicked will not escape God's
punishment.
Sinners will not worship God with
good people.
⁶This is because the Lord protects
good people.
But the wicked will be destroyed.

Today's Prayer

Dear God, thank you for
giving us the Bible. Help me
to share you and your word
with others so our world will
be a happier place. In the
name of your son, Jesus,
amen.

Memory Verse
"The Lord is my shepherd. I have everything I
need." Psalm 23:1

God Is My Shepherd

The shepherd loves his flock. He leads them to good pastures and fresh water. He protects them from danger and finds them shelter. In many ways, God is like a shepherd to His people.

23 The Lord is my shepherd.
I have everything I need.
²He gives me rest in green
pastures.
He leads me to calm water.
³ He gives me new strength.
For the good of his name,
he leads me on paths that are
right.
⁴Even if I walk
through a very dark valley,
I will not be afraid
because you are with me.
Your rod and your walking stick
comfort me.

⁵You prepare a meal for me
in front of my enemies.
You pour oil on my head.
You give me more than I can
hold.
⁶Surely your goodness and love will
be with me
all my life.
And I will live in the house of the
Lord forever.

Today's Prayer

Dear Lord in heaven, I am happy because I know you love me and will take care of me. Let me depend on you as a sheep depends on its shepherd. I pray in Jesus' name, amen.

Memory Verse
"The Lord is my shepherd. I have everything I need." Psalm 23:1

Trust in God

This psalm is a song of trust in God. He hears when his people pray. He protects us and helps us to be strong and brave.

27The Lord is my light and the one who saves me.
I fear no one.
The Lord protects my life.
I am afraid of no one.
²Evil people may try to destroy my body.
My enemies and those who hate me attack me.
But they are overwhelmed and defeated.
³If an army surrounds me,
I will not be afraid.
If war breaks out,
I will trust the Lord.

⁴I ask only one thing from the Lord.

This is what I want:
Let me live in the Lord's house
    all my life.
Let me see the Lord's beauty.
    Let me look around in his
        Temple.
⁷Lord, hear me when I call.
    Be kind and answer me.
⁸My heart said of you, "Go,
    worship him."
    So I come to worship you, Lord.
¹⁰If my father and mother leave me,
    the Lord will take me in.
¹¹Lord, teach me your ways.
    Guide me to do what is right
    because I have enemies.
¹²Do not let my enemies defeat me.
    They tell lies about me.
    They say they will hurt me.
¹³I truly believe
    I will live to see the Lord's
        goodness.
¹⁴Wait for the Lord's help.
    Be strong and brave
    and wait for the Lord's help.

Today's Prayer

Dear loving God, thank you for protecting me and being with me. When I pray to you for help, give me strength to wait for your answer. In Jesus' name I pray, amen.

Memory Verse
"The Lord is my shepherd. I have everything I need." Psalm 23:1

God Guards His People

Our God made everything in the world. He is powerful enough to protect us at all times. With God to guard us, we should be truly happy.

121 I look up to the hills.
But where does my help
come from?
²My help comes from the Lord.
He made heaven and earth.

³He will not let you be defeated.
He who guards you never
sleeps.
⁴He who guards Israel
never rests or sleeps.
⁵The Lord guards you.
The Lord protects you as the
shade protects you from the
sun.
⁶The sun cannot hurt you during
the day.
And the moon cannot hurt you
at night.
⁷The Lord will guard you from all
dangers.
He will guard your life.
⁸The Lord will guard you as you
come and go,
both now and forever.

Today's Prayer

Dear Lord, I am truly happy
that you guard me always.
Help me to thank you in
times of joy and trust you in
times of trouble. In the
name of Jesus, my
Savior, amen.

Memory Verse
"The Lord is my shepherd. I have everything I
need." Psalm 23:1

The Lord Knows Me

God knows everything about us. He is always there in every place we go. He guides us and holds us in his hand.

139 Lord, you have examined me.
    You know all about me.
²You know when I sit down and
        when I get up.
    You know my thoughts before I
        think them.
³You know where I go and where I
        lie down.
    You know well everything I do.
⁴Lord, even before I say a word,
        you already know what I am
        going to say.
⁵You are all around me—in front
        and in back.
    You have put your hand on me.
⁶Your knowledge is amazing to me.

It is more than I can
understand.

¹³You made my whole being.
You formed me in my mother's
body.
¹⁴I praise you because you made me
in an amazing and wonderful
way.
What you have done is
wonderful.
I know this very well.
¹⁵You saw my bones being formed
as I took shape in my mother's
body.
When I was put together there,
¹⁶ you saw my body as it was
formed.
All the days planned for me
were written in your book
before I was one day old.

²³God, examine me and know my
heart.
Test me and know my thoughts.
²⁴See if there is any bad thing in
me.
Lead me in the way you set
long ago.

Today's Prayer

Wonderful God, thank you
for holding me in your hand
all of the time. I am so glad
that you know everything
about me. In the name of
Christ, my Lord, amen.

Memory Verse
"The Lord is my shepherd. I have everything I
need." Psalm 23:1

A Time for Everything

Humans are able to understand time, but we aren't able to see into the future. We also can't understand everything that happens as God understands it.

3 There is a right time for everything.
Everything on earth has its special season.
²There is a time to be born
and a time to die.
There is a time to plant
and a time to pull up plants.
³There is a time to kill
and a time to heal.
There is a time to destroy
and a time to build.
⁴There is a time to cry
and a time to laugh.
There is a time to be sad
and a time to dance.

⁵There is a time to throw away stones
and a time to gather them.
There is a time to hug
and a time not to hug.
⁶There is a time to look for
something
and a time to stop looking for it.
There is a time to keep things
and a time to throw things
away.
⁷There is a time to tear apart
and a time to sew together.
There is a time to be silent
and a time to speak.
⁸There is a time to love
and a time to hate.
There is a time for war
and a time for peace.

¹¹God has also given us a desire to know the future. God certainly does everything at just the right time. But we can never completely understand what he is doing.

Today's Prayer

Dear God, give me patience and help me to accept change. Thank you for being an unchanging God. I know that you are always near and that you understand. I pray in Christ, amen.

Memory Verse
"The Lord gives strength to those who are tired. He gives more power to those who are weak."
Isaiah 40:29

A Savior Is Coming

The nation of Israel was about to be captured and Jerusalem, its capital, destroyed. Isaiah, God's prophet, brought a message of hope to the people. God told him that Jesus Christ, the Prince of Peace, was coming.

[2]Now those people live in darkness.
     But they will see a great light.
They live in a place that is very dark.
     But a light will shine on them.
[3]God, you will cause the nation to
          grow.
     You will make the people happy.
And they will show their happiness
          to you.

It will be like the joy during
    harvest time.
It will be like the joy of people taking
  what they have won in war.

⁶A child will be born to us.
    God will give a son to us.
    He will be responsible for leading
      the people.
His name will be Wonderful
      Counselor, Powerful God,
    Father Who Lives Forever, Prince
    of Peace.
⁷Power and peace will be in his
    kingdom.
    It will continue to grow.
He will rule as king on David's throne
  and over David's kingdom.
He will make it strong,
    by ruling with goodness and fair
      judgment.
    He will rule it forever and ever.
The Lord of heaven's armies will do
    this
  because of his strong love for his
    people.

Today's Prayer

Mighty Lord, thank you for your love, your promises and the hope that Jesus brings me. May I always remember that I am your child. In Jesus' name, amen.

Memory Verse
"The Lord gives strength to those who are tired. He gives more power to those who are weak."
Isaiah 40:29

A Savior's Peace

Although David's kingdom, Israel, was going to be cut down like a tree, there was still hope. God was sending a new king, Jesus Christ, to save and bring peace to God's people.

11 A branch will grow from a stump of a tree that was cut down.
So a new king will come
    from the family of Jesse.
²The Spirit of the Lord will rest upon
    that king.
    The Spirit gives him wisdom,
      understanding, guidance and
      power.
    And the Spirit teaches him to know
      and respect the Lord.
³This king will be glad to obey the
    Lord.
He will not judge by the way things
    look.

He will not judge by what
people say.
⁴He will judge the poor honestly.
He will be fair in his decisions for
the poor people of the land.
At his command evil people will be
punished.
By his words the wicked will be
put to death.
⁵Goodness and fairness will give him
strength.
They will be like a belt around his
waist.

⁶Then wolves will live in peace with
lambs.
And leopards will lie down to rest
with goats.
Calves, lions and young bulls will eat
together.
And a little child will lead them.
⁹They will not hurt or destroy each
other
on all my holy mountain.
The earth will be full of the
knowledge of the Lord,
as the sea is full of water.

Today's Prayer

Dear God, when life is hard,
help me remember that
Christ is king of my life. I
know he can give me
peace and strength to face
each day. In him I pray,
amen.

Memory Verse
"The Lord gives strength to those who are tired.
He gives more power to those who are weak."
Isaiah 40:29

God Gives Strength

When we look up into the sky, we see the strength of the Lord in his creation. God is never tired. He gives power to the weak, and he is able to give strength to all who trust him.

22God sits on his throne above the circle of the earth.
    And compared to him, people are like grasshoppers.
He stretches out the skies like a piece of cloth.
    He spreads them out like a tent to sit under.
25God, the Holy One, says, "Can you compare me to anyone?
    Is anyone equal to me?
26Look up to the skies.
    Who created all these stars?
He leads out all the army of heaven one by one.
    He calls all the stars by name.
He is very strong and full of power.

So not one of them is missing."
²⁸Surely you know.

Surely you have heard.

The Lord is the God who lives forever.

He created all the world.

He does not become tired or need to rest.

No one can understand how great his wisdom is.

²⁹The Lord gives strength to those who are tired.

He gives more power to those who are weak.

³⁰Even boys become tired and need to rest.

Even young men trip and fall.

³¹But the people who trust the Lord will become strong again.

They will be able to rise up as an eagle in the sky.

They will run without needing rest.

They will walk without becoming tired.

Today's Prayer

Holy Lord, when I see the moon and stars, help me to remember you made them all. I know you have great power. Give me more trust in you. I pray in Jesus' name, amen.

Memory Verse
"The Lord gives strength to those who are tired. He gives more power to those who are weak."
Isaiah 40:29

The Lord's Servant

God promised to bless the world's people. Isaiah said that God's special servant, Jesus Christ, would make that promise come true.

42 "Here is my servant, the one I support.
He is the one I chose, and I am
pleased with him.
I will put my Spirit in him.
And he will bring justice to all
nations.
²He will not cry out or yell.
He will not speak loudly in the
streets.
³He will not break a crushed blade of
grass.
He will not put out even a weak
flame.
He will bring justice and find what is
true.
⁴   He will not lose hope or give up

until he brings justice to the
world.
And people far away will trust his
teachings."

⁵God, the Lord, said these things.
He created the skies and stretched
them out.
He spread out the earth and
everything on it.
He gives life to all people on earth.
He gives life to everyone who
walks on the earth.
⁶The Lord says, "I called you to do
right.
And I will hold your hand.
I will protect you.
You will be the sign of my
agreement with the people.
You will be a light to shine for all
people.
⁷You will help the blind to see.
You will free those who are in
prison.
You will lead those who live in
darkness out of their prison."

Today's Prayer

Dear Lord, thank you for keeping your promise to send Jesus to bless the people of the world. Thank you for sending him to love me. Through Jesus' name I pray, amen.

Memory Verse
"The Lord gives strength to those who are tired. He gives more power to those who are weak."
Isaiah 40:29

God Calls Jeremiah

Jeremiah lived in exciting but dangerous times. Two great nations, Babylon and Egypt, were threatening God's people in Judah. Since Jeremiah was the son of a priest, he could have lived in comfort in the king's court. But instead, he chose to preach God's word.

⁴The Lord spoke these words to me:

⁵"Before I made you in your mother's womb, I chose you.
Before you were born, I set you apart for a special work.
I appointed you as a prophet to the nations."

⁶Then I said, "But Lord God, I don't know how to speak. I am only a boy."

⁷But the Lord said to me, "Don't say, 'I am only a boy.' You must go everywhere that I send you. You must say everything I tell you to say. ⁸Don't be afraid of anyone, because I am with you. I will protect you," says the Lord.

⁹Then the Lord reached out with his hand and touched my mouth. He said to me, "See, I am putting my words in your mouth. ¹⁰Today I have put you in charge of nations and kingdoms. You will pull up and tear down, destroy and overthrow. You will build up and plant.

¹⁷"Jeremiah, get ready. Stand up and speak to the people. Tell them everything I tell you to say. Don't be afraid of the people. If you are afraid of them, I will give you good reason to be afraid of them. ¹⁸Today I am going to make you a strong city, an iron pillar, a bronze wall. You will be able to stand against everyone in the land: Judah's kings, officers, priests and the people of the land. ¹⁹They will fight against you. But they will not defeat you. This is because I am with you, and I will save you!" says the Lord.

Today's Prayer

Dear God, thank you for great men like Jeremiah who show me how to live bravely. Give me the courage to stand for right and live for you. I pray in Christ's name, amen.

Memory Verse

"Your word is like a lamp for my feet and a light for my way." Psalm 119:105

A New Agreement

The people of Israel had been taken as captives by Assyria. The people of Judah were being threatened by mighty Babylon. But Jeremiah knew a better time was coming. The Lord would make a new agreement with his people.

³¹"Look, the time is coming," says the Lord,
  "when I will make a new agreement.
It will be with the people of Israel and the people of Judah.
³³I will make this agreement with the people of Israel," says the Lord.
"I will put my teachings in their minds.
  And I will write them on their hearts.
I will be their God,
  and they will be my people.
³⁴People will no longer have to

teach their neighbors and
relatives
to know the Lord.
This is because all people will
know me,
from the least to the most
important," says the Lord.
"I will forgive them for the wicked
things they did.
I will not remember their sins
anymore."

³⁵This is what the Lord says:
"The Lord makes the sun shine in
the day.
And he makes the moon and
stars shine at night.
He stirs up the sea so that its
waves crash on the shore.
The Lord of heaven's armies is
his name.

³⁶"Only if these laws should ever
fail,"
says the Lord,
"will Israel's descendants stop
being a nation before me."

Today's Prayer

Help me, Lord, to see
beyond my present
problems. Help me to
remember Jesus and to be
glad that he is with me.
Thank you for your
promises to bless me. In his
name, amen.

Memory Verse
"Your word is like a lamp for my feet and a light
for my way." Psalm 119:105

Jeremiah in the Well

Jeremiah warned the people about what would happen if they didn't serve God. Although he was trying to save the nation, he was often treated like an enemy.

38 Some of the officers heard what Jeremiah was prophesying. ⁴Then the officers said to the king, "Jeremiah must be put to death! He is making the soldiers who are still in the city become discouraged. He is discouraging everyone by the things he is saying. He does not want good to happen to us. He wants to ruin the people of Jerusalem."

⁵King Zedekiah said to them, "Jeremiah is in your control. I cannot do anything to stop you!"

⁶So the officers took Jeremiah and put him into the well of Malkijah, the king's son. That well was in the courtyard of the guards. The officers used

ropes to lower Jeremiah into the well. It did not have any water in it, only mud. And Jeremiah sank down into the mud.

[7]But Ebed-Melech heard that the officers had put Jeremiah into the well. Ebed-Melech was a Cushite, and he was a eunuch in the palace. King Zedekiah was sitting at the Benjamin Gate. [8]So Ebed-Melech left the palace and went to the king. Ebed-Melech said, [9]"My master and king, the rulers have acted in an evil way. They have treated Jeremiah the prophet badly! They have thrown him into a well! They have left him there to die! When there is no more bread in the city, he will starve."

[10]Then King Zedekiah commanded Ebed-Melech the Cushite: "Ebed-Melech, take 30 men from the palace with you. Go and lift Jeremiah the prophet out of the well before he dies."

[13]The men pulled Jeremiah up with the ropes and lifted him out of the well. And Jeremiah stayed under guard in the courtyard.

Today's Prayer

Dear God, help me love those around me, even when they seem to be my enemies. Like Jeremiah, help me have the faith to share your word. I pray in Jesus' name, amen.

Memory Verse

"Your word is like a lamp for my feet and a light for my way." Psalm 119:105

A Vision of Bones

The nation of Israel had been destroyed and its people had become slaves. They had lost all hope. But Ezekiel told them that God can give life, even to skeletons. He would make the nation of Israel live again, too.

37 I felt the power of the Lord was on me. He brought me out by the Spirit of the Lord. And he put me down in the middle of a valley. It was full of bones. ²The Lord led me around among the bones. There were many bones on the bottom of the valley. I saw the bones were very dry. ³Then he asked me, "Human being, can these bones live?"

I answered, "Lord God, only you know."

⁴The Lord said to me, "Prophesy to these bones. Say to them, 'Dry bones, hear the word of the Lord. ⁵This is what the Lord God says to the bones: I will cause breath to enter you. Then

you will live. ⁶I will put muscles on you. I will put flesh on you. I will cover you with skin. Then I will put breath in you, and you will live. Then you will know that I am the Lord.' "

⁷So I prophesied as I was commanded. While I prophesied, there was a noise and a rattling. The bones came together, bone to bone. ⁸I looked and saw muscles come on the bones. Flesh grew, and skin covered the bones. But there was no breath in them.

⁹Then the Lord said to me, "Prophesy to the wind. Prophesy, human being, and say to the wind: 'This is what the Lord God says: Wind, come from the four winds. Breathe on these people who were killed so they can live again.' " ¹⁰So I prophesied as the Lord commanded me. And the breath came into them, and they came to life. They stood on their feet. They were a very large army.

Today's Prayer

God in heaven, sometimes I feel like Israel—destroyed and hopeless. Help me to remember that your power is greater than any problem I have. In Jesus' name, amen.

Memory Verse
"Your word is like a lamp for my feet and a light for my way." Psalm 119:105

A Prayer for Protection

The psalms are filled with prayers and songs to God. Some praise God. Some ask for God's help. Others ask for forgiveness and strength. Psalm 46 talks about God's power and protection.

46God is our protection and our strength.
  He always helps in times of
    trouble
²So we will not be afraid if the
    earth shakes,
  or if the mountains fall into
    the sea.
³We will not fear even if the
    oceans roar and foam,
  or if the mountains shake at the
    raging sea.
⁶Nations tremble, and kingdoms
    shake.
  God shouts, and the earth
    crumbles.

⁷The Lord of heaven's armies is
   with us.
   The God of Jacob is our
   protection.

⁸Come and see what the Lord has
   done.
   He has done amazing things on
   the earth.

⁹He stops wars everywhere on the
   earth.
   He breaks all bows and spears
   and burns up the chariots with
   fire.

¹⁰God says, "Be quiet and know
   that I am God.
   I will be supreme over all the
   nations.
   I will be supreme in the earth."

¹¹The Lord of heaven's armies is
   with us.
   The God of Jacob is our
   protection.

Today's Prayer

O God, help me pray to you
in times of trouble. I know
you are always ready to
listen to me and to answer
my prayers. I praise you and
your mighty power. In Jesus'
name, amen.

Memory Verse
"Your word is like a lamp for my feet and a light
for my way." Psalm 119:105

The Golden Statue

When King Nebuchadnezzar captured Jerusalem, he chose some of the best educated young men to work in his government. All went well until the king made a golden statue ninety feet high and nine feet wide. Then he called all the officers together for an announcement.

⁴Then the man who made announcements for the king spoke in a loud voice. He said, "People, nations and men of every language, this is what you are commanded to do: ⁶Everyone must bow down and worship this gold statue. Anyone who doesn't will be quickly thrown into a blazing furnace."

⁸Then some Babylonians came up to the king. They began speaking against the men of Judah. ¹²"Our king, there are some men of Judah who did not pay attention to your order. You made them important officers in the area of Babylon. Their names are Shadrach, Meshach and Abednego.

They do not serve your gods. And they do not worship the gold statue you have set up."

[13]Nebuchadnezzar became very angry. He called for Shadrach, Meshach and Abednego. So those men were brought to the king. [14]And Nebuchadnezzar said, "Shadrach, Meshach and Abednego, is it true that you do not serve my gods? And is it true that you did not worship the gold statue I have set up?"

[16]Shadrach, Meshach and Abednego answered the king. They said, "Nebuchadnezzar, we do not need to defend ourselves to you. [17]You can throw us into the blazing furnace. The God we serve is able to save us from the furnace and your power. If he does this, it is good. [18]But even if God does not save us, we want you, our king, to know this: We will not serve your gods. We will not worship the gold statue you have set up."

Today's Prayer

I praise your name, O Lord. I want to always put you first in my life. Give me the courage to say no to anything that does not honor you. In Jesus' name, amen.

Memory Verse

"When a person is tempted and still continues strong, he should be happy. After he has proved his faith, God will reward him with life forever." James 1:12

The Fiery Furnace

When Shadrach, Meshach, and Abednego refused to worship the golden statue, King Nebuchadnezzar was very angry. He ordered the furnace to be heated seven times hotter!

[23]Firmly tied, Shadrach, Meshach and Abednego fell into the blazing furnace.

[24]Then King Nebuchadnezzar was very surprised and jumped to his feet. He asked the men who advised him, "Didn't we tie up only three men? Didn't we throw them into the fire?"

They answered, "Yes, our king."

[25]The king said, "Look! I see four men. They are walking around in the fire. They are not tied up, and they are not burned. The fourth man looks like a son of the gods."

[26]Then Nebuchadnezzar went to the opening of the blazing furnace. He

shouted, "Shadrach, Meshach and Abednego, come out! Servants of the Most High God, come here!"

So Shadrach, Meshach and Abednego came out of the fire. [27]When they came out, the princes, assistant governors, governors and royal advisers crowded around them. They saw that the fire had not harmed their bodies. Their hair was not burned. Their robes were not burned. And they didn't even smell like smoke.

[28]Then Nebuchadnezzar said, "Praise the God of Shadrach, Meshach and Abednego. Their God has sent his angel and saved his servants from the fire! These three men trusted their God. They refused to obey my command. And they were willing to die rather than serve or worship any god other than their own."

Today's Prayer

Dear God, give me a faith like Shadrach, Meshach, and Abednego had. I want to serve only you. Help me to say no to temptations. I praise you in Jesus' name, amen.

Memory Verse

"When a person is tempted and still continues strong, he should be happy. After he has proved his faith, God will reward him with life forever." James 1:12

Handwriting on the Wall

When Belshazzar was king of Babylon, he gave a great feast. He used the golden cups taken from the Temple in Jerusalem to honor his gods. As the people drank, a hand appeared and wrote a mysterious message on the palace wall.

[5]Then suddenly a person's hand appeared. The fingers wrote words on the plaster on the wall. This was near the lampstand in the royal palace. The king watched the hand as it wrote. [6]King Belshazzar was very frightened. His face turned white, and his knees knocked together. He could not stand up because his legs were too weak. [7]The king called for the magicians and wise men to be brought to him. He said to the wise men of Babylon, "I will give a reward to anyone who can read this writing and explain it. I will give him purple clothes fit for a king. I will put a gold chain around

his neck. And I will make him the third highest ruler in the kingdom."

8So all the king's wise men came in. But they could not read the writing. And they could not tell the king what it meant.

13So they brought Daniel to the king. The king said to him, "Is your name Daniel? Are you one of the captives my father the king brought from Judah? 14I have heard that the spirit of the gods is in you. And I have heard that you are very smart and have knowledge and understanding. 15The wise men and magicians were brought to me to read this writing on the wall. I wanted those men to explain to me what it means. But they could not explain it. 16I have heard that you are able to explain what things mean. And you can find the answers to hard problems. Read this writing on the wall and explain it to me. If you can, I will give you purple clothes fit for a king. And I will put a gold chain around your neck. And you will become the third highest ruler in the kingdom."

Today's Prayer

Heavenly Father, I praise you. Forgive me when I am proud. All things belong to you, even my very life. I want to honor you in everything I think and say and do. In Jesus' holy name I pray, amen.

Memory Verse
"When a person is tempted and still continues strong, he should be happy. After he has proved his faith, God will reward him with life forever." James 1:12

Daniel Reads the Message

When the king's wise men could not read the message on the wall, he called Daniel. Daniel was one of the men who had been brought from Jerusalem as a captive. The king asked Daniel what the message meant.

¹⁷Then Daniel answered the king, "You may keep your gifts for yourself. Or you may give those rewards to someone else. I will read the writing on the wall for you. And I will explain to you what it means.

²³"You have turned against the Lord of heaven. You ordered the drinking cups from the Temple of the Lord to be brought to you. Then you and your royal guests drank wine from them. Your wives and your slave women also drank wine from them. You praised the gods of silver, gold, bronze, iron, wood and stone. They are not really gods. They cannot see or hear or understand anything. But

you did not honor God. He is the One who has power over your life and everything you do. [24]So God sent the hand that wrote on the wall.

[25]"These are the words that were written on the wall: 'Mene, mene, tekel, parsin.'

[26]"This is what these words mean: Mene: God has counted the days until your kingdom will end. [27]Tekel: You have been weighed on the scales and found not good enough. [28]Parsin: Your kingdom is being divided. It will be given to the Medes and the Persians."

[29]Then Belshazzar gave an order for Daniel to be dressed in purple clothes. A gold chain was put around his neck. And he was announced to be the third highest ruler in the kingdom. [30]That very same night Belshazzar, king of the Babylonian people, was killed. [31]A man named Darius the Mede became the new king. Darius was 62 years old.

Today's Prayer

Dear Lord, give me the courage to be like Daniel. Help me tell others about you. Thank you for giving me the things I need. I pray in Jesus' name, amen.

Memory Verse

"When a person is tempted and still continues strong, he should be happy. After he has proved his faith, God will reward him with life forever." James 1:12

The Lions' Den

After Belshazzar's death, Darius became king. He kept Daniel as one of his supervisors. Jealous men tricked the king into making an evil law. It said that for thirty days the people could pray only to the king. Anyone who broke the law would be thrown into a den of lions.

[13]Then those men spoke to the king. They said, "Daniel is one of the captives from Judah. And he is not paying attention to the law you wrote. Daniel still prays to his God three times every day." [14]The king became very upset when he heard this. He decided he had to save Daniel. He worked until sunset trying to think of a way to save him.

[15]Then those men went as a group to the king. They said, "Remember, our king, the law of the Medes and Persians. It says that no law or command given by the king can be changed."

[16]So King Darius gave the order.

They brought Daniel and threw him into the lions' den. The king said to Daniel, "May the God you serve all the time save you!" [17]A big stone was brought. It was put over the opening of the lions' den. Then the king used his signet ring to put his special seal on the rock.

[18]Then King Darius went back to his palace. He did not eat that night. He did not have any entertainment brought to entertain him. And he could not sleep.

[19]The next morning King Darius got up at dawn. He hurried to the lions' den. [20]As he came near the den, he was worried. He called out to Daniel. He said, "Daniel, servant of the living God! Has your God that you always worship been able to save you from the lions?"

[21]Daniel answered, "My king, live forever! [22]My God sent his angel to close the lions' mouths. They have not hurt me, because my God knows I am innocent. I never did anything wrong to you, my king."

Today's Prayer

Holy Lord, protect me from jealous people and those who would hurt me. Give me courage to face their threats and always praise your name. Thank you for watching over me. Through Christ I pray, amen.

Memory Verse

"When a person is tempted and still continues strong, he should be happy. After he has proved his faith, God will reward him with life forever." James 1:12

Jonah Runs from God

God told his prophet Jonah to go to the evil city of Nineveh and to preach against it. Jonah wanted God to destroy the city instead, so he got on a ship and tried to run away from the Lord. When God sent a storm, the sailors found out what Jonah had done.

¹⁴So the men cried to the Lord, "Lord, please don't let us die because of taking this man's life. Please don't think we are guilty of killing an innocent man. Lord, you have caused all this to happen. You wanted it this way." ¹⁵Then the men picked up Jonah and threw him into the sea. So the sea became calm. ¹⁶Then they began to fear the Lord very much. They offered a sacrifice to the Lord. They also made promises to him.

¹⁷And the Lord caused a very big fish to swallow Jonah. Jonah was in the stomach of the fish three days and three nights.

2 While Jonah was in the stomach of the fish, he prayed to the Lord his God. Jonah said,

²"I was in danger.
>   So I called to the Lord,
>   and he answered me.
I was about to die.
>   So I cried to you,
>   and you heard my voice.
³You threw me into the sea.
>   I went down, down into the
>   deep sea.
The water was all around me.
>   Your powerful waves flowed
>   over me.

⁷"When my life had almost gone,
>   I remembered the Lord.
Lord, I prayed to you.
>   And you heard my prayers in your
>   Holy Temple.
⁹Lord, I will praise and thank you
>   while I give sacrifices to you.
I will make promises to you.
>   And I will do what I promise.
Salvation comes from the Lord!"

¹⁰Then the Lord spoke to the fish. And the fish spit Jonah out of its stomach onto the dry land.

Today's Prayer

Holy God, you see and know everything I do. Thank you for watching over me and guiding my footsteps. I want to do your will and never try to hide from you. In Jesus' name, amen.

Memory Verse

"Jesus answered, 'If anyone loves me, then he will obey my teaching. My Father will love him, and we will come to him and make our home with him.'" John 14:23

Jonah Obeys God

After three days in the stomach of a big fish, Jonah was ready to listen when God spoke to him again.

3 Then the Lord spoke his word to Jonah again. The Lord said, ²"Get up. Go to the great city Nineveh. Preach against it what I tell you."

³So Jonah obeyed the Lord. He got up and went to Nineveh. It was a very large city. It took a person three days just to walk across it. ⁴Jonah entered the city. When he had walked for one day, he preached to the people. He said, "After 40 days, Nineveh will be destroyed!"

⁵The people of Nineveh believed in God. They announced they would stop eating for a while. They put on rough cloth to show how sad they were. All the people in the city wore

the cloth. People from the most important to the least important did this.

[6]When the king of Nineveh heard this news, he got up from his throne. He took off his robe. He covered himself with rough cloth and sat in ashes to show how upset he was.

[7]He made an announcement and sent it through the city. The announcement said: "By command of the king and his important men: No person or animal should eat anything. No herd or flock will be allowed to taste anything. Do not let them eat food or drink water. [8]But every person and animal should be covered with rough cloth. People should cry loudly to God. Everyone must turn away from his evil life. Everyone must stop doing harm. [9]Maybe God will change his mind. Maybe he will stop being angry. Then we will not die."

[10]God saw what the people did. He saw that they stopped doing evil things. So God changed his mind and did not do what he had warned. He did not punish them.

Today's Prayer

Dear Lord in heaven, thank you for never forgetting me, no matter what I do. When I disobey you, as Jonah did, turn me around and help me go the right direction. I pray in Christ's name, amen.

Memory Verse

"Jesus answered, 'If anyone loves me, then he will obey my teaching. My Father will love him, and we will come to him and make our home with him.'" John 14:23

God's Blessing

Micah was a prophet of God. Many years ahead of time he said that the people would return from captivity. Even more important, he said the Savior would be born in Bethlehem.

²"But you, Bethlehem Ephrathah,
    are one of the smallest towns in
        Judah.
But from you will come one who will
        rule Israel for me.
    He comes from very old times,
    from days long ago."

³The Lord will leave his people in
        Babylon
    until Jerusalem, who is in labor,
        gives birth to her children.
Then his brothers who are in captiv-
        ity will return.
    They will come back to the people
        of Israel living in Judah.
⁴Then the ruler of Israel will stand
    and take care of his people.
He will lead them with the Lord's
        power.
    He will lead them in the wonderful
        name of the Lord his God.
They will live in safety.
    And his greatness will be known
        all over the earth.
⁵   He will bring peace.

Today's Prayer

Dear loving God, thank you
for sending your son, Jesus,
to be the Savior of the
world. Help me to know
Jesus better and to tell
others about him. In his
name, amen.

Memory Verse
"Jesus answered, 'If anyone loves me, then he will
obey my teaching. My Father will love him, and
we will come to him and make our home with
him.'" John 14:23

A Happy Song

Zephaniah was a prophet in the days of King Josiah. He knew that Jerusalem was to be destroyed because of evil. He also knew the people would someday be brought back and God would love and bless them. So he wrote a song of joy.

[14]Sing, Jerusalem.
 Israel, shout for joy!
Jerusalem, be happy.
 Rejoice with all your heart.
[15]The Lord has stopped punish-
 ing you.
 He has sent your enemies away.
The King of Israel, the Lord, is
 with you.
 You will never again be afraid of
 being harmed.
[16]On that day Jerusalem will be told,
 "Don't be afraid, city of
 Jerusalem.
 Don't be so discouraged that you
 can't do anything.
[17]The Lord your God is with you.

The mighty One will save you.
The Lord will be happy with you.
    You will rest in his love.
    He will sing and be joyful
        about you."

[18]"I will take away the sadness
        planned for you.
    It would have made you very
        ashamed.
[19]At that time I will punish
    all those who harmed you.
I will save my people who are hurt.
    I will gather my people who are
        scattered.
I will give them praise and honor
    in every place where they were
        disgraced.
[20]At that time I will gather you.
    At that time I will bring you back
        home.
I will give you honor and praise
    from people everywhere.
That will happen when I give you
        back your riches.
    You will see this with your own
        eyes," says the Lord.

Today's Prayer

Lord, my God, you have given me wonderful promises. Thank you for the joy that comes from obeying you. Help me sing your praises everywhere. I pray in Jesus' name, amen.

Memory Verse
"Jesus answered, 'If anyone loves me, then he will obey my teaching. My Father will love him, and we will come to him and make our home with him.'" John 14:23

Following the Lord

The Old Testament ends with sadness. The great kingdom of Israel had been destroyed because the people would not obey God's teachings. Psalm 119 tells about the happiness that comes from obeying the Lord.

119 Happy are the people who live pure lives.
  They follow the Lord's teachings.
²Happy are the people who keep his rules.
  They ask him for help with their whole heart.
³They don't do what is wrong.
  They follow his ways.
⁴Lord, you gave your orders
  to be followed completely.
⁷When I learned that your laws are fair,
  I praised you with an honest heart.
⁸I will meet your demands.
  So please don't ever leave me.

⁹How can a young person live a pure
     life?
  He can do it by obeying your word.
¹⁰With all my heart I try to obey
     you, God.
  Don't let me break your
     commands.
¹¹I have taken your words to heart
  so I would not sin against you.
¹²Lord, you should be praised.
  Teach me your demands.
¹³My lips will tell about
  all the laws you have spoken.
¹⁴I enjoy living by your rules
  as people enjoy great riches.
¹⁵I think about your orders
  and study your ways.
¹⁶I enjoy obeying your demands.
  And I will not forget your word.

¹⁷Do good to me, your servant, so I
     can live,
  so I can obey your word.
¹⁸Open my eyes to see the wonderful
     things
  in your teachings.

Today's Prayer

Dear God, I want to follow you completely. Thank you for the rules you have given to guide me. In the Savior's name, amen.

Memory Verse
"Jesus answered, 'If anyone loves me, then he will obey my teaching. My Father will love him, and we will come to him and make our home with him.'" John 14:23

Zechariah Has a Vision

Over four hundred years have passed since the last prophet told about the coming of the Messiah. Then one day God sent a special messenger to a priest named Zechariah as he was burning incense inside the Temple.

[12]When he saw the angel, Zechariah was confused and frightened. [13]But the angel said to him, "Zechariah, don't be afraid. Your prayer has been heard by God. Your wife, Elizabeth, will give birth to a son. You will name him John. [14]You will be very happy. Many people will be happy because of his birth. [15]John will be a great man for the Lord. He will never drink wine or beer. Even at the time John is born, he will be filled with the Holy Spirit. [16]He will help many people of Israel return to the Lord their God. [17]He himself will go first before the Lord. John will be powerful in spirit like Elijah. He will make peace between

fathers and their children. He will bring those who are not obeying God back to the right way of thinking. He will make people ready for the coming of the Lord."

18Zechariah said to the angel, "How can I know that what you say is true? I am an old man, and my wife is old, too."

19The angel answered him, "I am Gabriel. I stand before God. God sent me to talk to you and to tell you this good news. 20Now, listen! You will not be able to talk until the day these things happen. You will lose your speech because you did not believe what I told you. But these things will really happen."

22Then Zechariah came outside, but he could not speak to them.

24Later, Zechariah's wife, Elizabeth, became pregnant.

Today's Prayer

Dear God, your promises are wonderful. Thank you for sending John to make the world ready for Jesus. Help me prepare myself to tell others the good news about Jesus also. In his name, amen.

Memory Verse
"Today your Savior was born in David's town. He is Christ, the Lord." Luke 2:11

Mary and the Angel

Elizabeth was so happy that she would at last have a son who would be a special servant to God. While she waited for the child to be born, God sent another messenger to a young woman in the small town of Nazareth.

26-27During Elizabeth's sixth month of pregnancy, God sent the angel Gabriel to a virgin who lived in Nazareth, a town in Galilee. She was engaged to marry a man named Joseph from the family of David. Her name was Mary. 28The angel came to her and said, "Greetings! The Lord has blessed you and is with you."

²⁹But Mary was very confused by what the angel said. Mary wondered, "What does this mean?"

³⁰The angel said to her, "Don't be afraid, Mary, because God is pleased with you. ³¹Listen! You will become pregnant. You gill give birth to a son, and you will name him Jesus. ³²He will be great, and people will call him the Son of the Most High. The Lord God will give him the throne of King David, his ancestor. ³³He will rule over the people of Jacob forever. His kingdom will never end."

³⁴Mary said to the angel, "How will this happen? I am a virgin!"

³⁵The angel said to Mary, "The Holy Spirit will come upon you, and the power of the Most High will cover you. The baby will be holy. He will be called the Son of God. ³⁶Now listen! Elizabeth, your relative, is very old. But she is also pregnant with a son. Everyone thought she could not have a baby, but she has been pregnant for six months. ³⁷God can do everything!"

³⁸Mary said, "I am the servant girl of the Lord. Let this happen to me as you say!" Then the angel went away.

Today's Prayer

Dear heavenly Father, your power is awesome. Help me accept your word, just as Mary believed and accepted your promise long ago. Thank you for sending your son. I pray in his name, amen.

Memory Verse

"Today your Savior was born in David's town. He is Christ, the Lord." Luke 2:11

Jesus Is Born

Joseph, Mary's husband, was from Bethlehem. He had to return to that city to be counted in the census. When he and Mary arrived there, the only room they could find in the crowded city was a small space in a shelter for animals.

⁶While Joseph and Mary were in Bethlehem, the time came for her to have the baby. ⁷She gave birth to her first son. There were no rooms left in the inn. So she wrapped the baby with cloths and laid him in a box where animals are fed.

⁸That night, some shepherds were in the fields nearby watching their sheep. ⁹An angel of the Lord stood before them. The glory of the Lord was shining around them, and suddenly they became very frightened. ¹⁰The angel said to them, "Don't be afraid, because I am bringing you some good news. It will be a joy to all the people. ¹¹Today your Savior was born in

David's town. He is Christ, the Lord. [12]This is how you will know him: You will find a baby wrapped in cloths and lying in a feeding box."

[13]Then a very large group of angels from heaven joined the first angel. All the angels were praising God, saying:
[14]"Give glory to God in heaven,
  and on earth let there be
    peace to the people who
    please God."

[16]So the shepherds went quickly and found Mary and Joseph. [17]And the shepherds saw the baby lying in a feeding box. Then they told what the angels had said about this child. [18]Everyone was amazed when they heard what the shepherds said to them. [20]Then the shepherds went back to their sheep, praising God and thanking him for everything that they had seen and heard. It was just as the angel had told them.

Today's Prayer

Dear Lord, I know Jesus was born in Bethlehem just as you promised he would be. Thank you for your love which made this possible. Help me to appreciate your wonderful gift. In the Savior's name, amen.

Memory Verse
"Today your Savior was born in David's town. He is Christ, the Lord." Luke 2:11

Wise Men Come

When Jesus was born, a great star appeared in the eastern sky. After seeing the star, three wise men came to Jerusalem. They were looking for the baby who was to become the king of the Jews.

2 Jesus was born in the town of Bethlehem in Judea during the time when Herod was king. After Jesus was born, some wise men from the east came to Jerusalem. ²They asked, "Where is the baby who was born to be the king of the Jews? We saw his star in the east. We came to worship him."

³When King Herod heard about this new king of the Jews, he was troubled. And all the people in Jerusalem were worried too.

⁷Then Herod had a secret meeting with the wise men from the east. He learned from them the exact time they first saw the star. ⁸Then Herod

sent the wise men to Bethlehem. He said to them, "Go and look carefully to find the child. When you find him, come tell me. Then I can go worship him too."

⁹The wise men heard the king and then left. They saw the same star they had seen in the east. It went before them until it stopped above the place where the child was. ¹⁰When the wise men saw the star, they were filled with joy. ¹¹They went to the house where the child was and saw him with his mother, Mary. They bowed down and worshiped the child. They opened the gifts they brought for him. They gave him treasures of gold, frankincense, and myrrh. ¹²But God warned the wise men in a dream not to go back to Herod. So they went home to their own country by a different way.

Today's Prayer

Dear God in heaven, help me to worship you as the wise men did. You have given me everything. So I want to give my life to you. In the name of Jesus, my Savior, amen.

Memory Verse
"Today your Savior was born in David's town. He is Christ, the Lord." Luke 2:11

Escape to Egypt

King Herod was very upset. He was afraid this new baby would grow up and become king instead of him. Herod made an evil plan to keep this from happening, but the Lord was watching over Jesus.

[13]After they left, an angel of the Lord came to Joseph in a dream. The angel said, "Get up! Take the child and his mother and escape to Egypt. Herod will start looking for the child to kill him. Stay in Egypt until I tell you to return."

[14]So Joseph got up and left for Egypt during the night with the child

and his mother. [15]Joseph stayed in Egypt until Herod died. This was to make clear the full meaning of what the Lord had said through the prophet. The Lord said, "I called my son out of Egypt."

[19]After Herod died, an angel of the Lord came to Joseph in a dream. This happened while Joseph was in Egypt. [20]The angel said, "Get up! Take the child and his mother and go to Israel. The people who were trying to kill the child are now dead."

[21]So Joseph took the child and his mother and went to Israel. [22]But he heard that Archelaus was now king in Judea. Archelaus became king when his father Herod died. So Joseph was afraid to go there. After being warned in a dream, he went to the area of Galilee. [23]He went to a town called Nazareth and lived there. And so what God had said through the prophets came true: "He will be called a Nazarene."

Today's Prayer

Dear loving God, thank you for watching over the baby Jesus just as you watch over me. Protect me from harm. In his name I pray, amen.

Memory Verse
"Today your Savior was born in David's town. He is Christ, the Lord." Luke 2:11

Jesus Grows Up

Joseph and Mary lived in Nazareth with the baby Jesus. God blessed Jesus, and he grew and became strong and wise.

⁴¹Every year Jesus' parents went to Jerusalem for the Passover Feast. ⁴²When Jesus was 12 years old, they went to the feast as they always did. ⁴³When the feast days were over, they went home. The boy Jesus stayed behind in Jerusalem, but his parents did not know it. ⁴⁴Joseph and Mary traveled for a whole day. They thought that Jesus was with them in the group. Then they began to look for him among their family and friends, ⁴⁵but they did not find him. So they went back to Jerusalem to look for him there. ⁴⁶After three days they found him. Jesus was sitting in the Temple with the religious teachers,

listening to them and asking them questions. ⁴⁷All who heard him were amazed at his understanding and wise answers. ⁴⁸When Jesus' parents saw him, they were amazed. His mother said to him, "Son, why did you do this to us? Your father and I were very worried about you. We have been looking for you."

⁴⁹Jesus asked, "Why did you have to look for me? You should have known that I must be where my Father's work is!" ⁵⁰But they did not understand the meaning of what he said.

⁵¹Jesus went with them to Nazareth and obeyed them. His mother was still thinking about all that had happened. ⁵²Jesus continued to learn more and more and to grow physically. People liked him, and he pleased God.

Today's Prayer

Thank you, Lord, for sending Jesus to live and grow up on this earth. Help me to remember that he was once my age and had problems to face just as I do. I am thankful he understands. In his name I pray, amen.

Memory Verse
"Jesus continued to learn more and more and to grow physically. People liked him, and he pleased God." Luke 2:52

John the Baptist

Zechariah and Elizabeth's son John was six months older than Jesus. As he grew up, he began telling the people that the Lord was coming.

1 This is the beginning of the Good News about Jesus Christ, the Son of God, ²as the prophet Isaiah wrote:

> "I will send my messenger ahead
>   of you.
> He will prepare your way."

³"There is a voice of a man who
    calls out in the desert:
'Prepare the way for the Lord.
    Make the road straight for him.'"

⁴John was baptizing people in the desert. He preached a baptism of changed hearts and lives for the forgiveness of sins. ⁵All the people from Judea and Jerusalem were going out to John. They told about the sins they had done. Then they were baptized by him in the Jordan River. ⁶John wore clothes made from camel's hair and had a leather belt around his waist. He ate locusts and wild honey. ⁷This is what John preached to the people: "There is one coming later who is greater than I. I am not good enough even to kneel down and untie his sandals. ⁸I baptize you with water. But the one who is coming will baptize you with the Holy Spirit."

Today's Prayer

I am thankful, God in heaven, that you sent Jesus to be my savior. Help me, like John the Baptist, to put Jesus first in my life and tell others about his love. In his name I pray, amen.

Memory Verse
"Jesus continued to learn more and more and to grow physically. People liked him, and he pleased God." Luke 2:52

Jesus Is Baptized

Even though the people of Israel did not realize who Jesus was, John the Baptist knew. One day while John was preaching, Jesus came to see him.

⁷Crowds of people came to be baptized by John. He said to them, "You poisonous snakes! Who warned you to run away from God's anger that is coming? ⁸You must do the things that will show that you really have changed your hearts. Don't say, 'Abraham is our father.' I tell you that God can make children for Abraham from these rocks here. ⁹The ax is now ready to cut down the trees. Every tree that does not produce good fruit will be cut down and thrown into the fire."

¹⁰The people asked John, "What should we do?"

¹¹John answered, "If you have two

shirts, share with the person who does not have one. If you have food, share that too."

¹²Even tax collectors came to John to be baptized. They said to John, "Teacher, what should we do?"

¹³John said to them, "Don't take more taxes from people than you have been ordered to take."

¹⁴The soldiers asked John, "What about us? What should we do?"

John said to them, "Don't force people to give you money. Don't lie about them. Be satisfied with the pay you get."

¹⁵All the people were hoping for the Christ to come, and they wondered about John. They thought, "Maybe he is the Christ."

²¹When all the people were being baptized by John, Jesus also was baptized. While Jesus was praying, heaven opened and ²²the Holy Spirit came down on him. The Spirit was in the form of a dove. Then a voice came from heaven and said, "You are my Son and I love you. I am very pleased with you."

Today's Prayer

Dear Lord, as I grow up, help me to serve you better. Help me live so you will be pleased with me. This I pray in Jesus' name, amen.

Memory Verse

"Jesus continued to learn more and more and to grow physically. People liked him, and he pleased God." Luke 2:52

Jesus Is Tested

John the Baptist was not the only one to recognize who Jesus was. The devil also knew. God allowed the devil to test Jesus.

4Then the Spirit led Jesus into the desert to be tempted by the devil. ²Jesus ate nothing for 40 days and nights. After this, he was very hungry. ³The devil came to Jesus to tempt him. The devil said, "If you are the Son of God, tell these rocks to become bread."

⁴Jesus answered, "It is written in the Scriptures, 'A person does not live only by eating bread. But a person lives by everything the Lord says.'"

⁵Then the devil led Jesus to the holy city of Jerusalem. He put Jesus on a very high place of the Temple. ⁶The devil said, "If you are the Son of

God, jump off. It is written in the Scriptures,

'He has put his angels in charge
of you.
They will catch you with their
hands.
And you will not hit your foot on a
rock.' "

[7]Jesus answered him, "It also says in the Scriptures, 'Do not test the Lord your God.' "

[8]Then the devil led Jesus to the top of a very high mountain. He showed Jesus all the kingdoms of the world and all the great things that are in those kingdoms. [9]The devil said, "If you will bow down and worship me, I will give you all these things."

[10]Jesus said to the devil, "Go away from me, Satan! It is written in the Scriptures, 'You must worship the Lord your God. Serve only him!' "

[11]So the devil left Jesus. And then some angels came to Jesus and helped him.

Today's Prayer

Holy Lord, thank you for Jesus. It gives me strength to know that he too was tempted by Satan. When I am tempted, help me to remember Jesus' answers and turn away from Satan. In Jesus' name I pray, amen.

Memory Verse
"Jesus continued to learn more and more and to grow physically. People liked him, and he pleased God." Luke 2:52

Jesus' First Miracle

Jesus, his followers, and his mother Mary were all invited to a wedding. Mary noticed that the host had no more wine for the guests. Then Jesus did his first miracle.

2 Two days later there was a wedding in the town of Cana in Galilee. Jesus' mother was there. [2]Jesus and his followers were also invited to the wedding. [3]When all the wine was gone, Jesus' mother said to him, "They have no more wine."

[4]Jesus answered, "Dear woman, why come to me? My time has not yet come."

[5]His mother said to the servants, "Do whatever he tells you to do."

[6]In that place there were six stone water jars. The Jews used jars like these in their washing ceremony. Each jar held about 20 or 30 gallons.

[7]Jesus said to the servants, "Fill the

jars with water." So they filled the jars to the top.

[8]Then he said to them, "Now take some out and give it to the master of the feast."

So the servants took the water to the master. [9]When he tasted it, the water had become wine. He did not know where the wine came from. But the servants who brought the water knew. The master of the wedding called the bridegroom [10]and said to him, "People always serve the best wine first. Later, after the guests have been drinking a lot, they serve the cheaper wine. But you have saved the best wine till now."

[11]So in Cana of Galilee, Jesus did his first miracle. There he showed his glory, and his followers believed in him.

Today's Prayer

Dear Father, thank you for Jesus, his power and his love. Thank you for my friends. Help me to live so they can see Jesus' power in my life and believe he is your son. I pray in Christ, amen.

Memory Verse
"Jesus continued to learn more and more and to grow physically. People liked him, and he pleased God." Luke 2:52

Jesus Chooses Followers

More and more people began to believe in Jesus. The time had come for him to begin telling everyone about God's plan. To do this, Jesus chose a special group of followers to help him.

⁴⁰These two men followed Jesus after they heard about him from John. One of the men was Andrew. He was Simon Peter's brother. ⁴¹The first thing Andrew did was to find his brother, Simon. He said to Simon, "We have found the Messiah." ("Messiah" means "Christ.")

⁴²Then Andrew took Simon to Jesus. Jesus looked at Simon and said, "You are Simon son of John. You will be called Cephas." ("Cephas" means "Peter.")

⁴³The next day Jesus decided to go to Galilee. He found Philip and said to him, "Follow me." ⁴⁴Philip was from the town of Bethsaida, where Andrew

and Peter lived. ⁴⁵Philip found Nathanael and told him, "Remember that Moses wrote in the law about a man who was coming, and the prophets also wrote about him. We have found him. He is Jesus, the son of Joseph. He is from Nazareth."

⁴⁶But Nathanael said to Philip, "Nazareth! Can anything good come from Nazareth?"

Philip answered, "Come and see."

⁴⁷Jesus saw Nathanael coming toward him. He said, "Here is truly a person of Israel. There is nothing false in him."

⁴⁸Nathanael asked, "How do you know me?"

Jesus answered, "I saw you when you were under the fig tree. That was before Philip told you about me."

⁴⁹Then Nathanael said to Jesus, "Teacher, you are the Son of God. You are the King of Israel."

⁵⁰Jesus said to Nathanael, "You believe in me because I told you I saw you under the fig tree. But you will see greater things than that!"

Today's Prayer

Dear loving God, thank you for giving me special friends just as you had special followers. Help me to share the good news of Jesus with my friends and family. In the name of Jesus I pray, amen.

Memory Verse
"Whoever serves me must follow me. Then my servant will be with me everywhere I am. My Father will honor anyone who serves me." John 12:26

A Miracle of Fish

One day a great crowd of people followed Jesus to the edge of Lake Galilee. It was so crowded that Jesus got into Simon's boat and asked him to push out into the water. After Jesus finished his teaching, an amazing thing happened.

5 One day Jesus was standing beside Lake Galilee. Many people were pressing all around him. They wanted to hear the word of God. ²Jesus saw two boats at the shore of the lake. The fishermen had left them and were washing their nets. ³Jesus got into one of the boats, the one which belonged to Simon. Jesus asked Simon to push off a little from the land. Then Jesus sat down in the boat and continued to teach the people on the shore.

⁴When Jesus had finished speaking, he said to Simon, "Take the boat into deep water. If you will put your nets

in the water, you will catch some fish."

⁵Simon answered, "Master, we worked hard all night trying to catch fish, but we caught nothing. But you say to put the nets in the water; so I will." ⁶The fishermen did as Jesus told them. And they caught so many fish that the nets began to break. ⁷They called to their friends in the other boat to come and help them. The friends came, and both boats were filled so full that they were almost sinking.

⁸⁻⁹The fishermen were all amazed at the many fish they caught. When Simon Peter saw what had happened, he bowed down before Jesus and said, "Go away from me, Lord. I am a sinful man!" ¹⁰James and John, the sons of Zebedee, were amazed too. (James and John were Simon's partners.)

Jesus said to Simon, "Don't be afraid. From now on you will be fishermen for men." ¹¹When the men brought their boats to the shore, they left everything and followed Jesus.

Today's Prayer

Dear Lord, thank you for Peter and the others who followed Jesus and told the world about him. Help me be a fisherman for people and bring others to Christ as they did. In Jesus' name, amen.

Memory Verse
"Whoever serves me must follow me. Then my servant will be with me everywhere I am. My Father will honor anyone who serves me." John 12:26

The Man on the Roof

After Jesus had traveled through Galilee preaching, teaching and healing the people, he returned to his home in Capernaum. The house was soon filled with people who came to hear him.

2 A few days later, Jesus came back to Capernaum. The news spread that he was home. ²So many people gathered to hear him preach that the house was full. There was no place to stand, not even outside the door. Jesus was teaching them. ³Some people came, bringing a paralyzed man to Jesus. Four of them were carrying the paralyzed man. ⁴But they could not get to Jesus because of the crowd. So they went to the roof above Jesus and made a hole in the roof. Then they lowered the mat with the paralyzed man on it. ⁵Jesus saw that these men had great faith. So he said to the paralyzed man, "Young man, your sins are forgiven."

⁶Some of the teachers of the law were sitting there. They saw what Jesus did, and they said to themselves, ⁷"Why does this man say things like that? He is saying things that are against God. Only God can forgive sins."

⁸At once Jesus knew what these teachers of the law were thinking. So he said to them, "Why are you thinking these things? ⁹Which is easier: to tell this paralyzed man, 'Your sins are forgiven,' or to tell him, 'Stand up. Take your mat and walk'? ¹⁰But I will prove to you that the Son of Man has authority on earth to forgive sins." So Jesus said to the paralyzed man, ¹¹"I tell you, stand up. Take your mat and go home." ¹²Immediately the paralyzed man stood up. He took his mat and walked out while everyone was watching him.

The people were amazed and praised God. They said, "We have never seen anything like this!"

Today's Prayer

Almighty God, thank you for Jesus' power to save. Give me faith to bring all my problems to you through Jesus. I pray in his name, amen.

Memory Verse

"Whoever serves me must follow me. Then my servant will be with me everywhere I am. My Father will honor anyone who serves me." John 12:26

Sermon on the Mount

Great crowds followed Jesus around. They wanted to hear him teach and to have him heal their diseases. Sometimes he had to get in a boat or go up on a mountain so they could hear him.

5 Jesus saw the crowds who were there. He went up on a hill and sat down. His followers came to him. ²Jesus taught the people and said:
³"Those people who know they have
        great spiritual needs are
        happy.
    The kingdom of heaven belongs to
        them.
⁴Those who are sad now are happy.
    God will comfort them.
⁵Those who are humble are happy.
    The earth will belong to them.
⁶Those who want to do right more
        than anything else are happy.
    God will fully satisfy them.

[7]Those who give mercy to others are happy.
Mercy will be given to them.
[8]Those who are pure in their thinking are happy.
They will be with God.
[9]Those who work to bring peace are happy.
God will call them his sons.
[10]Those who are treated badly for doing good are happy.
The kingdom of heaven belongs to them.
[11]"People will say bad things about you and hurt you. They will lie and say all kinds of evil things about you because you follow me. But when they do these things to you, you are happy. [12]Rejoice and be glad. You have a great reward waiting for you in heaven. People did the same evil things to the prophets who lived before you."

Today's Prayer

Dear God in heaven, thank you for the teachings of your son, Jesus. Help me understand his teachings and how he wants me to be. In the name of Jesus I pray, amen.

Memory Verse

"Whoever serves me must follow me. Then my servant will be with me everywhere I am. My Father will honor anyone who serves me." John 12:26

The Lord's Prayer

As the crowds followed Jesus, he taught them how to live better lives and how to get along with others. Then he taught them how to worship and pray.

[7]"And when you pray, don't be like those people who don't know God. They continue saying things that mean nothing. They think that God will hear them because of the many things they say. [8]Don't be like them. Your Father knows the things you need before you ask him. [9]So when you pray, you should pray like this:

'Our Father in heaven,
we pray that your name will
     always be kept holy.
¹⁰We pray that your kingdom will
     come.
We pray that what you want will
     be done,
     here on earth as it is in heaven.
¹¹Give us the food we need for
     each day.
¹²Forgive the sins we have done,
     just as we have forgiven those
     who did wrong to us.
¹³Do not cause us to be tested;
     but save us from the Evil One.'
¹⁴Yes, if you forgive others for the things they do wrong, then your Father in heaven will also forgive you for the things you do wrong. ¹⁵But if you don't forgive the wrongs of others, then your Father in heaven will not forgive the wrong things you do."

Today's Prayer

Dear Lord our God, help me to pray in that way that Jesus taught. Thank you for listening when I talk to you, and forgive me when I am not a good follower. In Jesus' name, amen.

Memory Verse
"Whoever serves me must follow me. Then my servant will be with me everywhere I am. My Father will honor anyone who serves me." John 12:26

A Soldier's Servant

Jesus spent many days healing the sick and teaching the twelve men he had chosen to help him. Then he and his followers returned to his home in Capernaum.

²In Capernaum there was an army officer. He had a servant who was so sick he was nearly dead. The officer loved the servant very much. ³When the officer heard about Jesus, he sent some older Jewish leaders to him. The officer wanted the leaders to ask Jesus to come and heal his servant. ⁴The men went to Jesus and begged

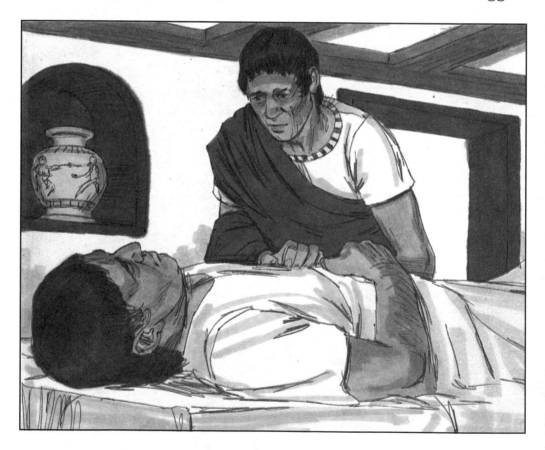

him saying, "This officer is worthy of your help. [5]He loves our people, and he built us a synagogue."

[6]So Jesus went with the men. He was getting near the officer's house when the officer sent friends to say, "Lord, you don't need to come into my house. I am not good enough for you to be under my roof. [7]That is why I did not come to you myself. You only need to say the word, and my servant will be healed. [8]I, too, am a man under the authority of other men. And I have soldiers under my command. I tell one soldier, 'Go,' and he goes. And I tell another soldier, 'Come,' and he comes. And I say to my servant, 'Do this,' and my servant obeys me."

[9]When Jesus heard this, he was amazed. He turned to the crowd following him and said, "I tell you, this is the greatest faith I have seen anywhere, even in Israel."

[10]The men who had been sent to Jesus went back to the house. There they found that the servant was healed.

Today's Prayer

God, I am so thankful for your son, Jesus. He understands how I feel when I hurt or when I am sad. I want to be like him and help others who are hurt or sad. In his name I pray, amen.

Memory Verse
"Jesus said to them, 'Let the little children come to me. Don't stop them. The kingdom of God belongs to people who are like these little children.'" Mark 10:14

A Son Lives Again

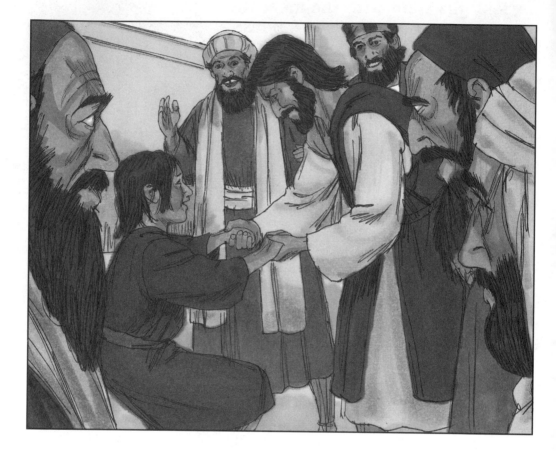

The day after Jesus healed the soldier's servant, Jesus led his followers and a great crowd of people to a town called Nain. There he saw something very sad.

¹¹The next day Jesus went to a town called Nain. His followers and a large crowd were traveling with him. ¹²When he came near the town gate, he saw a funeral. A mother, who was a widow, had lost her only son. A large crowd from the town was with the mother while her son was being carried out. ¹³When the Lord saw her, he felt very sorry for her. Jesus said to her, "Don't cry." ¹⁴He went up to the coffin and touched it. The men who were carrying it stopped. Jesus said, "Young man, I tell you, get up!" ¹⁵And the son sat up and began to talk. Then Jesus gave him back to his mother.

¹⁶All the people were amazed. They began praising God. They said, "A great prophet has come to us! God is taking care of his people."

¹⁷This news about Jesus spread through all Judea and into all the places around there.

Today's Prayer

Thank you Lord for the healing power of Jesus. Thank you for his concern and care for me. Let me follow Christ's example and show love to others. In Jesus' name, amen.

Memory Verse

"Jesus said to them, 'Let the little children come to me. Don't stop them. The kingdom of God belongs to people who are like these little children.'" Mark 10:14

Forgive Each Other

Peter came to Jesus and asked if he should forgive someone as many as seven times. Jesus told Peter that the person should be forgiven seventy-seven times! Jesus told a story to teach this lesson.

[23]"The kingdom of heaven is like a king who decided to collect the money his servants owed him. [24]So the king began to collect his money. One servant owed him several million dollars. [25]But the servant did not have enough money to pay his master, the king. So the master ordered that everything the servant owned should be sold, even the servant's wife and children. The money would be used to pay the king what the servant owed.

[26]"But the servant fell on his knees and begged, 'Be patient with me. I will pay you everything I owe.' [27]The master felt sorry for his servant. So the

master told the servant he did not have to pay. He let the servant go free.

²⁸"Later, that same servant found another servant who owed him a few dollars. The servant grabbed the other servant around the neck and said, 'Pay me the money you owe me!'

²⁹"The other servant fell on his knees and begged him, 'Be patient with me. I will pay you everything I owe.'

³⁰"But the first servant refused to be patient. He threw the other servant into prison until he could pay everything he owed. ³¹All the other servants saw what happened. They were very sorry. So they went and told their master all that had happened.

³²"Then the master called his servant in and said, 'You evil servant! You begged me to forget what you owed. So I told you that you did not have to pay anything. ³³I had mercy on you. You should have had the mercy on that other servant.' "

Today's Prayer

Dear God, when people are unfair or treat me badly, it is easy to be angry. Teach me to forgive. Help me remember that I am a sinner and that you forgive me as I forgive others. Through Christ I pray, amen.

Memory Verse
"Jesus said to them, 'Let the little children come to me. Don't stop them. The kingdom of God belongs to people who are like these little children.'" Mark 10:14

Jesus Heals a Boy

Jesus did his miracles, not to make himself famous, but to help people believe he was the Son of God. For a second time in Cana, Jesus performed a miracle.

⁴⁶Jesus went to visit Cana in Galilee again. This is where Jesus had changed the water into wine. One of the king's important officers lived in the city of Capernaum. This man's son was sick. ⁴⁷The man heard that Jesus had come from Judea and was now in Galilee. He went to Jesus and begged him to come to Capernaum

and heal his son. His son was almost dead. [48]Jesus said to him, "You people must see signs and miracles before you will believe in me."

[49]The officer said, "Sir, come before my child dies."

[50]Jesus answered, "Go. Your son will live."

The man believed what Jesus told him and went home. [51]On the way the man's servants came and met him. They told him, "Your son is well."

[52]The man asked, "What time did my son begin to get well?"

They answered, "It was about one o'clock yesterday when the fever left him."

[53]The father knew that one o'clock was the exact time that Jesus had said, "Your son will live." So the man and all the people of his house believed in Jesus.

[54]That was the second miracle that Jesus did after coming from Judea to Galilee.

Today's Prayer

Holy Lord, I didn't see the miracles Jesus did, but I believe he is your son. Help me share my faith with others so they also will believe in him. In his name I pray, amen.

Memory Verse
"Jesus said to them, 'Let the little children come to me. Don't stop them. The kingdom of God belongs to people who are like these little children.'" Mark 10:14

A Story of a Farmer

As people began to hear about what Jesus did and said, they came from many places to hear him teach. Often Jesus taught lessons using stories.

[5]"A farmer went out to plant his seed. While he was planting, some seed fell beside the road. People walked on the seed, and the birds ate all this seed. [6]Some seed fell on rock. It began to grow but then died because it had no water. [7]Some seed fell among thorny weeds. This seed grew, but later the weeds choked the good plants. [8]And some seed fell on good ground. This seed grew and made 100 times more grain."

Jesus finished the story. Then he called out, "You people who hear me, listen!"

[9]Jesus' followers asked him, "What does this story mean?"

[11]"This is what the story means: The seed is God's teaching. [12]What is the seed that fell beside the road? It is like the people who hear God's teaching, but then the devil comes and takes it away from their hearts. So they cannot believe the teaching and be saved. [13]What is the seed that fell on rock? It is like those who hear God's teaching and accept it gladly. But they don't have deep roots. They believe for a while, but then trouble comes. They stop believing and turn away from God. [14]What is the seed that fell among the thorny weeds? It is like those who hear God's teaching, but they let the worries, riches, and pleasures of this life keep them from growing. So they never produce good fruit. [15]And what is the seed that fell on the good ground? That is like those who hear God's teaching with a good, honest heart. They obey God's teaching and patiently produce good fruit."

Today's Prayer

Dear God in heaven, help me understand the teachings of Jesus. Give me an honest heart so I will be like the good ground and produce good fruit. In Christ I pray, amen.

Memory Verse
"Jesus said to them, 'Let the little children come to me. Don't stop them. The kingdom of God belongs to people who are like these little children.'" Mark 10:14

The Man by the Pool

While in Jerusalem Jesus went by the Pool of Bethzatha. People believed that the first person who got into the pool after the waters moved would be healed. On this Sabbath day, many blind, crippled and paralyzed people were waiting by the pool.

5 Later Jesus went to Jerusalem for a special Jewish feast. ²In Jerusalem there is a pool with five covered porches. In the Jewish language it is called Bethzatha. This pool is near the Sheep Gate. ³Many sick people were lying on the porches beside the pool. Some were blind, some were crippled, and some were paralyzed. ⁵There was a man lying there who had been sick for 38 years. ⁶Jesus saw the man and knew that he had been sick for a very long time. So Jesus asked him, "Do you want to be well?"

⁷The sick man answered, "Sir, there is no one to help me get into the pool when the water starts moving. I try to

be the first one into the water. But when I try, someone else always goes in before I can."

⁸Then Jesus said, "Stand up. Pick up your mat and walk." ⁹And immediately the man was well. He picked up his mat and began to walk.

The day all this happened was a Sabbath day. ¹⁰So the Jews said to the man who had been healed, "Today is the Sabbath. It is against our law for you to carry your mat on the Sabbath day."

¹¹But he answered, "The man who made me well told me, 'Pick up your mat and walk.'"

¹⁶Jesus was doing this on the Sabbath day. So the Jews began to do bad things to him. ¹⁷But Jesus said to them, "My Father never stops working. And so I work, too."

¹⁸This made the Jews try harder to kill him. They said, "First Jesus was breaking the law about the Sabbath day. Then he said that God is his own Father! He is making himself equal with God!"

Today's Prayer

Oh Lord, my God, thank you for loving me so much. I thank you and your son, Jesus, for always caring for me and for people everywhere. In Jesus' name, amen.

Memory Verse
"Praise the Lord! Thank the Lord because he is good. His love continues forever." Psalm 106:1

Jesus Stops a Storm

Sometimes Jesus went with his followers in a boat to get away from the crowds. One night he showed them his power over nature.

³⁵That evening, Jesus said to his followers, "Come with me across the lake." ³⁶He and the followers left the people there. They went in the boat that Jesus was already sitting in. There were also other boats with them. ³⁷A very strong wind came up on the lake. The waves began coming over the sides and into the boat. It was almost full of water. ³⁸Jesus was at the back of the boat, sleeping with his head on a pillow. The followers went to him and woke him. They said, "Teacher, do you care about us? We will drown!"

³⁹Jesus stood up and commanded the wind and the waves to stop. He said, "Quiet! Be still!" Then the wind stopped, and the lake became calm.

⁴⁰Jesus said to his followers, "Why are you afraid? Do you still have no faith?"

⁴¹The followers were very afraid and asked each other, "What kind of man is this? Even the wind and the waves obey him!"

Today's Prayer

Wonderful God, help me to understand that the power of Jesus has no limits. Because you love me, I won't be afraid. In the name of Christ Jesus I pray, amen.

Memory Verse

"Praise the Lord! Thank the Lord because he is good. His love continues forever." Psalm 106:1

A Man with Demons

On the other side of the lake was the country of the Gerasenes. Here, Jesus met a man who had many demons in him. No one could heal him, except Jesus.

5Jesus and his followers went across the lake to the region of the Gerasene people. ²When Jesus got out of the boat, a man came to him from the caves where dead people were buried. This man, who lived in the caves, had an evil spirit living in him. ³No one could tie him up, not even with a chain. ⁴Many times people had used chains to tie the man's hands and feet. But he always broke the chains off. No one was strong enough to control him. ⁵Day and night he would wander around the burial caves and on the hills, screaming and cutting himself with stones. ⁶While Jesus was still far away, the man saw

him. He ran to Jesus and knelt down before him. [7-8]Jesus said to the man, "You evil spirit, come out of that man."

But the man shouted in a loud voice, "What do you want with me, Jesus, Son of the Most High God? I beg you, promise God that you will not punish me!"

[9]Then Jesus asked the man, "What is your name?"

The man answered, "My name is Legion, because I have many spirits in me." [10]The man begged Jesus again and again not to send the spirits out of that area.

[11]A large herd of pigs was eating on a hill near there. [12]The evil spirits begged Jesus, "Send us to the pigs. Let us go into them." [13]So Jesus allowed them to do this. The evil spirits left the man and went into the pigs. Then the herd of pigs rushed down the hill into the lake and were drowned. There were about 2,000 pigs in that herd.

Today's Prayer

Dear God, I am glad that you are stronger than Satan. Thank you for showing us your great power. In Jesus' holy name, amen.

Memory Verse
"Praise the Lord! Thank the Lord because he is good. His love continues forever." Psalm 106:1

Jesus Heals a Girl

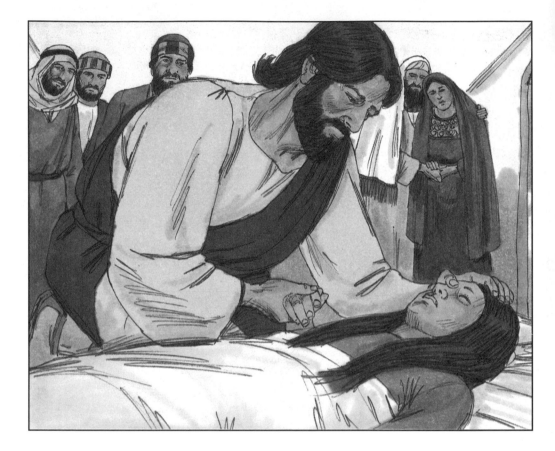

Jesus had great love and pity for those who were ill or who were sad. One day while Jesus was teaching, an important religious leader came to him, asking for his help.

¹⁸While Jesus was saying these things, a ruler of the synagogue came to him. The ruler bowed down before Jesus and said, "My daughter has just died. But come and touch her with your hand, and she will live again."

¹⁹So Jesus stood up and went with the ruler. Jesus' followers went too.

²⁰Then a woman who had been bleeding for 12 years came behind Jesus and touched the edge of his coat. ²¹She was thinking, "If I can touch his coat, then I will be healed."

²²Jesus turned and saw the woman. He said, "Be happy, dear woman. You are made well because you believed." And the woman was healed at once.

²³Jesus continued along with the ruler and went into the ruler's house. Jesus saw people there who play music for funerals. And he saw many people there crying. ²⁴Jesus said, "Go away. The girl is not dead. She is only asleep." But the people laughed at Jesus. ²⁵After the crowd had been put outside, Jesus went into the girl's room. He took her hand, and she stood up. ²⁶The news about this spread all around the area.

Today's Prayer

Dear God, thank you for Jesus' great love and pity for those who are sick or sad. Give me a loving heart so that I can comfort my friends and family. I pray in the name of Jesus, amen.

Memory Verse
"Praise the Lord! Thank the Lord because he is good. His love continues forever." Psalm 106:1

His Love Endures Forever

We must be thankful for God's love. We can see it in the wonders of our universe and in everything around us. God's love will never end.

136 Give thanks to the Lord because he is good.
His love continues forever.
²Give thanks to the God over all gods.
His love continues forever.
³Give thanks to the Lord of all lords.
His love continues forever.

⁴Only he can do great miracles.

His love continues forever.
⁵With his wisdom he made the skies.
His love continues forever.
⁶He spread out the earth on the seas.
His love continues forever.
⁷He made the sun and the moon.
His love continues forever.
⁸He made the sun to rule the day.
His love continues forever.
⁹He made the moon and stars to rule
the night.
His love continues forever.

²³He remembered us when we were in
trouble.
His love continues forever.
²⁴He freed us from our enemies.
His love continues forever.
²⁵He gives food to every living
creature.
His love continues forever.

²⁶Give thanks to the God of heaven.
His love continues forever.

Today's Prayer

Holy Lord, I am so glad that
your love continues forever.
Help me always to show
love to those around me.
I pray in the name of Jesus
who loves me, amen.

Memory Verse
"Praise the Lord! Thank the Lord because he is
good. His love continues forever." Psalm 106:1

Jesus Feeds 5,000

Jesus had sent his twelve special followers out to other towns. He wanted them to tell people about God's kingdom and to heal the sick. They had many things to share when they returned.

¹⁰When the apostles returned, they told Jesus all the things they had done on their trip. Then Jesus took them away to a town called Bethsaida. There, Jesus and his apostles could be alone together. ¹¹But the people learned where Jesus went and followed him. Jesus welcomed them and talked with them about God's kingdom. He healed those who needed to be healed.

¹²Late in the afternoon, the 12 apostles came to Jesus and said, "No one lives in this place. Send the people away. They need to find food and places to sleep in the towns and countryside around here."

[13]But Jesus said to them, "You give them something to eat."

They said, "We have only five loaves of bread and two fish. Do you want us to go buy food for all these people?" [14](There were about 5,000 men there.)

Jesus said to his followers, "Tell the people to sit in groups of about 50 people."

[15]So the followers did this, and all the people sat down. [16]Then Jesus took the five loaves of bread and two fish. He looked up to heaven and thanked God for the food. Then Jesus divided the food and gave it to the followers to give to the people. [17]All the people ate and were satisfied. And there was much food left. Twelve baskets were filled with pieces of food that were not eaten.

Today's Prayer

Dear God in heaven, help me to see your power all around me. I know Jesus is your son and that he wants to help me with his great power. I pray in his name, amen.

Memory Verse

"Jesus said to her, 'I am the resurrection and the life. He who believes in me will have life even if he dies.'" John 11:25

Jesus Walks on Water

Jesus had sent his followers away in a boat. Later, he came to join them, but they thought he was a ghost!

²²Then Jesus made his followers get into the boat. He told them to go ahead of him to the other side of the lake. Jesus stayed there to tell the people they could go home. ²³After he said good-bye to them, he went alone up into the hills to pray. It was late, and Jesus was there alone. ²⁴By this time, the boat was already far away on the lake. The boat was having trouble because of the waves, and the wind was blowing against it.

²⁵Between three and six o'clock in the morning, Jesus' followers were still in the boat. Jesus came to them. He was walking on the water. ²⁶ When the followers saw him walking on the

water, they were afraid. They said, "It's a ghost!" and cried out in fear.

²⁷But Jesus quickly spoke to them. He said, "Have courage! It is I! Don't be afraid."

²⁸Peter said, "Lord, if that is really you, then tell me to come to you on the water."

²⁹Jesus said, "Come."

And Peter left the boat and walked on the water to Jesus. ³⁰But when Peter saw the wind and the waves he became afraid and began to sink. He shouted, "Lord, save me!"

³¹Then Jesus reached out his hand and caught Peter. Jesus said, "Your faith is small. Why did you doubt?"

³²After Peter and Jesus were in the boat, the wind became calm. ³³Then those who were in the boat worshiped Jesus and said, "Truly you are the Son of God!"

Today's Prayer

Holy Father, sometimes, like Peter, I am afraid and I forget to trust you. Help me know that Jesus is always with me when I follow him. I praise you in his name, amen.

Memory Verse

"Jesus said to her, 'I am the resurrection and the life. He who believes in me will have life even if he dies.'" John 11:25

Jesus Helps a Woman

At the time Jesus lived, Jewish people had little to do with people who were not Jews. But on this day a woman who wasn't a Jew came to Jesus, begging him for help. And she didn't give up.

²¹Jesus left that place and went to the area of Tyre and Sidon. ²²A Canaanite woman from that area came to Jesus. The woman cried out, "Lord, Son of David, please help me! My daughter has a demon, and she is suffering very much."

²³But Jesus did not answer the woman. So the followers came to Jesus and begged him, "Tell the woman to go away. She is following us and shouting."

²⁴Jesus answered, "God sent me only to the lost sheep, the people of Israel."

²⁵Then the woman came to Jesus again. She bowed before him and said, "Lord, help me!"

²⁶Jesus answered, "It is not right to take the children's bread and give it to the dogs."

²⁷The woman said, "Yes, Lord, but even the dogs eat the pieces of food that fall from their masters' table."

²⁸Then Jesus answered, "Woman, you have great faith! I will do what you asked me to do." And at that moment the woman's daughter was healed.

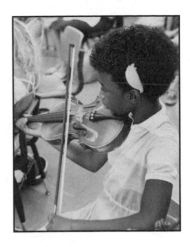

Today's Prayer

Dear Lord, Jesus helped a woman who wasn't from his race because he loves all people. As Christ's follower, teach me to love and help all people, even those who are different from me. In Jesus' name, amen.

Memory Verse
"Jesus said to her, 'I am the resurrection and the life. He who believes in me will have life even if he dies.'" John 11:25

Peter's Faith

Many people followed Jesus as he taught. Some were just curious. Some thought he was just a prophet. But a few believed he was truly the Son of God. One day Jesus asked his followers two questions. Peter's answer was very important.

¹³Jesus went to the area of Caesarea Philippi. He said to his followers, "I am the Son of Man. Who do the people say I am?"

¹⁴They answered, "Some people say you are John the Baptist. Others say you are Elijah. And others say that you are Jeremiah or one of the prophets."

¹⁵Then Jesus asked them, "And who do you say I am?"

¹⁶Simon Peter answered, "You are the Christ, the Son of the living God."

¹⁷Jesus answered, "You are blessed, Simon son of Jonah. No person taught you that. My Father in heaven showed you who I am. ¹⁸So I tell you, you are Peter. And I will build my church on this rock. The power of death will not be able to defeat my church. ¹⁹I will give you the keys of the kingdom of heaven. The things you don't allow on earth will be the things that God does not allow. The things you allow on earth will be the things that God allows." ²⁰Then Jesus warned his followers not to tell anyone that he was the Christ.

Today's Prayer

Holy Lord, I believe that Jesus is the Son of God. Give me courage to always believe that and to share my love for him with others. In Jesus' name I pray, amen.

Memory Verse

"Jesus said to her, 'I am the resurrection and the life. He who believes in me will have life even if he dies.'" John 11:25

Moses and Elijah Appear

Even Jesus' closest followers had a hard time understanding that Jesus was the Son of God. One day God spoke to them from a cloud to help them understand.

²⁸About eight days after Jesus said these things, he took Peter, James, and John and went up on a mountain to pray. ²⁹While Jesus was praying, his face was changed, and his clothes became shining white. ³⁰Then two men were talking with Jesus. The men were Moses and Elijah. ³¹They appeared in heavenly glory, talking with

Jesus about his death which would happen in Jerusalem. ³²Peter and the others were asleep. But they woke up and saw the glory of Jesus. They also saw the two men who were standing with him. ³³When Moses and Elijah were about to leave, Peter said, "Master, it is good that we are here. We will put three tents here—one for you, one for Moses, and one for Elijah." (Peter did not know what he was saying.)

³⁴While Peter was saying these things, a cloud came down all around them. Peter, James, and John became afraid when the cloud covered them. ³⁵A voice came from the cloud. The voice said, "This is my Son. He is the One I have chosen. Obey him."

³⁶When the voice finished speaking, only Jesus was there. Peter, James, and John said nothing. At that time they told no one about what they had seen.

Today's Prayer

Lord in heaven, I want to put Jesus first in my life above all others. I know he is your chosen son. I praise you for sending him to show us how to obey your will. In Christ I pray, amen.

Memory Verse

"Jesus said to her, 'I am the resurrection and the life. He who believes in me will have life even if he dies.'" John 11:25

A Good Samaritan

A Jewish teacher tried to test Jesus. He asked, "Who is my neighbor?" To answer his question Jesus told a story about a man from Samaria, a people the Jews hated.

[30]To answer this question, Jesus said, "A man was going down the road from Jerusalem to Jericho. Some robbers attacked him. They tore off his clothes and beat him. Then they left him lying there, almost dead. [31]It happened that a Jewish priest was going down the road. When the priest saw the man, he walked by on the

other side of the road. ³²Next, a Levite came there. He went over and looked at the man. Then he walked by on the other side of the road. ³³Then a Samaritan traveling down the road came to where the hurt man was lying. He saw the man and felt very sorry for him. ³⁴The Samaritan went to him and poured olive oil and wine on his wounds and bandaged them. He put the hurt man on his own donkey and took him to an inn. At the inn, the Samaritan took care of him. ³⁵The next day, the Samaritan brought out two silver coins and gave them to the innkeeper. The Samaritan said, 'Take care of this man. If you spend more money on him, I will pay it back to you when I come again.' "

³⁶Then Jesus said, "Which one of these three men do you think was a neighbor to the man who was attacked by the robbers?"

³⁷The teacher of the law answered, "The one who helped him."

Jesus said to him, "Then go and do the same thing he did!"

Today's Prayer

Dear God, help me show Jesus' love to all people, even those I don't like as much. Thank you for loving me. In Jesus' name I pray, amen.

Memory Verse
"Always remember what you have been taught. Don't let go of it. Keep safe all that you have learned. It is the most important thing in your life."
Proverbs 4:13

The Lost Sheep

Jesus told two stories, one about a lost sheep and one about a lost coin. He wanted the people to understand that God cares about every person.

15Many tax collectors and "sinners" came to listen to Jesus. ²The Pharisees and the teachers of the law began to complain: "Look! This man welcomes sinners and even eats with them!"

³Then Jesus told them this story: ⁴"Suppose one of you has 100 sheep, but he loses 1 of them. Then he will

leave the other 99 sheep alone and go out and look for the lost sheep. The man will keep on searching for the lost sheep until he finds it. [5]And when he finds it, the man is very happy. He puts it on his shoulders [6]and goes home. He calls to his friends and neighbors and says, 'Be happy with me because I found my lost sheep!' [7]In the same way, I tell you there is much joy in heaven when 1 sinner changes his heart. There is more joy for that 1 sinner than there is for 99 good people who don't need to change.

[8]"Suppose a woman has ten silver coins, but she loses one of them. She will light a lamp and clean the house. She will look carefully for the coin until she finds it. [9]And when she finds it, she will call her friends and neighbors and say, 'Be happy with me because I have found the coin that I lost!' [10]In the same way, there is joy before the angels of God when 1 sinner changes his heart."

Today's Prayer

Dear God, from the stories Jesus told, help me learn to love all people as he did. Help me to care about people I know who don't follow him. Use me to lead them to Christ. In Jesus' name, amen.

Memory Verse

"Always remember what you have been taught. Don't let go of it. Keep safe all that you have learned. It is the most important thing in your life."
Proverbs 4:13

A Son Leaves Home

Jesus told a story about a man with two sons. The younger one wanted his share of his father's property. But when his father gave it to him, he went away and wasted it. Then he found himself in trouble.

¹³"Then the younger son gathered up all that was his and left. He traveled far away to another country. There he wasted his money in foolish living. ¹⁴He spent everything that he had. Soon after that, the land became very dry, and there was no rain. There was not enough food to eat anywhere in the country. The son was hungry and needed money. ¹⁵So he got a job with one of the citizens there. The man sent the son into the fields to feed pigs. ¹⁶The son was so hungry that he was willing to eat the food the pigs were eating. But no one gave him anything. ¹⁷The son realized that he had been very foolish. He

thought, 'All of my father's servants have plenty of food. But I am here, almost dying with hunger. [18]I will leave and return to my father. I'll say to him: Father, I have sinned against God and have done wrong to you. [19]I am not good enough to be called your son. But let me be like one of your servants.' [20]So the son left and went to his father.

"While the son was still a long way off, his father saw him coming. He felt sorry for his son. So the father ran to him, and hugged and kissed him. [21]The son said, 'Father, I have sinned against God and have done wrong to you. I am not good enough to be called your son.' [22]But the father said to his servants, 'Hurry! Bring the best clothes and put them on him. Also, put a ring on his finger and sandals on his feet. [23]And get our fat calf and kill it. Then we can have a feast and celebrate! [24]My son was dead, but now he is alive again! He was lost, but now he is found!' So they began to celebrate."

Today's Prayer

God in heaven, thank you for loving me even when I have done wrong. Thank you for forgiving me. Help me to love and trust you more. In Jesus' name, I pray, amen.

Memory Verse

"Always remember what you have been taught. Don't let go of it. Keep safe all that you have learned. It is the most important thing in your life."
Proverbs 4:13

A Son Is Angry

Jesus continued his story about the boy who left home. The younger son who returned home was forgiven. He was even welcomed back with a celebration. When the older brother came home and found a party going on, he was angry.

²⁵"The older son was in the field. As he came closer to the house, he heard the sound of music and dancing. ²⁶So he called to one of the servants and asked, 'What does all this mean?'

²⁷The servant said, 'Your brother has come back. Your father killed the fat calf to eat because your brother came home safely!'

²⁸The older son was angry and would not go in to the feast. So his father went out and begged him to come in. ²⁹The son said to his father, 'I have served you like a slave for many years! I have always obeyed your commands. But you never even killed a young goat for me to have a feast with my friends. ³⁰But your other son has wasted all your money on prostitutes. Then he comes home, and you kill the fat calf for him!'

³¹The father said to him, 'Son, you are always with me. All that I have is yours. ³²We had to celebrate and be happy because your brother was dead, but now he is alive. He was lost, but now he is found.'"

Today's Prayer

Dear God, sometimes I am jealous of what another person has. Help me, instead, to be happy for the blessings you give others. I pray in Jesus' name, amen.

Memory Verse

"Always remember what you have been taught. Don't let go of it. Keep safe all that you have learned. It is the most important thing in your life."
Proverbs 4:13

Jesus Heals Lazarus

Jesus' friend Lazarus had died. By the time Jesus got there, many people had come to comfort his sisters, Martha and Mary.

³³Jesus saw that Mary was crying and that the Jews who came with her were crying, too. Jesus felt very sad in his heart and was deeply troubled. ³⁴He asked, "Where did you bury him?"

"Come and see, Lord," they said.

³⁵Jesus cried.

³⁶So the Jews said, "See how much he loved him."

³⁷But some of them said, "If Jesus healed the eyes of the blind man, why didn't he keep Lazarus from dying?"

³⁸Again Jesus felt very sad in his heart. He came to the tomb. The tomb was a cave with a large stone

covering the entrance. ³⁹Jesus said, "Move the stone away."

Martha said, "But, Lord, it has been four days since he died. There will be a bad smell." Martha was the sister of the dead man.

⁴⁰Then Jesus said to her, "Didn't I tell you that if you believed, you would see the glory of God?"

⁴¹So they moved the stone away from the entrance. Then Jesus looked up and said, "Father, I thank you that you heard me. ⁴²I know that you always hear me. But I said these things because of the people here around me. I want them to believe that you sent me." ⁴³After Jesus said this, he cried out in a loud voice, "Lazarus, come out!" ⁴⁴The dead man came out. His hands and feet were wrapped with pieces of cloth, and he had a cloth around his face.

Jesus said to them, "Take the cloth off of him and let him go."

⁴⁵There were many Jews who had come to visit Mary. They saw what Jesus did. And many of them believed in him.

Today's Prayer

Thank you, my God, for giving me a savior like Jesus who understands me when I am sad. I know he has power over death so that I can live with him forever. In his name I pray, amen.

Memory Verse

"Always remember what you have been taught. Don't let go of it. Keep safe all that you have learned. It is the most important thing in your life."
Proverbs 4:13

Jesus Heals Ten Men

As they traveled from place to place, Jesus taught his followers many things. They learned from what he taught, from the stories he told, and from the things he did. One lesson was about the importance of being thankful.

¹¹Jesus was on his way to Jerusalem. Traveling from Galilee to Samaria, ¹²he came into a small town. Ten men met him there. These men did not come close to Jesus, because they all had a harmful skin disease. ¹³But they called to him, "Jesus! Master! Please help us!"

¹⁴When Jesus saw the men, he said, "Go and show yourselves to the priests."

While the ten men were going, they were healed. ¹⁵When one of them saw that he was healed, he went back to Jesus. He praised God in a loud voice. ¹⁶Then he bowed down at Jesus' feet and thanked him. (This man was a Samaritan.) ¹⁷Jesus asked, "Ten men were healed: where are the other nine? ¹⁸Is this Samaritan the only one who came back to thank God?" ¹⁹Then Jesus said to him, "Stand up and go on your way. You were healed because you believed."

Today's Prayer

Loving God, help me remember to be thankful. Sometimes I complain and ask for your help. Then when you have helped me, I may forget to thank you. Forgive me, I pray, in Jesus' name, amen.

Memory Verse
"If anyone belongs to Christ, then he is made new. The old things have gone; everything is made new!" 2 Corinthians 5:17

Two Different Prayers

Jesus wanted his followers to learn about prayer and about being right with God. So he told them a story about a proud man and a tax collector. To the Jews, a tax collector was a very evil person.

⁹There were some people who thought that they were very good and looked down on everyone else. Jesus used this story to teach them: ¹⁰"One day there was a Pharisee and a tax collector. Both went to the Temple to pray. ¹¹The Pharisee stood alone, away from the tax collector. When the Pharisee prayed, he said, 'God, I thank you that I am not as bad as other people. I am not like men who steal, cheat, or take part in adultery. I thank you that I am better than this tax collector. ¹²I give up eating twice a week, and I give one-tenth of everything I earn!'

¹³"The tax collector stood at a distance. When he prayed, he would not even look up to heaven. He beat on his chest because he was so sad. He said, 'God, have mercy on me. I am a sinner!' ¹⁴I tell you, when this man went home, he was right with God. But the Pharisee was not right with God. Everyone who makes himself great will be made humble. But everyone who makes himself humble will be made great."

Today's Prayer

My Lord, forgive me when I am proud. Help me understand that only you are truly good. Change my heart and make me right with you. I pray in Jesus' name, amen.

Memory Verse

"If anyone belongs to Christ, then he is made new. The old things have gone; everything is made new!" 2 Corinthians 5:17

A Rich Man's Question

A Jewish leader came to Jesus with a question. He wanted to know what to do to get the life that continues forever. Jesus' answer made the rich man very sad.

[18]A Jewish leader asked Jesus, "Good Teacher, what must I do to get the life that continues forever?"

[19]Jesus said to him, "Why do you call me good? Only God is good. [20]You know the commands: 'You must not be guilty of adultery. You must not murder anyone. You must not steal. You must not tell lies about your neighbor in court. Honor your father and mother.'"

[21]But the leader said, "I have obeyed all these commands since I was a boy!"

[22]When Jesus heard this, he said to him, "But there is still one more thing you need to do. Sell everything you

have and give the money to the poor. You will have a reward in heaven. Then come and follow me!" ²³But when the man heard this, he became very sad because he was very rich.

²⁴When Jesus saw that the man was sad, he said, "It will be very hard for rich people to enter the kingdom of God! ²⁵It would be easier for a camel to go through the eye of a needle than for a rich person to enter the kingdom of God!"

²⁶When the people heard this, they asked, "Then who can be saved?"

²⁷Jesus answered, "God can do things that are not possible for men to do!"

²⁸Peter said, "Look, we left everything we had and followed you!"

²⁹Jesus said, "I tell you the truth. Everyone who has left his house, wife, brothers, parents, or children for God's kingdom ³⁰will get much more than he left. He will receive many times more in this life. And after he dies, he will live with God forever."

Today's Prayer

Holy Lord, help me to follow Jesus. Don't let money be more important to me than following Jesus. Help me obey your commands. I pray in Christ, amen.

Memory Verse
"If anyone belongs to Christ, then he is made new. The old things have gone; everything is made new!" 2 Corinthians 5:17

Jesus Heals a Blind Man

Jesus called his special followers to him and told them they were going to Jerusalem. As they were walking toward the city, a blind man called out to Jesus for help.

⁴⁶Then they came to the town of Jericho. As Jesus was leaving there with his followers and a large crowd, a blind beggar named Bartimaeus (son of Timaeus) was sitting by the road. ⁴⁷He heard that Jesus from Nazareth was walking by. The blind man cried out, "Jesus, Son of David, please help me!"

⁴⁸Many people scolded the blind man and told him to be quiet. But he shouted more and more, "Son of David, please help me!"

⁴⁹Jesus stopped and said, "Tell the man to come here."

So they called the blind man. They said, "Cheer up! Get to your feet. Jesus is calling you." ⁵⁰The blind man stood up quickly. He left his coat there and went to Jesus.

⁵¹Jesus asked him, "What do you want me to do for you?"

The blind man answered, "Teacher, I want to see again."

⁵²Jesus said, "Go. You are healed because you believed." At once the man was able to see again, and he followed Jesus on the road.

Today's Prayer

Great Lord of heaven and earth, thank you for the power of Jesus in my life. Help me not to give up when others try to stop me from following Jesus. Show me how to grow as I follow him. Thank you for answering my prayers. In him I pray, amen.

Memory Verse
"If anyone belongs to Christ, then he is made new. The old things have gone; everything is made new!" 2 Corinthians 5:17

Jesus Meets Zaccheus

The Jewish leaders of Jesus' time disliked tax collectors. Many of the tax collectors were dishonest and charged the people too much. But Jesus was kind to them. His kindness and his teaching often changed their lives.

19 Jesus was going through the city of Jericho. ²In Jericho there was a man named Zaccheus. He was a wealthy, very important tax collector. ³He wanted to see who Jesus was, but he was too short to see above the crowd. ⁴He ran ahead to a place where he knew Jesus would come. He climbed a sycamore tree so he could

see Jesus. [5]When Jesus came to that place, he looked up and saw Zacchaeus in the tree. He said to him, "Zacchaeus, hurry and come down! I must stay at your house today."

[6]Zacchaeus came down quickly. He was pleased to have Jesus in his house. [7]All the people saw this and began to complain, "Look at the kind of man Jesus stays with. Zacchaeus is a sinner!"

[8]But Zacchaeus said to the Lord, "I will give half of my money to the poor. If I have cheated anyone, I will pay that person back four times more!"

[9]Jesus said, "Salvation has come to this house today. This man truly belongs to the family of Abraham. [10]The Son of Man came to find lost people and save them."

Today's Prayer

Loving Father, I am thankful for Jesus' kindness and love. Help me show his kindness to my friends and family. In Jesus' name I pray, amen.

Memory Verse
"If anyone belongs to Christ, then he is made new. The old things have gone; everything is made new!" 2 Corinthians 5:17

Jesus Is with His Friends

Jesus was visiting his friends Mary, Martha and Lazarus. While he was there, a woman gave Jesus a very expensive gift.

12Six days before the Passover Feast, Jesus went to Bethany, where Lazarus lived. (Lazarus is the man Jesus raised from death.) ²There they had a dinner for Jesus. Martha served the food. Lazarus was one of the people eating with Jesus. ³Mary brought in a pint of very expensive perfume made from pure nard. She

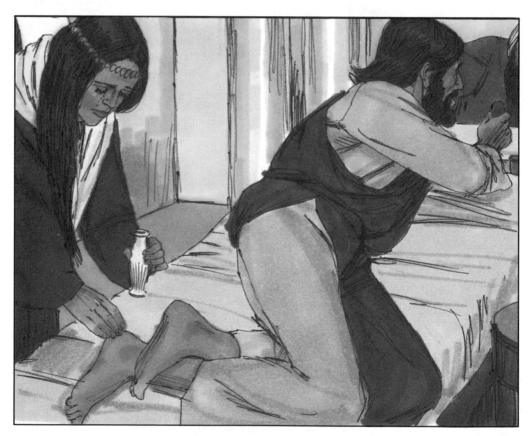

poured the perfume on Jesus' feet, and then she wiped his feet with her hair. And the sweet smell from the perfume filled the whole house.

[4]Judas Iscariot, one of Jesus' followers, was there. (He was the one who would later turn against Jesus.) Judas said, [5]"This perfume was worth 300 silver coins. It should have been sold and the money given to the poor." [6]But Judas did not really care about the poor. He said this because he was a thief. He was the one who kept the money box, and he often stole money from it.

[7]Jesus answered, "Let her alone. It was right for her to save this perfume for today—the day for me to be prepared for burial. [8]The poor will always be with you, but you will not always have me."

Today's Prayer

Thank you, Lord, for sending Jesus to be my friend. Like Mary, Martha and Lazarus, I want to honor Jesus in everything I do. I pray in his name, amen.

Memory Verse

"Obey your leaders and be under their authority. These men are watching you because they are responsible for your souls." Hebrews 13:17

Jesus Enters Jerusalem

Jesus and his followers had almost reached Jerusalem. When they came to Bethphage, a nearby town, Jesus sent two followers to find a very special colt.

11 Jesus and his followers were coming closer to Jerusalem. They came to the towns of Bethphage and Bethany near the Mount of Olives. There Jesus sent two of his followers. ²He said to them, "Go to the town you see there. When you enter it, you will find a colt tied which no one has ever ridden. Untie it and bring it here to me. ³If anyone asks you why you are doing this, tell him, 'The Master needs the colt. He will send it back soon.' "

⁴The followers went into the town. They found a colt tied in the street near the door of a house, and they untied it. ⁵Some people were standing

there and asked, "What are you doing? Why are you untying that colt?" [6]The followers answered the way Jesus told them to answer. And the people let them take the colt.

[7]The followers brought the colt to Jesus. They put their coats on the colt, and Jesus sat on it. [8]Many people spread their coats on the road. Others cut branches in the fields and spread the branches on the road. [9]Some of the people were walking ahead of Jesus. Others were following him. All of them were shouting,
"Praise God!
God bless the One who comes in
the name of the Lord!

[10]God bless the kingdom of our
father David!
That kingdom is coming!
Praise to God in heaven!"

[11]Jesus entered Jerusalem and went into the Temple. When he had looked at everything, and since it was already late, he went out to Bethany with the 12 apostles.

Today's Prayer

God in heaven, I praise you for Jesus, who came to earth to be king of kings and lord of lords. Help me always to honor him as king of my life. In his name I pray, amen.

Memory Verse
"Obey your leaders and be under their authority. These men are watching you because they are responsible for your souls." Hebrews 13:17

Merchants in the Temple

Jewish leaders allowed merchants to do business in the outer court of the Temple. They would exchange foreign money for local money and would sell animals for sacrifices. They charged the people too much and made a big profit.

¹⁵Jesus returned to Jerusalem and went into the Temple. He began to throw out those who were buying and selling things there. He overturned the tables that belonged to the men who were exchanging different kinds of money. And he turned over the benches of the men who were selling doves. ¹⁶Jesus refused to allow anyone to carry goods through the Temple courts. ¹⁷Then Jesus taught the people. He said, "It is written in the Scriptures, 'My Temple will be a house where people from all nations will pray.' But you are changing God's house into a 'hideout for robbers.' "

¹⁸The leading priests and the teachers of the law heard all this. They began trying to find a way to kill Jesus. They were afraid of him because all the people were amazed at his teaching. ¹⁹That night, Jesus and his followers left the city.

Today's Prayer

Dear Lord in heaven, give me the strength to stand against wrong, as Jesus did in the Temple. Help me to be fair to others. I pray in Jesus' name, amen.

Memory Verse

"Obey your leaders and be under their authority. These men are watching you because they are responsible for your souls." Hebrews 13:17

The Wicked Farmers

While teaching in the Temple, Jesus told a story. When the teachers of the law and the priests heard the story, they became very angry. They understood that Jesus meant they were like the wicked farmers.

[9]Then Jesus told the people this story: "A man planted a vineyard. The man leased the land to some farmers. Then he went away for a long time. [10]Later, it was time for the grapes to be picked. So the man sent a servant to those farmers to get his share of the grapes. But they beat the servant and sent him away with nothing.

¹¹Then he sent another servant. They beat this servant too. They showed no respect for him and sent him away with nothing. ¹²So the man sent a third servant. The farmers hurt this servant badly and threw him out. ¹³The owner of the vineyard said, 'What will I do now? I will send my son whom I love very much. Maybe they will respect him!' ¹⁴When they saw the son, they said to each other, 'This is the owner's son. This vineyard will be his. If we kill him, then it will be ours!' ¹⁵So the farmers threw the son out of the vineyard and killed him.

"What will the owner of this vineyard do? ¹⁶He will come and kill those farmers! Then he will give the vineyard to other farmers."

The people heard this story. They said, "No! Let this never happen!"

¹⁹The teachers of the law and the priests heard this story that Jesus told. They knew the story was about them. So they wanted to arrest Jesus at once. But they were afraid of what the people would do.

Today's Prayer

O Lord, my God, open my heart and mind that I may learn from Jesus' teachings. May I always be willing to listen. Forgive me when I am wrong. In his name I pray, amen.

Memory Verse

"Obey your leaders and be under their authority. These men are watching you because they are responsible for your souls." Hebrews 13:17

Money for Taxes

The religious leaders became more and more determined to kill Jesus. They tried all kinds of plans. One plan was to trick him into speaking against the Roman rulers so they could arrest him.

¹⁵Then the Pharisees left the place where Jesus was teaching. They made plans to trap Jesus with a question. ¹⁶They sent some of their own followers and some men from the group called Herodians. These men said, "Teacher, we know that you are an honest man. We know that you teach the truth about God's way. You are not afraid of what other people think about you. All men are the same to you. ¹⁷So tell us what you think. Is it right to pay taxes to Caesar or not?"

¹⁸But Jesus knew that these men were trying to trick him. So he said, "You hypocrites! Why are you trying to trap me? ¹⁹Show me a coin used for paying the tax." The men showed him a silver coin. ²⁰Then Jesus asked, "Whose picture is on the coin? And whose name is written on the coin?"

²¹The men answered, "Caesar's."

Then Jesus said to them, "Give to Caesar the things that are Caesar's. And give to God the things that are God's."

²²The men heard what Jesus said, and they were amazed. They left him and went away.

Today's Prayer

Dear God, when people try to trick me into doing wrong, as they tried to trick Jesus long ago, give me wisdom, show me what to say and do. In Jesus' name, amen.

Memory Verse
"Obey your leaders and be under their authority. These men are watching you because they are responsible for your souls." Hebrews 13:17

Important Commands

A teacher of the law asked Jesus which command was the most important. Jesus gave a wise answer.

²⁸One of the teachers of the law came to Jesus. He heard Jesus arguing with the Sadducees and the Pharisees. He saw that Jesus gave good answers to their questions. So he asked Jesus, "Which of the commands is most important?"

²⁹Jesus answered, "The most important command is this: 'Listen,

people of Israel! The Lord our God, he is the only Lord. ³⁰Love the Lord your God. Love him with all your heart, all your soul, all your mind, and all your strength.' ³¹The second most important command is this: 'Love your neighbor as you love yourself.' These two commands are the most important commands."

³²The man answered, "That was a good answer, Teacher. You were right when you said these things. God is the only Lord, and there is no other God besides him. ³³One must love God with all his heart, all his mind, and all his strength. And one must love his neighbor as he loves himself. These commands are more important than all the animals and sacrifices we offer to God."

³⁴Jesus saw that the man answered him wisely. So Jesus said to him, "You are close to the kingdom of God." And after that, no one was brave enough to ask Jesus any more questions.

Today's Prayer

God, my heavenly Father, help me to love you with my heart, my mind and my strength. Help me love others as much as I love myself. Thank you for loving me. In Jesus' name, amen.

Memory Verse
"Love the Lord your God. Love him with all your heart, all your soul, all your strength, and all your mind." Also, "You must love your neighbor as you love yourself." Luke 10:27

A Poor Woman's Gift

Jesus patiently and wisely answered all the questions the religious leaders asked. Even though they looked religious, they just wanted to trick Jesus. Then Jesus pointed out a poor widow who truly worshiped God.

³⁸Jesus continued teaching. He said, "Beware of the teachers of the law. They like to walk around wearing clothes that look important. And they love for people to show respect to them in the marketplaces. ³⁹They love to have the most important seats in the synagogues. And they love to have the most important seats at the

feasts. [40]They cheat widows and steal their homes. Then they try to make themselves look good by saying long prayers. God will punish these people terribly."

[41]Jesus sat near the Temple money box where people put their gifts. He watched the people put in their money. Many rich people gave large sums of money. [42]Then a poor widow came and gave two very small copper coins. These coins were not worth even a penny.

[43]Jesus called his followers to him. He said, "I tell you the truth. This poor widow gave only two small coins. But she really gave more than all those rich people. [44]The rich have plenty; they gave only what they did not need. This woman is very poor. But she gave all she had. And she needed that money to help her live."

Today's Prayer

Dear Lord, help me to share whatever I have, whether it is much or little. May I learn to give of myself to help others. I thank you that Jesus was willing to give himself for me. In his name, amen.

Memory Verse
"Love the Lord your God. Love him with all your heart, all your soul, all your strength, and all your mind." Also, "You must love your neighbor as you love yourself." Luke 10:27

Oil for the Lamps

Jesus told a story about ten girls with lamps who were going to a wedding feast. The story teaches us to be always prepared for the coming of the Lord.

²"Five of the girls were foolish and five were wise. ³The five foolish girls took their lamps, but they did not take more oil for the lamps to burn. ⁴The wise girls took their lamps and more oil in jars. ⁵The bridegroom was very late. All the girls became sleepy and went to sleep.

⁶"At midnight someone cried out,

'The bridegroom is coming! Come and meet him!' [7]Then all the girls woke up and got their lamps ready. [8]But the foolish girls said to the wise, 'Give us some of your oil. Our lamps are going out.' [9]The wise girls answered, 'No! The oil we have might not be enough for all of us. Go to the people who sell oil and buy some for yourselves.'

[10]"So the five foolish girls went to buy oil. While they were gone, the bridegroom came. The girls who were ready went in with the bridegroom to the wedding feast. Then the door was closed and locked.

[11]"Later the others came back. They called, 'Sir, sir, open the door to let us in.' [12]But the bridegroom answered, 'I tell you the truth, I don't know you.'

[13]"So always be ready. You don't know the day or the time the Son of Man will come."

Today's Prayer

My Lord, forgive me when I sin, and keep my heart from wrong. Help me live so that I am always ready for the time when he will come again. In Jesus' name, I pray, amen.

Memory Verse
"Love the Lord your God. Love him with all your heart, all your soul, all your strength, and all your mind." Also, "You must love your neighbor as you love yourself." Luke 10:27

The King's Judgment

To teach the people about the coming judgment, Jesus told them another story. He said the King, Jesus, will come and divide people into two groups—good people and bad people.

³⁴"Then the King will say to the good people on his right, 'Come. My Father has given you his blessing. Come and receive the kingdom God has prepared for you since the world was made. ³⁵I was hungry, and you gave me food. I was thirsty, and you gave me something to drink. I was alone and away from home, and you invited me into your house. ³⁶I was without clothes, and you gave me something to wear. I was sick, and you cared for me. I was in prison, and you visited me.'

³⁷"Then the good people will answer, 'Lord, when did we see you hungry and give you food? When did

we see you thirsty and give you something to drink? [38]When did we see you alone and away from home and invite you into our house? When did we see you without clothes and give you something to wear? [39]When did we see you sick or in prison and care for you?'

[40]"Then the King will answer, 'I tell you the truth. Anything you did for any of my people here, you also did for me.'

[41]"Then the King will say to those on his left, 'Go away from me. God has said that you will be punished. Go into the fire that burns forever. That fire was prepared for the devil and his helpers. [42]I was hungry, and you gave me nothing to eat. I was thirsty, and you gave me nothing to drink. [43]I was alone and away from home, and you did not invite me into your house. I was without clothes, and you gave me nothing to wear. I was sick and in prison, and you did not care for me.' "

Today's Prayer

Dear God, make me remember that I can serve you by serving others and being kind to them. Teach me how to use my life in serving you. Thank you for the home in heaven you have promised. In his name, amen.

Memory Verse
"Love the Lord your God. Love him with all your heart, all your soul, all your strength, and all your mind." Also, "You must love your neighbor as you love yourself." Luke 10:27

Judas' Evil Plan

For several days before the Feast of Passover, Jesus had been teaching in the courtyard of the Temple. As more people began to follow him, the religious leaders became more and more angry. Then they made a plan.

26 After Jesus finished saying all these things, he told his followers, [2]"You know that the day after tomorrow is the day of the Passover Feast. On that day the Son of Man will be given to his enemies to be killed on a cross."

[3]Then the leading priests and the older Jewish leaders had a meeting at the palace of the high priest. The high priest's name was Caiaphas. [4]At the meeting, they planned to set a trap to arrest Jesus and kill him. [5]But they said, "We must not do it during the feast. The people might cause a riot."

[14]Then 1 of the 12 followers went to talk to the leading priests. This was the follower named Judas Iscariot. [15]He said, "I will give Jesus to you. What will you pay me for doing this?" The priests gave Judas 30 silver coins. [16]After that, Judas waited for the best time to give Jesus to the priests.

Today's Prayer

Holy Father, help me not to betray Jesus in anything I do. Give me the strength I need to be faithful to him. In Jesus' name, amen.

Memory Verse
"Love the Lord your God. Love him with all your heart, all your soul, all your strength, and all your mind." Also, "You must love your neighbor as you love yourself." Luke 10:27

Washing the Apostles' Feet

Jesus and his apostles came together to eat the Passover Meal. That evening he taught his followers about serving others as he, the Son of God, had served them.

13 It was almost time for the Jewish Passover Feast. Jesus knew that it was time for him to leave this world and go back to the Father. He had always loved those who were his own in the world, and he loved them all the way to the end. ²Jesus and his followers were at the evening meal. The devil had already persuaded Judas Iscariot to turn against Jesus. (Judas was the son of Simon.) ³Jesus knew that the Father had given him power over everything. He also knew that he had come from God and was going back to God. ⁴So during the meal Jesus stood up and took off his outer clothing. Taking a towel, he wrapped it around his waist. ⁵Then he poured water into a bowl and began to wash the followers' feet. He dried them with the towel that was wrapped around him.

¹²When he had finished washing their feet, he put on his clothes and sat down again. Jesus asked, "Do you understand what I have just done for you? ¹³You call me 'Teacher' and 'Lord.' And this is right, because that is what I am. ¹⁴I, your Lord and Teacher, have washed your feet. So you also should wash each other's feet. ¹⁵I did this as an example for you. So you should do as I have done for you. ¹⁶I tell you the truth. A servant is not greater than his master. A messenger is not greater than the one who sent him. ¹⁷If you know these things, you will be happy if you do them."

Today's Prayer

Dear Lord in heaven, thank you for sending Jesus to show me how to treat others. Give me a heart that is not selfish. Teach me how to serve others in your name. I pray in Christ, amen.

Memory Verse
"I give you a new command: Love each other. You must love each other as I have loved you."
John 13:34

The Lord's Supper

After Jesus had washed the apostles' feet, they were ready to eat the Passover meal. Jesus used it also to teach them.

¹⁴When the time came, Jesus and the apostles were sitting at the table. ¹⁵He said to them, "I wanted very much to eat this Passover meal with you before I die. ¹⁶I will never eat another Passover meal until it is given its true meaning in the kingdom of God."

¹⁷Then Jesus took a cup. He gave thanks to God for it and said, "Take this cup and give it to everyone here. ¹⁸I will not drink again from the fruit of the vine until God's kingdom comes."

¹⁹Then Jesus took some bread. He thanked God for it, broke it, and gave it to the apostles. Then Jesus said, "This bread is my body that I am giving for you. Do this to remember me." ²⁰In the same way, after supper, Jesus took the cup and said, "This cup shows the new agreement that God makes with his people. This new agreement begins with my blood which is poured out for you."

Today's Prayer

Holy Lord, give me courage to be like Jesus. Even when he was facing death, he thought about others. Help me understand the meaning of the Lord's Supper and let it remind me of his body and his blood. In him I pray, amen.

Memory Verse
"I give you a new command: Love each other. You must love each other as I have loved you."
John 13:34

Judas Leaves

As they were eating their last meal together Jesus said, "One of you will turn against me."

²¹After Jesus said this, he was very troubled. He said openly, "I tell you the truth. One of you will turn against me."

²²The followers all looked at each other. They did not know whom Jesus was talking about. ²³One of the followers was sitting next to Jesus. This was the follower Jesus loved. ²⁴Simon Pe-

ter made signs to him to ask Jesus who it was that he was talking about.

²⁵That follower leaned closer to Jesus and asked, "Lord, who is it that will turn against you?"

²⁶Jesus answered, "I will dip this bread into the dish. The man I give it to is the man who will turn against me." So Jesus took a piece of bread. He dipped it and gave it to Judas Iscariot, the son of Simon. ²⁷As soon as Judas took the bread, Satan entered him. Jesus said to Judas, "The thing that you will do — do it quickly!" ²⁸None of the men at the table understood why Jesus said this to Judas. ²⁹He was the one who kept the money box. So some of the followers thought that Jesus was telling Judas to buy what was needed for the feast. Or they thought that Jesus wanted Judas to give something to the poor.

³⁰Judas accepted the bread Jesus gave him and immediately went out. It was night.

Today's Prayer

Great God in heaven, be with me when I have to make hard choices. May I never betray you or Jesus. Give me courage to be strong. In Christ's name, amen.

Memory Verse
"I give you a new command: Love each other. You must love each other as I have loved you."
John 13:34

Peter Will Deny Jesus

After their meal, Jesus and the apostles sang a hymn and went out to a mountain overlooking the city. There were still things he needed to say to prepare his followers for his death.

³¹When Judas was gone, Jesus said, "Now the Son of Man receives his glory. And God receives glory through him. ³²If God receives glory through him, then God will give glory to the Son through himself. And God will give him glory quickly."

³³Jesus said, "My children, I will be with you only a little longer. You will look for me. And what I told the Jews, I tell you now: Where I am going you cannot come.

³⁴"I give you a new command: Love each other. You must love each other as I have loved you. ³⁵All people will know that you are my followers if you love each other."

³⁶Simon Peter asked Jesus, "Lord, where are you going?"

Jesus answered, "Where I am going you cannot follow now. But you will follow later."

³⁷Peter asked, "Lord, why can't I follow you now? I am ready to die for you!"

³⁸Jesus answered, "Will you really die for me? I tell you the truth. Before the rooster crows, you will say three times that you don't know me."

Today's Prayer

O Lord, when my faith is tested as Peter's was, be with me so that I will never deny Jesus. I want to tell others that I am one of his followers. In his name, amen.

Memory Verse
"I give you a new command: Love each other. You must love each other as I have loved you."
John 13:34

Jesus Prays Alone

To find strength for what was soon to happen, Jesus wanted to talk with God. He took his followers, Peter, James and John, with him.

³²Jesus and his followers went to a place called Gethsemane. He said to his followers, "Sit here while I pray." ³³Jesus told Peter, James, and John to come with him. Then Jesus began to be very sad and troubled. ³⁴He said to them, "I am full of sorrow. My heart is breaking with sadness. Stay here and watch."

³⁵Jesus walked a little farther away from them. Then he fell on the ground and prayed. He prayed that, if possible, he would not have this time of suffering. ³⁶He prayed, "Abba, Father! You can do all things. Let me not have this cup of suffering. But do what you want, not what I want."

³⁷Then Jesus went back to his followers. He found them asleep. He said to Peter, "Simon, why are you sleeping? You could not stay awake with me for one hour? ³⁸Stay awake and pray that you will not be tempted. Your spirit wants to do what is right, but your body is weak."

³⁹Again Jesus went away and prayed the same thing. ⁴⁰Then he went back to the followers. Again he found them asleep because their eyes were very heavy. And they did not know what to say to Jesus.

⁴¹After Jesus prayed a third time, he went back to his followers. He said to them, "You are still sleeping and resting? That's enough! The time has come for the Son of Man to be given to sinful people. ⁴²Get up! We must go. Here comes the man who has turned against me."

Today's Prayer

I thank you Lord in heaven that I can pray to you and find strength as Jesus did. When I am sad and worried, comfort and strengthen me. In all things, may your will be done. I pray in Christ, amen.

Memory Verse
"I give you a new command: Love each other. You must love each other as I have loved you."
John 13:34

Jesus Is Arrested

When Jesus finished praying, he led his followers across a valley to a garden of olive trees.

²Judas knew where this place was, because Jesus met there often with his followers. Judas was the one who turned against Jesus. ³So Judas led a group of soldiers to the garden. Judas also brought some guards from the leading priests and the Pharisees. They were carrying torches, lanterns, and weapons.

⁴Jesus knew everything that would happen to him. Jesus went out and asked, "Who is it you are looking for?"

⁵The men answered, "Jesus from Nazareth."

Jesus said, "I am Jesus." (Judas, the one who turned against Jesus, was standing there with them.) ⁶When Jesus said, "I am Jesus," the men moved back and fell to the ground.

⁷Jesus asked them again, "Who is it you are looking for?"

They said, "Jesus of Nazareth."

⁸Jesus said, "I told you that I am he. So if you are looking for me, then let these other men go." ⁹This happened so that the words Jesus said before might come true: "I have not lost any of the men you gave me."

¹⁰Simon Peter had a sword. He took out the sword and struck the servant of the high priest, cutting off his right ear. (The servant's name was Malchus.) ¹¹Jesus said to Peter, "Put your sword back. Shall I not drink of the cup the Father has given me?"

¹²Then the soldiers with their commander and the Jewish guards arrested Jesus.

Today's Prayer

Thank you, Lord, for the courage of Jesus. When I face enemies or those who lie about me, I pray that I may remember Christ and be like him. In his name, amen.

Memory Verse
"For God loved the world so much that he gave his only Son. God gave his Son so that whoever believes in him may not be lost, but have eternal life." John 3:16

People Accuse Jesus

Those who arrested Jesus took him to the house of the high priest. There they tried to find something he had done wrong.

⁵³The people who arrested Jesus led him to the house of the high priest. All the leading priests, the older Jewish leaders, and the teachers of the law were gathered there. ⁵⁴Peter followed far behind and entered the courtyard of the high priest's house. There he sat with the guards, warming himself by the fire.

⁵⁵The leading priests and all the Jewish council tried to find something that Jesus had done wrong so they could kill him. But the council could find no proof against him. ⁵⁶Many people came and told false things about him. But all said different things—none of them agreed.

⁵⁷Then some men stood up and lied about Jesus. They said, ⁵⁸"We heard this man say, 'I will destroy this Temple that men made. And three days later, I will build another Temple—a Temple not made by men.'" ⁵⁹But even the things these men said did not agree.

⁶⁰Then the high priest stood before them and said to Jesus, "Aren't you going to answer the charges these men bring against you?" ⁶¹But Jesus said nothing. He did not answer.

The high priest asked Jesus another question: "Are you the Christ, the Son of the blessed God?"

⁶²Jesus answered, "I am. And in the future you will see the Son of Man sitting at the right side of the Powerful One. And you will see the Son of Man coming on clouds in the sky."

⁶³When the high priest heard this, he was very angry. He tore his clothes and said, "We don't need any more witnesses! ⁶⁴You all heard him say these things against God. What do you think?"

They all said that Jesus was guilty and should be killed.

Today's Prayer

My Lord, how cruel and unfairly Christ was treated. Help me never to behave this way. Help me always to tell the truth about others. I pray in the name of Jesus, amen.

Memory Verse
"For God loved the world so much that he gave his only Son. God gave his Son so that whoever believes in him may not be lost, but have eternal life." John 3:16

Peter Denies Jesus

Peter had followed behind the crowd that took Jesus to the priest's house. As they questioned Jesus, Peter waited outside in the courtyard to see what would happen.

[66]Peter was still in the courtyard when a servant girl of the high priest came there. [67]She saw Peter warming himself at the fire. She looked closely at him.

Then the girl said, "You were with Jesus, that man from Nazareth."

[68]But Peter said that he was never with Jesus. He said, "I don't know or

understand what you are talking about." Then Peter left and went toward the entrance of the courtyard.

[69]The servant girl saw Peter there. Again she said to the people who were standing there, "This man is one of those who followed Jesus." [70]Again Peter said that it was not true.

A short time later, some people were standing near Peter. They said, "We know you are one of those who followed Jesus. You are from Galilee, too."

[71]Then Peter began to curse. He said, "I swear that I don't know this man you're talking about!"

[72]As soon as Peter said this, the rooster crowed the second time. Then Peter remembered what Jesus had told him: "Before the rooster crows twice, you will say three times that you don't know me." Then Peter was very sad and began to cry.

Today's Prayer

Dear God, thank you for your grace and mercy. Help me always to be ready to tell others that I belong to Jesus. When I am weak, I know you will forgive me as you did Peter. In Jesus' name, amen.

Memory Verse

"For God loved the world so much that he gave his only Son. God gave his Son so that whoever believes in him may not be lost, but have eternal life." John 3:16

Pilate's Questions

The Jewish leaders found Jesus guilty of saying he was the Son of God. To them, this was a sin that should receive the death penalty. Since only the Roman government could sentence someone to death, they took Jesus to Pilate, a Roman officer.

23 Then the whole group stood up and led Jesus to Pilate. ²They began to accuse Jesus. They told Pilate, "We caught this man telling things that were confusing our people. He says that we should not pay taxes to Caesar. He calls himself the Christ, a king."

³Pilate asked Jesus, "Are you the king of the Jews?"

Jesus answered, "Yes, that is right."

⁴Pilate said to the leading priests and the people, "I find nothing wrong with this man."

⁵They said again and again, "But Jesus is making trouble with the people! He teaches all around Judea. He

began in Galilee, and now he is here!" ⁶Pilate heard this and asked if Jesus was from Galilee. ⁷If so, Jesus was under Herod's authority. Herod was in Jerusalem at that time; so Pilate sent Jesus to him. ⁸When Herod saw Jesus, he was very glad. He had heard about Jesus and had wanted to meet him for a long time. Herod was hoping to see Jesus work a miracle. ⁹Herod asked Jesus many questions, but Jesus said nothing. ¹⁰The leading priests and teachers of the law were standing there. They were shouting things against Jesus. ¹¹Then Herod and his soldiers made fun of Jesus. They dressed him in a kingly robe and then sent him back to Pilate. ¹²In the past, Pilate and Herod had always been enemies. But on that day they became friends.

Today's Prayer

Dear Lord in heaven, give me patience with people who don't understand your ways. Thank you for Jesus who faced pain and cruelty with patience and courage. In his name, amen.

Memory Verse

"For God loved the world so much that he gave his only Son. God gave his Son so that whoever believes in him may not be lost, but have eternal life." John 3:16

Jesus Is Sentenced

Pilate sent Jesus to King Herod. He made fun of Jesus and then sent him back to Pilate. Pilate had to decide what to do with Jesus.

¹³Pilate called all the people together with the leading priests and the Jewish leaders. ¹⁴He said to them, "You brought this man to me. You said that he was making trouble among the people. But I have questioned him before you all, and I have not found him guilty of the things you say. ¹⁵Also, Herod found nothing wrong with him: he sent him back to us. Look, he has done nothing for which he should die. ¹⁶So, after I punish him, I will let him go free."

¹⁸But all the people shouted, "Kill him! Let Barabbas go free!" ¹⁹(Barabbas was a man who was in prison because he started a riot in

the city. He was guilty of murder.)

²⁰Pilate wanted to let Jesus go free. So he told this to the crowd. ²¹But they shouted again, "Kill him! Kill him on a cross!"

²²A third time Pilate said to them, "Why? What wrong has he done? I can find no reason to kill him. So I will have him punished and set him free."

²³But they continued to shout. They demanded that Jesus be killed on the cross. Their yelling became so loud that ²⁴Pilate decided to give them what they wanted. ²⁵They wanted Barabbas to go free, the man who was in jail for starting a riot and for murder. Pilate let Barabbas go free and gave Jesus to them to be killed.

²⁶The soldiers led Jesus away. At that time, there was a man coming into the city from the fields. His name was Simon, and he was from the city of Cyrene. The soldiers forced Simon to carry Jesus' cross and walk behind him.

Today's Prayer

My God and Father, teach me to be honest and to be fair with others. Help me do what is right even when that is difficult. I pray in the Savior's name, amen.

Memory Verse
"For God loved the world so much that he gave his only Son. God gave his Son so that whoever believes in him may not be lost, but have eternal life." John 3:16

Jesus Dies on a Cross

After his trial before Pilate, Jesus was taken away by a group of soldiers. They made Simon, a farmer, carry the cross they would use to crucify Jesus.

³²There were also two criminals led out with Jesus to be killed. ³³Jesus and the two criminals were taken to a place called the Skull. There the soldiers nailed Jesus to his cross. They also nailed the criminals to their crosses, one beside Jesus on the right and the other beside Jesus on the left. ³⁴Jesus said, "Father, forgive them.

They don't know what they are doing."

The soldiers threw lots to decide who would get his clothes. [35]The people stood there watching. The Jewish leaders made fun of Jesus. They said, "If he is God's Chosen One, the Christ, then let him save himself. He saved other people, didn't he?"

[36]Even the soldiers made fun of him. They came to Jesus and offered him some vinegar. [37]They said, "If you are the king of the Jews, save yourself!"

[44]It was about noon, and the whole land became dark until three o'clock in the afternoon. [45]There was no sun! The curtain in the Temple was torn into two pieces. [46]Jesus cried out in a loud voice, "Father, I give you my life." After Jesus said this, he died.

[47]The army officer there saw what happened. He praised God, saying, "I know this was a good man!"

Today's Prayer

Dear God, I am sad when I think of Jesus dying on the cross, but I am thankful for his promise of life after death. Teach me to forgive my enemies as he did. In his name I pray, amen.

Memory Verse
"After I go and prepare a place for you, I will come back. Then I will take you to be with me so that you may be where I am." John 14:3

Jesus Lives Again!

Those who loved Jesus took his body and placed it in a tomb. The tomb was sealed, and Roman soldiers were sent to guard it. Three days passed.

28The day after the Sabbath day was the first day of the week. At dawn on the first day, Mary Magdalene and another woman named Mary went to look at the tomb. [2]At that time there was a strong earthquake. An angel of the Lord came down from heaven. The angel went to the tomb and rolled the stone away from the entrance. Then he sat on the stone. [3]He was shining as bright as lightning. His clothes were white as snow. [4]The soldiers guarding the tomb were very frightened of the angel. They shook with fear and then became like dead men.

[5]The angel said to the women,

"Don't be afraid. I know that you are looking for Jesus, the one who was killed on the cross. ⁶But he is not here. He has risen from death as he said he would. Come and see the place where his body was. ⁷And go quickly and tell his followers. Say to them: 'Jesus has risen from death. He is going to Galilee. He will be there before you. You will see him there.'" Then the angel said, "Now I have told you."

⁸The women left the tomb quickly. They were afraid, but they were also very happy. They ran to tell Jesus' followers what had happened. ⁹Suddenly, Jesus met them and said, "Greetings." The women came up to Jesus, took hold of his feet, and worshiped him. ¹⁰Then Jesus said to them, "Don't be afraid. Go and tell my brothers to go on to Galilee. They will see me there."

Today's Prayer

Dear Lord in heaven, thank you for raising Jesus from the dead. Thank you for promising that I will live in heaven with him if I follow his way. Help me share this promise with others. In Jesus' name, amen.

Memory Verse

"After I go and prepare a place for you, I will come back. Then I will take you to be with me so that you may be where I am." John 14:3

Jesus Appears to Thomas

Jesus' friends gathered together on Sunday evening. They locked the doors of the house because they were afraid. Jesus came and showed them he really was the Christ who had been crucified.

[19]It was the first day of the week. That evening the followers were together. The doors were locked, because they were afraid of the Jews. Then Jesus came and stood among them. He said, "Peace be with you!" [20]After he said this, he showed them his hands and his side. The followers were very happy when they saw the Lord.

[21]Then Jesus said again, "Peace be with you! As the Father sent me, I now send you." [22]After he said this, he breathed on them and said, "Receive the Holy Spirit. [23]If you forgive anyone his sins, they are forgiven. If you

don't forgive them, they are not forgiven."

²⁴Thomas (called Didymus) was not with the followers when Jesus came. Thomas was 1 of the 12. ²⁵The other followers told Thomas, "We saw the Lord."

But Thomas said, "I will not believe it until I see the nail marks in his hands. And I will not believe until I put my finger where the nails were and put my hand into his side."

²⁶A week later the followers were in the house again. Thomas was with them. The doors were locked, but Jesus came in and stood among them. He said, "Peace be with you!" ²⁷Then he said to Thomas, "Put your finger here. Look at my hands. Put your hand here in my side. Stop doubting and believe."

²⁸Thomas said to him, "My Lord and my God!"

²⁹Then Jesus told him, "You believe because you see me. Those who believe without seeing me will be truly happy."

Today's Prayer

My Lord and my God, I am glad that Jesus lives and is always with me. Thank you for forgiveness and the happiness that comes from knowing Jesus. May I never doubt him. In Jesus' name I pray, amen.

Memory Verse

"After I go and prepare a place for you, I will come back. Then I will take you to be with me so that you may be where I am." John 14:3

Jesus Talks to Peter

When trouble came, Peter had said three times that he didn't know who Jesus was. He felt very sad about his sin. When Peter and some friends had gone fishing in Lake Galilee, Jesus gave Peter another chance.

[15]When they finished eating, Jesus said to Simon Peter, "Simon son of John do you love me more than these?"

He answered, "Yes, Lord, you know that I love you."

Jesus said, "Take care of my lambs."

[16]Again Jesus said, "Simon son of

John do you love me?"

He answered, "Yes, Lord, you know that I love you."

Jesus said, "Take care of my sheep."

[17]A third time he said, "Simon son of John do you love me?"

Peter was hurt because Jesus asked him the third time, "Do you love me?" Peter said, "Lord, you know everything. You know that I love you!"

He said to him, "Take care of my sheep. [18]I tell you the truth. When you were younger, you tied your own belt and went where you wanted. But when you are old, you will put out your hands and someone else will tie them. They will take you where you don't want to go." [19](Jesus said this to show how Peter would die to give glory to God.) Then Jesus said to Peter, "Follow me!"

[25]There are many other things that Jesus did. If every one of them were written down, I think the whole world would not be big enough for all the books that would be written.

Today's Prayer

Dear heavenly Father, thank you for loving me and sending Jesus to be my savior. When my faith is weak, forgive me as you forgave Peter. Help me always to follow you and share my faith. I pray in Christ, amen.

Memory Verse
"After I go and prepare a place for you, I will come back. Then I will take you to be with me so that you may be where I am." John 14:3

Jesus Returns to Heaven

Jesus' time on earth was almost over. He told his followers to go into all the world and make believers of the people. They didn't understand that he was about to leave the earth.

[3]After his death, he showed himself to them and proved in many ways that he was alive. The apostles saw Jesus during the 40 days after he was raised from death. He spoke to them about the kingdom of God. [4]Once when he was eating with them, he told them not to leave Jerusalem. He said, "The Father has made you a promise which I told you about before. Wait here to receive this promise. [5]John baptized people with water, but in a few days you will be baptized with the Holy Spirit."

[6]The apostles were all together. They asked Jesus, "Lord, are you at

this time going to give the kingdom back to Israel?"

[7]Jesus said to them, "The Father is the only One who has the authority to decide dates and times. These things are not for you to know. [8]But the Holy Spirit will come to you. Then you will receive power. You will be my witnesses—in Jerusalem, in all of Judea, in Samaria, and in every part of the world."

[9]After he said this, as they were watching, he was lifted up. A cloud hid him from their sight. [10]As he was going, they were looking into the sky. Suddenly, two men wearing white clothes stood beside them. [11]They said, "Men of Galilee, why are you standing here looking into the sky? You saw Jesus taken away from you into heaven. He will come back in the same way you saw him go."

Today's Prayer

Dear God in heaven, I am thankful that Jesus is alive today. Thank you for his promise to come again to take me to heaven too. Help me live so that I will be ready for his coming. I pray in Jesus' name, amen.

Memory Verse
"After I go and prepare a place for you, I will come back. Then I will take you to be with me so that you may be where I am." John 14:3

The Holy Spirit Comes

After Jesus went back to heaven, the apostles waited in Jerusalem as Jesus had told them. They chose another apostle, named Matthias, to replace Judas, who had killed himself. Then something very special happened.

2When the day of Pentecost came, they were all together in one place. ²Suddenly a noise came from heaven. It sounded like a strong wind blowing. This noise filled the whole house where they were sitting. ³They saw something that looked like flames of fire. The flames were separated and stood over each person there. ⁴They

were all filled with the Holy Spirit, and they began to speak different languages. The Holy Spirit was giving them the power to speak these languages.

[5]There were some religious Jews staying in Jerusalem who were from every country in the world. [6]When they heard this noise, a crowd came together. They were all surprised, because each one heard them speaking in his own language. [7]They were completely amazed at this. They said, "Look! Aren't all these men that we hear speaking from Galilee? [8]But each of us hears them in his own language. How is this possible? We are from different places: [9]Parthia, Media, Elam, Mesopotamia, Judea, Cappadocia, Pontus, Asia, [10]Phrygia, Pamphylia, Egypt, the areas of Libya near Cyrene, Rome [11](both Jews and those who had become Jews), Crete and Arabia. But we hear these men telling in our own languages about the great things God has done!" [12]They were all amazed and confused. They asked each other, "What does this mean?"

Today's Prayer

Mighty God, thank you for your Holy Spirit and the power that he gives. May your Spirit live in me and give me courage to tell others the good news about Jesus. I pray in Christ, amen.

Memory Verse
"Finally, be strong in the Lord and in his great power." Ephesians 6:10

Peter Preaches

The coming of the Holy Spirit caused a great crowd to gather. Some people didn't understand. Some even said the apostles were drunk. But Peter began speaking to the Jews. He told them to change their hearts and lives.

[22]"Men of Israel, listen to these words: Jesus from Nazareth was a very special man. God clearly showed this to you by the miracles, wonders, and signs God did through him. You all know this, because it happened right here among you. [23]Jesus was given to you, and you killed him. With the help of evil men you nailed him to a cross. But God knew all this would happen. This was God's plan which he had made long ago. [24]God raised Jesus from death. God set him free from the pain of death. Death could not hold him.

[32]"So Jesus is the One who God raised from death! And we are all wit-

nesses to this. [33]Jesus was lifted up to heaven and is now at God's right side. The Father has given the Holy Spirit to Jesus as he promised. So now Jesus has poured out that Spirit. This is what you see and hear.

[36]"So, all the people of Israel should know this truly: God has made Jesus both Lord and Christ. He is the man you nailed to the cross!"

[37]When the people heard this, they were sick at heart. They asked Peter and the other apostles, "What shall we do?"

[38]Peter said to them, "Change your hearts and lives and be baptized, each one of you, in the name of Jesus Christ for the forgiveness of your sins. And you will receive the gift of the Holy Spirit."

[41]Then those people who accepted what Peter said were baptized. About 3,000 people were added to the number of believers that day.

Today's Prayer

Holy Lord, thank you for the power of the gospel of Christ. It brings hope, joy and peace. Help me to obey. I thank you that I can believe like those Christians long ago. In Christ's name I pray, amen.

Memory Verse

"Finally, be strong in the Lord and in his great power." Ephesians 6:10

The Believers Share

Three thousand people believed Peter's teaching and became followers of Christ. Many who had been Christ's enemies now followed his teachings.

[42]They spent their time learning the apostles' teaching. And they continued to share, to break bread, and to pray together.

[43]The apostles were doing many miracles and signs. And everyone felt great respect for God. [44]All the believers stayed together. They shared everything. [45]They sold their land and

the things they owned. Then they divided the money and gave it to those people who needed it. [46]The believers met together in the Temple every day. They all had the same purpose. They broke bread in their homes, happy to share their food with joyful hearts. [47]They praised God, and all the people liked them. More and more people were being saved every day; the Lord was adding those people to the group of believers.

[32]The group of believers were joined in their hearts, and they had the same spirit. No person in the group said that the things he had were his own. Instead, they shared everything. [33]With great power the apostles were telling people that the Lord Jesus was truly raised from death. And God blessed all the believers very much. [34]They all received the things they needed. Everyone that owned fields or houses sold them. They brought the money [35]and gave it to the apostles. Then each person was given the things he needed.

Today's Prayer

Dear God in heaven, create in me a sharing heart like the hearts of those first Christians. Help me live so others will see Jesus living in me and praise your name. In Jesus' name I pray, amen.

Memory Verse
"Finally, be strong in the Lord and in his great power." Ephesians 6:10

Peter Heals a Man

More and more people believed in Christ. The apostles, who were filled with special power, taught the people of Jerusalem just as Jesus told them to do.

3 One day Peter and John went to the Temple. It was three o'clock in the afternoon. This was the time for the daily prayer service. ²There, at the Temple gate called Beautiful Gate, was a man who had been crippled all his life. Every day he was carried to this gate to beg. He would ask

for money from the people going into the Temple.

³The man saw Peter and John going into the Temple and asked them for money. ⁴Peter and John looked straight at him and said, "Look at us!" ⁵The man looked at them; he thought they were going to give him some money. ⁶But Peter said, "I don't have any silver or gold, but I do have something else I can give you: By the power of Jesus Christ from Nazareth—stand up and walk!"

⁷Then Peter took the man's right hand and lifted him up. Immediately the man's feet and ankles became strong. ⁸He jumped up, stood on his feet, and began to walk. He went into the Temple with them, walking and jumping, and praising God.

⁹⁻¹⁰All the people recognized him. They knew he was the crippled man who always sat by the Beautiful Gate begging for money. Now they saw this same man walking and praising God. The people were amazed. They could not understand how this could happen.

Today's Prayer

Holy Lord, even though I don't have the power to heal as Peter did, help me use the power I do have to share the good news about Jesus. Teach me how to help others in any way I can. I ask in Jesus' name, amen.

Memory Verse
"Finally, be strong in the Lord and in his great power." Ephesians 6:10

Peter and John in Jail

The Jewish leaders who had caused Jesus to be put to death were upset with Peter and John. They didn't like Peter and John telling everyone about the power of Jesus who had been brought back to life.

³The Jewish leaders grabbed Peter and John and put them in jail. It was already night, so they kept them in jail until the next day. ⁴But many of those who heard Peter and John preach believed the things they said. There were now about 5,000 men in the group of believers.

⁵The next day the Jewish leaders, the older Jewish leaders, and the teachers of the law met in Jerusalem. ⁶Annas the high priest, Caiaphas, John, and Alexander were there. Everyone from the high priest's family was there. ⁷They made Peter and John stand before them. The Jewish leaders asked them: "By what power

or authority did you do this?"

[8]Then Peter was filled with the Holy Spirit. He said to them, "Rulers of the people and you older leaders, [9]are you questioning us about a good thing that was done to a crippled man? Are you asking us who made him well? [10]We want all of you and all the Jewish people to know that this man was made well by the power of Jesus Christ from Nazareth! You nailed him to a cross, but God raised him from death. This man was crippled, but he is now well and able to stand here before you because of the power of Jesus! [11]Jesus is

'the stone that you builders did
not want.
It has become the cornerstone.'

[12]Jesus is the only One who can save people. His name is the only power in the world that has been given to save people. And we must be saved through him!"

Today's Prayer

Thank you, God, for the faith and joy of the early Christians. Thank you for their courage to teach about Jesus even when they were punished for it. Give me courage to share my faith. I pray in his name, amen.

Memory Verse
"Finally, be strong in the Lord and in his great power." Ephesians 6:10

Peter and John Are Freed

Peter and John were under arrest for preaching about Christ and for healing a crippled man. In defending themselves, they told the leaders more about Jesus.

[13]The Jewish leaders saw that Peter and John were not afraid to speak. They understood that these men had no special training or education. So they were amazed. Then they realized that Peter and John had been with Jesus. [14]They saw the crippled man standing there beside the two apostles. They saw that the man was healed. So they could say nothing against them.

[15]The Jewish leaders told them to leave the meeting. Then the leaders talked to each other about what they should do. [16]They said, "What shall we do with these men? Everyone in Jerusalem knows that they have done

a great miracle! We cannot say it is not true. [17]But we must warn them not to talk to people anymore using that name. Then this thing will not spread among the people."

[18]So they called Peter and John in again. They told them not to speak or to teach at all in the name of Jesus. [19]But Peter and John answered them, "What do you think is right? What would God want? Should we obey you or God? [20]We cannot keep quiet. We must speak about what we have seen and heard."

[21-22]The Jewish leaders could not find a way to punish them because all the people were praising God for what had been done. (This miracle was a proof from God. The man who was healed was more than 40 years old!) So the Jewish leaders warned the apostles again and let them go free.

Today's Prayer

Dear Lord, thank you for the early Christians who were not afraid to speak out for Jesus. Help me to be brave as they were. In the Savior's name I pray, amen.

Memory Verse
"Jesus said, 'It is more blessed to give than to receive.'" Acts 20:35

The Believers Pray

For the first time since Jesus went back to heaven, the Jewish leaders had put his followers in jail. Peter and John were thankful to be freed, but they knew they would need courage for what was ahead.

²³Peter and John left the meeting of Jewish leaders and went to their own group. They told them everything that the leading priests and the older Jewish leaders had said to them. ²⁴When the believers heard this, they prayed to God with one purpose. They prayed, "Lord, you are the One who made the sky, the earth, the sea, and everything in the world. ²⁵Our father David was your servant. With the help of the Holy Spirit he said:

'Why are the nations so angry?
Why are the people making
useless plans?

²⁶The kings of the earth prepare to fight.
  Their leaders make plans together
against the Lord
  and against his Christ.'
²⁷"These things really happened when Herod, Pontius Pilate, the non-Jewish people, and the Jewish people all came together against Jesus here in Jerusalem. Jesus is your holy Servant. He is the One you made to be the Christ. ²⁸These people made your plan happen; it happened because of your power and your will. ²⁹And now, Lord, listen to what they are saying. They are trying to make us afraid! Lord, we are your servants. Help us to speak your word without fear. ³⁰Help us to be brave by showing us your power; make sick people well, give proofs, and make miracles happen by the power of Jesus, your holy servant."

³¹After they had prayed, the place where they were meeting was shaken. They were all filled with the Holy Spirit, and they spoke God's word without fear.

Today's Prayer

Dear loving God, I am thankful that I can pray to you when I am afraid. Give me courage to show not only my friends but also my enemies how good it is to serve you. In Jesus' name, amen.

Memory Verse
"Jesus said, 'It is more blessed to give than to receive.'" Acts 20:35

An Angel Rescue

The church was growing fast. The apostles used their special powers to heal the sick and to show people they had God's power. But the Jewish leaders didn't like it.

[17]The high priest and all his friends (a group called the Sadducees) became very jealous. [18]They took the apostles and put them in jail. [19]But during the night, an angel of the Lord opened the doors of the jail. He led the apostles outside and said, [20]"Go and stand in the Temple. Tell the people everything about this new life." [21]When the apostles heard this, they obeyed and went into the Temple. It was early in the morning, and they began to teach.

The high priest and his friends arrived. They called a meeting of the Jewish leaders and all the important older men of the Jews. They sent

some men to the jail to bring the apostles to them. ²²When the men went to the jail, they could not find the apostles. So they went back and told the Jewish leaders about this. ²³They said, "The jail was closed and locked. The guards were standing at the doors. But when we opened the doors, the jail was empty!" ²⁴Hearing this, the captain of the Temple guards and the leading priests were confused. They wondered, "What will happen because of this?"

²⁵Then someone came and told them, "Listen! The men you put in jail are standing in the Temple. They are teaching the people!" ²⁶Then the captain and his men went out and brought the apostles back. But the soldiers did not use force, because they were afraid that the people would kill them with stones.

Today's Prayer

Dear heavenly Father, help me to defend the name of Jesus even when it means I may lose my friends. Thank you for rescuing me from trouble. I pray in Jesus' name, amen.

Memory Verse
"Jesus said, 'It is more blessed to give than to receive.'" Acts 20:35

The Apostles Obey God

The Jewish leaders didn't understand why the apostles continued to preach about God. So the apostles told them what was most important to them.

²⁷The soldiers brought the apostles to the meeting and made them stand before the Jewish leaders. The high priest questioned them. ²⁸He said, "We gave you strict orders not to go on teaching in that name. But look what you have done! You have filled Jerusalem with your teaching. You are trying to make us responsible for this man's death."

²⁹Peter and the other apostles answered, "We must obey God, not men! ³⁰You killed Jesus. You hung him on a cross. But God, the same God our ancestors had, raised Jesus up from death! ³¹Jesus is the One whom God raised to be on his right side. God made Jesus our Leader and Savior. God did this so that all Jews could change their hearts and lives and have their sins forgiven. ³²We saw all these things happen. The Holy Spirit also proves that these things are true. God has given the Spirit to all who obey him."

³³When the Jewish leaders heard this, they became very angry and wanted to kill them.

Today's Prayer

Dear God, thank you for the example of the apostles obeying God. Help me to obey you at all times. In Jesus' name, amen.

Memory Verse

"Jesus said, 'It is more blessed to give than to receive.'" Acts 20:35

Gamaliel's Advice

When the Jewish leaders heard John and Peter, they became very angry and wanted to kill the apostles. But a Jewish teacher of the law gave them good advice.

[34]A Pharisee named Gamaliel stood up in the meeting. He was a teacher of the law, and all the people respected him. He ordered the apostles to leave the meeting for a little while. [35]Then he said to them, "Men of Israel, be careful of what you are planning to do to these men! [36]Remember when Theudas appeared? He said that he

was a great man, and about 400 men joined him. But he was killed. And all his followers were scattered. They were able to do nothing. ³⁷Later, a man named Judas came from Galilee at the time of the registration. He led a group of followers, too. He was also killed, and all his followers were scattered.

³⁸"And so now I tell you: Stay away from these men. Leave them alone. If their plan comes from men, it will fail. ³⁹But if it is from God, you will not be able to stop them. You might even be fighting against God himself!"

The Jewish leaders agreed with what Gamaliel said. ⁴⁰They called the apostles in again. They beat the apostles and told them not to speak in the name of Jesus again. Then they let them go free. ⁴¹The apostles left the meeting full of joy because they were given the honor of suffering disgrace for Jesus. ⁴²The apostles did not stop teaching people. Every day in the Temple and in people's homes they continued to tell the Good News — that Jesus is the Christ.

Today's Prayer

Dear Lord, thank you for your word, the Bible, that teaches me about you. Help me to tell others about you, as the apostles did. In Jesus' name, amen.

Memory Verse
"Jesus said, 'It is more blessed to give than to receive.'" Acts 20:35

Stephen Is Killed

Stephen, one of the believers, had special abilities from God. Jewish leaders couldn't argue with Stephen because he spoke with such power and wisdom from God. So they told lies about him and had him arrested.

[51]Stephen continued speaking: "You stubborn Jewish leaders! You have not given your hearts to God! You won't listen to him! You are always against what the Holy Spirit is trying to tell you. Your ancestors were like this, and you are just like them! [52]Your fathers tried to hurt every prophet who ever lived. Those prophets said long ago that the Righteous One would come. But your fathers killed them. And now you have turned against the Righteous One and killed him. [53]You received the law of Moses, which God gave you through his angels. But you don't obey it!"

[54]When the Jewish leaders heard

Stephen saying all these things, they became very angry. They were so mad that they were grinding their teeth at Stephen. ⁵⁵But Stephen was full of the Holy Spirit. He looked up to heaven and saw the glory of God. He saw Jesus standing at God's right side. ⁵⁶He said, "Look! I see heaven open. And I see the Son of Man standing at God's right side!"

⁵⁷Then the Jewish leaders all shouted loudly. They covered their ears with their hands and all ran at Stephen. ⁵⁸They took him out of the city and threw stones at him until he was dead. The men who told lies against Stephen left their coats with a young man named Saul. ⁵⁹While they were throwing stones, Stephen prayed, "Lord Jesus, receive my spirit!" ⁶⁰He fell on his knees and cried in a loud voice, "Lord, do not hold this sin against them!" After Stephen said this, he died.

8 Saul agreed that the killing of Stephen was a good thing.

Today's Prayer

Dear Lord, thank you for men like Stephen who have had the courage to teach about Jesus even when others threatened to kill them. Make me brave. Help me to forgive my enemies. In Jesus' name I pray, amen.

Memory Verse
"We can trust God. He does what is right. He will make us clean from all the wrongs we have done." 1 John 1:9

Simon, the Magician

After Stephen's death, Jewish leaders began to hurt the church in Jerusalem. One man, Saul, went from house to house arresting believers. The believers left Jerusalem to tell others their story. With them was a Christian named Philip.

⁵Philip went to the city of Samaria and preached about the Christ. ⁶The people there heard Philip and saw the miracles he was doing. They all listened carefully to the things he said. ⁷Many of these people had evil spirits in them. But Philip made the evil spirits leave them. The spirits made a loud noise when they came out.

There were also many weak and crippled people there. Philip healed them, too. ⁸So the people in that city were very happy.

⁹But there was a man named Simon in that city. Before Philip came there, Simon had practiced magic. He amazed all the people of Samaria with his magic. He bragged and called himself a great man. ¹⁰All the people—the least important and the most important—paid attention to what Simon said. They said, "This man has the power of God, called 'the Great Power'!" ¹¹Simon had amazed them with his magic tricks so long that the people became his followers.

¹²But Philip told them the Good News about the kingdom of God and the power of Jesus Christ. Men and women believed Philip and were baptized. ¹³Simon himself believed and was baptized. He stayed very close to Philip. When he saw the miracles and the very powerful things that Philip did, Simon was amazed.

Today's Prayer

Mighty Lord, thank you for the power of the gospel to change people's lives. Help me be a Christian and share the good news about the kingdom of God with others. In my Savior's name I pray, amen.

Memory Verse
"We can trust God. He does what is right. He will make us clean from all the wrongs we have done." 1 John 1:9

An Ethiopian Officer

While Philip was in Samaria, an angel of the Lord spoke to him. The angel wanted Philip to meet someone on the road to Gaza.

²⁶An angel of the Lord spoke to Philip. The angel said, "Get ready and go south. Go to the road that leads down to Gaza from Jerusalem—the desert road." ²⁷So Philip got ready and went. On the road he saw a man from Ethiopia, a eunuch. He was an important officer in the service of Candace, the queen of the Ethiopians. He was responsible for taking care of all her money. He had gone to Jerusalem to worship, and ²⁸now he was on his way home. He was sitting in his chariot and reading from the book of Isaiah, the prophet. ²⁹The Spirit said to Philip, "Go to that chariot and stay near it."

³⁰So Philip ran toward the chariot. He heard the man reading from Isaiah, the prophet. Philip asked, "Do you understand what you are reading?"

³¹He answered, "How can I understand? I need someone to explain it to me!" Then he invited Philip to climb in and sit with him.

³⁶While they were traveling down the road, they came to some water. The officer said, "Look! Here is water! What is stopping me from being baptized?" ³⁸Then the officer commanded the chariot to stop. Both Philip and the officer went down into the water, and Philip baptized him. ³⁹When they came up out of the water, the Spirit of the Lord took Philip away; the officer never saw him again. The officer continued on his way home, full of joy.

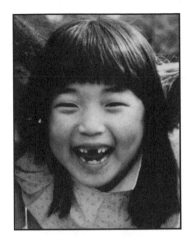

Today's Prayer

Dear God, help me, like the Ethiopian, to hear your truth and obey it. Help me also to be like Philip, always ready to share the good news about Jesus and your kingdom. In his name, amen.

Memory Verse

"We can trust God. He does what is right. He will make us clean from all the wrongs we have done." 1 John 1:9

Jesus Appears to Saul

Saul caused great trouble for the Christians in Jerusalem. He also planned to arrest Christians in other cities. But Saul didn't know that God had a plan for him.

9In Jerusalem Saul was still trying to frighten the followers of the Lord by saying he would kill them. So he went to the high priest ²and asked him to write letters to the synagogues in the city of Damascus. Saul wanted the high priest to give him the authority to find people in Damascus who were followers of Christ's Way. If he

found any there, men or women, he would arrest them and bring them back to Jerusalem.

³So Saul went to Damascus. As he came near the city, a bright light from heaven suddenly flashed around him. ⁴Saul fell to the ground. He heard a voice saying to him, "Saul, Saul! Why are you doing things against me?"

⁵Saul said, "Who are you, Lord?"

The voice answered, "I am Jesus. I am the One you are trying to hurt. ⁶Get up now and go into the city. Someone there will tell you what you must do."

⁷The men traveling with Saul stood there, but they said nothing. They heard the voice, but they saw no one. ⁸Saul got up from the ground. He opened his eyes, but he could not see. So the men with Saul took his hand and led him into Damascus. ⁹For three days Saul could not see, and he did not eat or drink.

Today's Prayer

How powerful is your love, dear Lord. It can change an enemy of Christ into a follower. Forgive me, change me and guide me. I pray in his name, amen.

Memory Verse
"We can trust God. He does what is right. He will make us clean from all the wrongs we have done." 1 John 1:9

Ananias Helps Saul

Christians everywhere knew what Saul had been doing. So they were afraid of him. Ananias, a Christian in Damascus, was chosen by God for a special visit to Saul.

¹⁰There was a follower of Jesus in Damascus named Ananias. The Lord spoke to Ananias in a vision, "Ananias!"

Ananias answered, "Here I am, Lord."

¹¹The Lord said to him, "Get up and go to the street called Straight Street. Find the house of Judas. Ask for a man named Saul from the city of Tarsus. He is there now, praying. ¹²Saul has seen a vision. In it a man named Ananias comes to him and lays his hands on him. Then he sees again."

¹³But Ananias answered, "Lord, many people have told me about this man and the terrible things he did to

your people in Jerusalem. [14]Now he has come here to Damascus. The leading priests have given him the power to arrest everyone who worships you."

[15]But the Lord said to Ananias, "Go! I have chosen Saul for an important work. He must tell about me to non-Jews, to kings, and to the people of Israel. [16]I will show him how much he must suffer for my name."

[17]So Ananias went to the house of Judas. He laid his hands on Saul and said, "Brother Saul, the Lord Jesus sent me. He is the one you saw on the road on your way here. He sent me so that you can see again and be filled with the Holy Spirit." [18]Immediately, something that looked like fish scales fell from Saul's eyes. He was able to see again! Then Saul got up and was baptized. [19]After eating some food, his strength returned.

Today's Prayer

Holy Lord, thank you for forgiveness. Even though Saul did terrible things to Christians, you forgave him when he obeyed you. Forgive me when I sin. Keep my heart right with you. In him I pray, amen.

Memory Verse
"We can trust God. He does what is right. He will make us clean from all the wrongs we have done." 1 John 1:9

Saul Preaches

Saul became a Christian. His belief in Christ brought great changes to his life. After a few days with the Christians in Damascus, Saul began to tell others about Jesus. He soon found himself in trouble with the Jews.

²⁰Soon he began to preach about Jesus in the synagogues, saying, "Jesus is the Son of God!"

²¹All the people who heard him were amazed. They said, "This is the man who was in Jerusalem. He was trying to destroy those who trust in this name! He came here to do the same thing. He came here to arrest the followers of Jesus and take them back to the leading priests."

²²But Saul became more and more powerful. His proofs that Jesus is the Christ were so strong that the Jews in Damascus could not argue with him.

²³After many days, the Jews made plans to kill Saul. ²⁴They were watch-

ing the city gates day and night. They wanted to kill him, but Saul learned about their plan. ²⁵One night some followers of Saul helped him leave the city. They lowered him in a basket through an opening in the city wall.

²⁶Then Saul went to Jerusalem. He tried to join the group of followers, but they were all afraid of him. They did not believe that he was really a follower. ²⁷But Barnabas accepted Saul and took him to the apostles. Barnabas told them that Saul had seen the Lord on the road. He explained how the Lord had spoken to Saul. Then he told them how boldly Saul had preached in the name of Jesus in Damascus.

²⁸And so Saul stayed with the followers. He went everywhere in Jerusalem, preaching boldly in the name of Jesus.

Today's Prayer

Mighty Lord, I praise you for the power of the gospel. It changed Saul's life, and it can change mine. Give me the power to tell others about your son, Jesus. In his name, amen.

Memory Verse

"I am proud of the Good News. It is the power God uses to save everyone who believes—to save the Jews first, and also to save the non-Jews." Romans 1:16

Tabitha Is Healed

Peter left Jerusalem and traveled to the city of Lydda where he healed a paralyzed man. Then he came to Joppa where Tabitha lived. She was a Christian who was always doing good and helping the poor.

³⁶In the city of Joppa there was a follower named Tabitha. (Her Greek name, Dorcas, means "a deer.") She was always doing good and helping the poor. ³⁷While Peter was in Lydda, Tabitha became sick and died. Her body was washed and put in a room upstairs. ³⁸The followers in Joppa heard that Peter was in Lydda.

(Lydda is near Joppa.) So they sent two men to Peter. They begged him, "Hurry, please come to us!"

[39]Peter got ready and went with them. When he arrived, they took him to the upstairs room. All the widows stood around Peter, crying. They showed him the shirts and coats that Tabitha had made when she was still alive.

[40]Peter sent everyone out of the room. He kneeled and prayed. Then he turned to the body and said, "Tabitha, stand up!" She opened her eyes, and when she saw Peter, she sat up. [41]He gave her his hand and helped her up. Then he called the saints and the widows into the room. He showed them Tabitha; she was alive!

[42]People everywhere in Joppa learned about this, and many believed in the Lord. [43]Peter stayed in Joppa for many days with a man named Simon who was a leatherworker.

Today's Prayer

Dear God in heaven, thank you for the power of prayer and for faithful Christians like Tabitha. Show me how to serve you better so others can see Jesus living in me. I pray in Jesus' name, amen.

Memory Verse
"I am proud of the Good News. It is the power God uses to save everyone who believes—to save the Jews first, and also to save the non-Jews."
Romans 1:16

Cornelius' Vision

The Jews were God's chosen people. Many of them believed that God did not care about other races. While Peter was in Joppa, something happened that showed God cares about all people everywhere.

10At Caesarea there was a man named Cornelius. He was an officer in the Italian group of the Roman army. ²Cornelius was a religious man. He and all the other people who lived in his house worshiped the true God. He gave much of his money to the poor and prayed to God often. ³One afternoon about three o'clock, Corne-

lius saw a vision clearly. In the vision an angel of God came to him and said, "Cornelius!"

[4]Cornelius stared at the angel. He became afraid and said, "What do you want, Lord?"

The angel said, "God has heard your prayers. He has seen what you give to the poor. And God remembers you. [5]Send some men now to Joppa to bring back a man named Simon. Simon is also called Peter. [6]Simon is staying with a man, also named Simon, who is a leatherworker. He has a house beside the sea." [7]Then the angel who spoke to Cornelius left.

Cornelius called two of his servants and a soldier. The soldier was a religious man who worked for Cornelius. [8]Cornelius explained everything to these three men and sent them to Joppa.

Today's Prayer

Holy Lord, help me understand that you love everyone. Help me to treat others with kindness and respect. In the name of Jesus I pray, amen.

Memory Verse

"I am proud of the Good News. It is the power God uses to save everyone who believes—to save the Jews first, and also to save the non-Jews."
Romans 1:16

Peter's Vision

The house where Peter stayed in Joppa had a flat roof with a wall around it. It was a quiet place to pray. As Peter was on the roof, the Lord sent him a vision. It was to show Peter that God also cares about people who aren't Jews.

⁹The next day as they came near Joppa, Peter was going up to the roof to pray. It was about noon. ¹⁰Peter was hungry and wanted to eat. But while the food was being prepared, he had a vision. ¹¹He saw heaven opened and something coming down. It looked like a big sheet being lowered to earth by its four corners. ¹²In it were all kinds of animals, reptiles, and birds. ¹³Then a voice said to Peter, "Get up, Peter; kill and eat."

¹⁴But Peter said, "No, Lord! I have never eaten food that is unholy or unclean."

¹⁵But the voice said to him again, "God has made these things clean.

Don't call them 'unholy'!" ¹⁶This happened three times. Then the sheet was taken back to heaven.

¹⁷While Peter was wondering what this vision meant, the men Cornelius sent had found Simon's house. They were standing at the gate. ¹⁸They asked, "Is Simon Peter staying here?"

¹⁹Peter was still thinking about the vision. But the Spirit said to him, "Listen! Three men are looking for you. ²⁰Get up and go downstairs. Go with them and don't ask questions. I have sent them to you."

²¹So Peter went down to the men. He said, "I am the man you are looking for. Why did you come here?"

²²They said, "A holy angel spoke to Cornelius, an army officer. He is a good man; he worships God. All the Jewish people respect him. The angel told Cornelius to ask you to his house so that he can hear what you have to say." ²³Peter asked the men to come in and spend the night.

Today's Prayer

Dear God and Father, thank you for loving us all. I want to love all races and people as you do. Help me not to think I am better than someone else. In Jesus' name I pray, amen.

Memory Verse
"I am proud of the Good News. It is the power God uses to save everyone who believes—to save the Jews first, and also to save the non-Jews."
Romans 1:16

Peter and Cornelius

Cornelius and his close friends and relatives were waiting for Peter when he arrived in Caesarea. Cornelius told Peter they were ready to hear the Lord's commands.

³⁴Peter began to speak: "I really understand now that to God every person is the same. ³⁵God accepts anyone who worships him and does what is right. It is not important what country a person comes from. ³⁶You know that God has sent his message to the people of Israel. That message is the Good News that peace has come through Jesus Christ. Jesus is the Lord of all people! ³⁷You know what has happened all over Judea. It began in Galilee after John preached to the people about baptism.

³⁸"You know about Jesus from Nazareth. God made him the Christ by giving him the Holy Spirit and power.

You know how Jesus went everywhere doing good. He healed those who were ruled by the devil, for God was with Jesus. [39]We saw all the things that Jesus did in Judea and in Jerusalem. But they killed him by nailing him to a cross."

[44]While Peter was still saying this, the Holy Spirit came down on all those who were listening. [45]The Jewish believers who came with Peter were amazed that the gift of the Holy Spirit had been given even to the non-Jewish people. [46]These Jewish believers heard them speaking in different languages and praising God. Then Peter said, [47]"Can anyone keep these people from being baptized with water? They have received the Holy Spirit just as we did!" [48]So Peter ordered that they be baptized in the name of Jesus Christ. Then they asked Peter to stay with them for a few days.

Today's Prayer

Holy Father, how wonderful and exciting it is when people obey your will and become Christians. What a joy it is to be your child. Help me to teach others so they too can share this joy. In Christ I pray, amen.

Memory Verse
"I am proud of the Good News. It is the power God uses to save everyone who believes—to save the Jews first, and also to save the non-Jews."
Romans 1:16

Peter Escapes from Prison

There was much good news. Non-Jewish people were following God. Far away in Antioch many people believed in the Lord. But in Jerusalem, King Herod killed James and put Peter in jail.

[4]After Herod arrested Peter, he put him in jail and handed him over to be guarded by 16 soldiers. Herod planned to bring Peter before the people for trial after the Passover Feast. [5]So Peter was kept in jail. But the church kept on praying to God for him.

[6]The night before Herod was to bring him to trial, Peter was sleeping. He was between two soldiers, bound with two chains. Other soldiers were guarding the door of the jail.

[7]Suddenly, an angel of the Lord stood there. A light shined in the room. The angel touched Peter on the side and woke him up. The angel

said, "Hurry! Get up!" And the chains fell off Peter's hands. ⁸The angel said to him, "Get dressed and put on your sandals." And so Peter did this. Then the angel said, "Put on your coat and follow me." ⁹So the angel went out, and Peter followed him. Peter did not know if what the angel was doing was real. He thought he might be seeing a vision.

¹⁰They went past the first and the second guard. They came to the iron gate that separated them from the city. The gate opened itself for them. They went through the gate and walked down a street. And the angel suddenly left him.

¹¹Then Peter realized what had happened. He thought, "Now I know that the Lord really sent his angel to me. He rescued me from Herod and from all the things the Jewish people thought would happen."

Today's Prayer

Dear Lord, thank you for listening to my prayers, as you heard the prayers for Peter when he was in prison. Help me remember to pray for others who need your help. I pray in Christ, amen.

Memory Verse

"If someone does wrong to you, do not pay him back by doing wrong to him. Try to do what everyone thinks is right." Romans 12:17

Paul Heals a Man

Paul and Barnabas, a Christian from Jerusalem, were sent on a preaching trip by the church in Antioch. They went to Lystra where the people worshiped Greek idols. A man lived in Lystra who had been born crippled and had never walked.

[8]In Lystra there sat a man who had been born crippled; he had never walked. [9]This man was listening to Paul speak. Paul looked straight at him and saw that the man believed God could heal him. [10]So he cried out, "Stand up on your feet!" The man jumped up and began walking around.

[11]When the crowds saw what Paul did, they shouted in their own Lycaonian language. They said, "The gods have become like men! They have come down to us!" [12]And the people began to call Barnabas "Zeus." They called Paul "Hermes," because he was the main speaker.

¹³The temple of Zeus was near the city. The priest of this temple brought some bulls and flowers to the city gates. The priest and the people wanted to offer a sacrifice to Paul and Barnabas. ¹⁴But when the apostles, Barnabas and Paul, understood what they were about to do, they tore their clothes in anger. Then they ran in among the people and shouted, ¹⁵"Men, why are you doing these things? We are only men, human beings like you! We are bringing you the Good News. We are telling you to turn away from these worthless things and turn to the true living God. He is the One who made the sky, the earth, the sea, and everything that is in them. ¹⁶In the past, God let all the nations do what they wanted. ¹⁷Yet he did things to prove he is real: He shows kindness to you. He gives you rain from heaven and crops at the right times. He gives you food and fills your hearts with joy." ¹⁸Even with these words, they were barely able to keep the crowd from offering sacrifices to them.

Today's Prayer

Mighty God, how great you are. How good are your gifts to us. Please heal those who are sick and hurt. Hear the prayer I offer in Jesus' holy name, amen.

Memory Verse
"If someone does wrong to you, do not pay him back by doing wrong to him. Try to do what everyone thinks is right." Romans 12:17

Paul Preaches in Europe

On Paul's second preaching trip, he took a man named Silas. They planned to go to Asia, but the Lord had other plans for them. When they came to the city of Troas, God sent a message to Paul.

⁹That night Paul had a vision. In the vision, a man from Macedonia came to him. The man stood there and begged, "Come over to Macedonia. Help us!" ¹⁰After Paul had seen the vision, we immediately prepared to leave for Macedonia. We understood that God had called us to tell the Good News to those people.

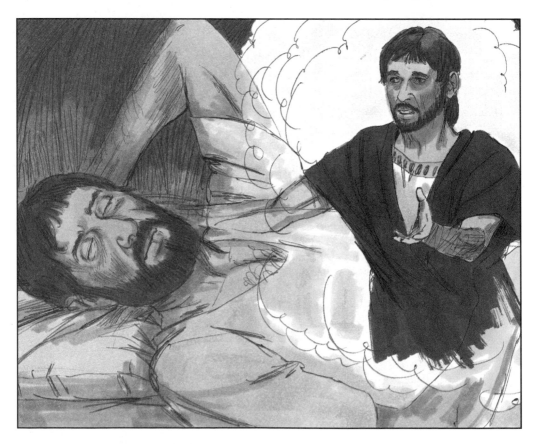

[11]We left Troas in a ship, and we sailed straight to the island of Samothrace. The next day we sailed to Neapolis. [12]Then we went by land to Philippi, the leading city in that part of Macedonia. It is also a Roman colony. We stayed there for several days.

[13]On the Sabbath day we went outside the city gate to the river. There we thought we would find a special place for prayer. Some women had gathered there, so we sat down and talked with them. [14]There was a woman named Lydia from the city of Thyatira. Her job was selling purple cloth. She worshiped the true God. The Lord opened her mind to pay attention to what Paul was saying. [15]She and all the people in her house were baptized. Then Lydia invited us to her home. She said, "If you think I am truly a believer in the Lord, then come stay in my house." And she persuaded us to stay with her.

Today's Prayer

Dear Lord, thank you for guiding Paul to preach the gospel to the other nations of the world. Guide me with your Holy Spirit so that I can tell the good news of Jesus to people all around me. In him I pray, amen.

Memory Verse
"If someone does wrong to you, do not pay him back by doing wrong to him. Try to do what everyone thinks is right." Romans 12:17

Paul and Silas in Jail

Paul was able to heal people. Usually people were happy when someone was healed, but this time it made them angry.

¹⁶Once, while we were going to the place for prayer, a servant girl met us. She had a special spirit in her. She earned a lot of money for her owners by telling fortunes. ¹⁷This girl followed Paul and us. She said loudly, "These men are servants of the Most High God! They are telling you how you can be saved!"

¹⁸She kept this up for many days. This bothered Paul, so he turned and said to the spirit, "By the power of Jesus Christ, I command you to come out of her!" Immediately, the spirit came out.

¹⁹The owners of the servant girl saw this. These men knew that now they could not use her to make money. So they grabbed Paul and Silas and dragged them before the city rulers in the marketplace. ²⁰Here they brought Paul and Silas to the Roman rulers and said, "These men are Jews and are making trouble in our city. ²¹They are teaching things that are not right for us as Romans to do."

²²The crowd joined the attack against them. The Roman officers tore the clothes of Paul and Silas and had them beaten with rods again and again. ²³Then Paul and Silas were thrown into jail. The jailer was ordered to guard them carefully. ²⁴When he heard this order, he put them far inside the jail. He pinned down their feet between large blocks of wood.

Today's Prayer

Father in heaven, give me a faith like that of Paul and Silas. When I am treated badly, help me sing your praise and pray. Help me know you are near. I pray in Christ, amen.

Memory Verse
"If someone does wrong to you, do not pay him back by doing wrong to him. Try to do what everyone thinks is right." Romans 12:17

The Jailer Is Saved

The jailer in Philippi had been told he must not let his prisoners escape or he would die. That is the reason he had locked Paul and Silas far inside the jail. Surely they couldn't escape from there!

²⁵About midnight Paul and Silas were praying and singing songs to God. The other prisoners were listening to them. ²⁶Suddenly, there was a big earthquake. It was so strong that it shook the foundation of the jail. Then all the doors of the jail broke open. All the prisoners were freed from their chains. ²⁷The jailer woke

up and saw that the jail doors were open. He thought that the prisoners had already escaped. So he got his sword and was about to kill himself. [28]But Paul shouted, "Don't hurt yourself! We are all here!"

[29]The jailer told someone to bring a light. Then he ran inside. Shaking with fear, he fell down before Paul and Silas. [30]Then he brought them outside and said, "Men, what must I do to be saved?"

[31]They said to him, "Believe in the Lord Jesus and you will be saved— you and all the people in your house." [32]So Paul and Silas told the message of the Lord to the jailer and all the people in his house. [33]At that hour of the night the jailer took Paul and Silas and washed their wounds. Then he and all his people were baptized immediately. [34]After this the jailer took Paul and Silas home and gave them food. He and his family were very happy because they now believed in God.

Today's Prayer

Dear Lord, thank you for the good news that can make enemies become friends in Jesus. May your word change my life as it did the jailer's life. In Christ's name, amen.

Memory Verse
"If someone does wrong to you, do not pay him back by doing wrong to him. Try to do what everyone thinks is right." Romans 12:17

Paul Heals Eutychus

Once, when Paul was preaching, a young man fell asleep and fell from a window.

⁶We sailed from Philippi after the Feast of Unleavened Bread and we met them in Troas five days later. We stayed there seven days.

⁷On the first day of the week, we all met together to break bread. Paul spoke to the group. Because he was planning to leave the next day, he kept on talking till midnight. ⁸We were all together in a room upstairs, and there were many lamps in the room.

⁹A young man named Eutychus was sitting in the window. As Paul continued talking, Eutychus was falling into a deep sleep. Finally, he went sound asleep and fell to the ground from the third floor. When they picked him up, he was dead.

¹⁰Paul went down to Eutychus. He knelt down and put his arms around him. He said, "Don't worry. He is alive now." ¹¹Then Paul went upstairs again, broke bread, and ate. He spoke to them a long time, until it was early morning. Then he left. ¹²They took the young man home alive and were greatly comforted.

Today's Prayer

Dear Lord my God, thank you for people who are able to preach your word. Teach me to be a good listener and to learn from them. In the name of Jesus, amen.

Memory Verse
"We are persecuted, but God does not leave us. We are hurt sometimes, but we are not destroyed." 2 Corinthians 4:9

Paul Is Arrested

When Paul entered the Temple at Jerusalem, Asian Jews told lies about him causing a riot. A Roman army commander rescued Paul and allowed him to speak to those in the Temple. Paul told about preaching to the people who weren't Jews.

²²The crowd listened to Paul until he said this. Then they began shouting, "Kill him! Get him out of the world! A man like this should not be allowed to live!" ²³They shouted and threw off their coats. They threw dust into the air.

²⁴Then the commander ordered the soldiers to take Paul into the army

building and beat him. The commander wanted to make Paul tell why the people were shouting against him like this. ²⁵So the soldiers were tying him up, preparing to beat him. But Paul said to an officer there, "Do you have the right to beat a Roman citizen who has not been proven guilty?"

²⁶When the officer heard this, he went to the commander and told him about it. The officer said, "Do you know what you are doing? This man is a Roman citizen!"

²⁷The commander came to Paul and said, "Tell me, are you really a Roman citizen?"

He answered, "Yes."

²⁸The commander said, "I paid a lot of money to become a Roman citizen."

But Paul said, "I was born a citizen."

²⁹The men who were preparing to question Paul moved away from him immediately. The commander was frightened because he had already tied Paul, and Paul was a Roman citizen.

Today's Prayer

Dear heavenly Lord, thank you for being with me when I am treated unfairly. Teach me to depend on you to lead me away from trouble as Paul did. I pray in Jesus' name, amen.

Memory Verse
"We are persecuted, but God does not leave us. We are hurt sometimes, but we are not destroyed." 2 Corinthians 4:9

Paul Before the Council

As a Roman citizen, Paul had the right to a fair trial. The commander could get into trouble for not respecting Paul's rights. The commander had to be careful to protect Paul.

[30]The next day the commander decided to learn why the Jews were accusing Paul. So he ordered the leading priests and the Jewish council to meet. The commander took Paul's chains off. Then he brought Paul out and stood him before their meeting.

23 Paul looked at the Jewish council and said, "Brothers, I have lived my life in a good way before God up to this day."

[6]Some of the men in the meeting were Sadducees, and others were Pharisees. So Paul shouted to them, "My brothers, I am a Pharisee and my father was a Pharisee! I am on trial

here because I hope that people will rise from death!"

⁷When Paul said this, there was an argument between the Pharisees and the Sadducees. The group was divided. ⁸(The Sadducees believe that after people die, they cannot live again. The Sadducees also teach that there are no angels or spirits. But the Pharisees believe in them all.) ⁹So there was a great uproar. Some of the teachers of the law, who were Pharisees, stood up and argued, "We find nothing wrong with this man! Maybe an angel or a spirit did speak to him."

¹⁰The argument was beginning to turn into a fight. The commander was afraid that the Jews would tear Paul to pieces. So the commander told the soldiers to go down and take Paul away and put him in the army building.

¹¹The next night the Lord came and stood by Paul. He said, "Be brave! You have told people in Jerusalem about me. You must do the same in Rome also."

A Plan to Kill Paul

Twice, the Roman commander had protected Paul from a mob. Now, once again, Jewish leaders were making plans to kill Paul.

[13]There were more than 40 Jews who made this plan. [14]They went and talked to the leading priests and the older Jewish leaders. They said, "We have made a promise to ourselves that we will not eat or drink until we have killed Paul! [15]So this is what we want you to do: Send a message to the commander to bring Paul out to you. Tell him you want to ask Paul more questions. We will be waiting to kill him while he is on the way here."

[16]But Paul's nephew heard about this plan. He went to the army building and told Paul about it. [17]Then Paul called one of the officers and said, "Take this young man to the com-

mander. He has a message for him."

[18]So the officer brought Paul's nephew to the commander. The officer said, "The prisoner, Paul, asked me to bring this young man to you. He wants to tell you something."

[19]The commander led the young man to a place where they could be alone. The commander asked, "What do you want to tell me?"

[20]The young man said, "The Jews have decided to ask you to bring Paul down to their council meeting tomorrow. They want you to think that they are going to ask him more questions. [21]But don't believe them! There are more than 40 men who are hiding and waiting to kill Paul. They have all made a promise not to eat or drink until they have killed him! Now they are waiting for you to agree."

[22]The commander sent the young man away. He said to him, "Don't tell anyone that you have told me about their plan."

Today's Prayer

Dear God in heaven, give me strength to follow you. Help me remember that even when I have troubles your way is best. In Jesus' name, amen.

Memory Verse
"We are persecuted, but God does not leave us. We are hurt sometimes, but we are not destroyed." 2 Corinthians 4:9

Paul Is Sent Away

When Claudius Lysias, the Roman commander, knew that Paul's life was in danger, he made a decision. He would send Paul to the Roman governor in Caesarea, 65 miles from Jerusalem.

²³Then the commander called two officers. He said to them, "I need some men to go to Caesarea. Get 200 soldiers ready. Also, get 70 horsemen and 200 men with spears. Be ready to leave at nine o'clock tonight. ²⁴Get some horses for Paul to ride. He must be taken to Governor Felix safely." ²⁵And he wrote a letter that said:

²⁶From Claudius Lysias.

To the Most Excellent Governor Felix:

Greetings.

²⁷The Jews had taken this man, and they planned to kill him. But I learned that he is a Roman citizen, so I went with my soldiers and saved him. ²⁸I

wanted to know why they were accusing him. So I brought him before their council meeting. ²⁹I learned that the Jews said Paul did some things that were wrong. But these charges were about their own laws. And no charge was worthy of jail or death. ³⁰I was told that some of the Jews were planning to kill Paul. So I sent him to you at once. I also told those Jews to tell you what they have against him.

³¹So the soldiers did what they were told. They took Paul and brought him to the city of Antipatris that night. ³²The next day the horsemen went with Paul to Caesarea. But the other soldiers went back to the army building in Jerusalem. ³³The horsemen came to Caesarea and gave the letter to the governor. Then they turned Paul over to him.

Today's Prayer

Dear God, I know that Paul didn't give up, even when others attacked him. I know you will help me also to be strong. In the Savior's name, amen.

Memory Verse
"We are persecuted, but God does not leave us. We are hurt sometimes, but we are not destroyed." 2 Corinthians 4:9

Paul Asks to See Caesar

In a trial before Governor Felix, Paul proved that he was innocent of breaking any law. But Felix kept Paul under arrest, hoping Paul would pay money for his freedom. Finally Festus became governor, and again the Jewish leaders tried to get Paul.

[6]Festus stayed in Jerusalem another eight or ten days. Then he went back to Caesarea. The next day he told the soldiers to bring Paul before him. Festus was seated on the judge's seat [7]when Paul came into the room. The Jews who had come from Jerusalem stood around him. They started making serious charges against Paul.

But they could not prove any of them. [8]This is what Paul said to defend himself: "I have done nothing wrong against the Jewish law, against the Temple, or against Caesar!"

[9]But Festus wanted to please the Jews. So he asked Paul, "Do you want to go to Jerusalem? Do you want me to judge you there on these charges?"

[10]Paul said, "I am standing at Caesar's judgment seat now. This is where I should be judged! I have done nothing wrong to the Jews; you know this is true. [11]If I have done something wrong and the law says I must die, I do not ask to be saved from death. But if these charges are not true, then no one can give me to them. No! I want Caesar to hear my case!"

[12]Festus talked about this with the people who advised him. Then he said, "You have asked to see Caesar; so you will go to Caesar!"

Today's Prayer

Dear God in heaven, help me be patient as Paul was patient. Thank you for guiding my life. In Jesus' name, amen.

Memory Verse
"With God's power working in us, God can do much, much more than anything we can ask or think of." Ephesians 3:20

A Storm at Sea

The king and the governor agreed that Paul was innocent. But since he had asked for Caesar to hear his case, they had to send him to Rome. So they put him on a ship going to Italy.

We sailed very close to the island of Crete. [14]But then a very strong wind named the "Northeaster" came from the island. [15]This wind took the ship and carried it away. The ship could not sail against it. So we stopped trying and let the wind blow us.

[16]We went below a small island named Cauda. Then we were able to bring in the lifeboat, but it was very hard to do. [17]After the men took the lifeboat in, they tied ropes around the ship to hold it together. The men were afraid that the ship would hit the sandbanks of Syrtis. So they lowered the sail and let the wind carry the ship.

[18]The next day the storm was blowing us so hard that the men threw out some of the cargo. [19]A day later they threw out the ship's equipment. [20]For many days we could not see the sun or the stars. The storm was very bad. We lost all hope of staying alive—we thought we would die.

[21]The men had gone without food for a long time. Then one day Paul stood up before them and said, "Men, I told you not to leave Crete. You should have listened to me. Then you would not have all this trouble and loss. [22]But now I tell you to cheer up. None of you will die! But the ship will be lost. [23]Last night an angel from God came to me. This is the God I worship. I am his. [24]God's angel said, 'Paul, do not be afraid! You must stand before Caesar. And God has given you this promise: He will save the lives of all those men sailing with you.' [25]So men, be cheerful! I trust in God. Everything will happen as his angel told me."

Today's Prayer

Dear Lord, remind me that you are with me even when I'm afraid. Give me faith. Please protect me and guard me just as you did Paul. In the Savior's name I pray, amen.

Memory Verse
"With God's power working in us, God can do much, much more than anything we can ask or think of." Ephesians 3:20

The Shipwreck

During the storm Paul told everyone they would be safe but that the boat would crash on an island. For two weeks the terrible storm blew the ship in front of it.

[33]Just before dawn Paul began persuading all the people to eat something. He said, "For the past 14 days you have been waiting and watching. You have not eaten. [34]Now I beg you to eat something. You need it to stay alive. None of you will lose even one hair off your heads."

[35]After he said this, Paul took some bread and thanked God for it before all of them. He broke off a piece and began eating. [36]All the men felt better. They all started eating too. [37](There were 276 people on the ship.) [38]We ate all we wanted. Then we began making the ship lighter by throwing the grain into the sea.

³⁹When daylight came, the sailors saw land. They did not know what land it was, but they saw a bay with a beach. They wanted to sail the ship to the beach, if they could. ⁴⁰So they cut the ropes to the anchors and left the anchors in the sea. At the same time, they untied the ropes that were holding the rudders. Then they raised the front sail into the wind and sailed toward the beach. ⁴¹But the ship hit a sandbank. The front of the ship stuck there and could not move. Then the big waves began to break the back of the ship to pieces.

⁴²The soldiers decided to kill the prisoners so that none of them could swim away and escape. ⁴³But Julius, the officer, wanted to let Paul live. He did not allow the soldiers to kill the prisoners. Instead he ordered everyone who could swim to jump into the water and swim to land. ⁴⁴The rest used wooden boards or pieces of the ship. And this is how all the people made it safely to land.

Today's Prayer

Dear loving God, thank you for guiding my life and letting me talk to you in prayer. I pray that you will lead me away from danger and keep me safe. In Jesus' name, amen.

Memory Verse
"With God's power working in us, God can do much, much more than anything we can ask or think of." Ephesians 3:20

A Snake Bites Paul

Everyone made it safely to land after the shipwreck, but Paul's troubles were not over.

28 When we were safe on land, we learned that the island was called Malta. ²It was raining and very cold. But the people who lived there were very good to us. They made us a fire and welcomed all of us. ³Paul gathered a pile of sticks for the fire. He was putting them on the fire when a poisonous snake came out because of the heat and bit him on the hand. ⁴The people living on the island saw the snake hanging from Paul's hand. They said to each other, "This man must be a murderer! He did not die in the sea, but Justice does not want him to live." ⁵But Paul shook the snake off into the fire. He was not

hurt. [6]The people thought that Paul would swell up or fall down dead. The people waited and watched him for a long time, but nothing bad happened to him. So they changed their minds about Paul. Now they said, "He is a god!"

[7]There were some fields around there owned by a very important man on the island. His name was Publius. He welcomed us into his home and was very good to us. We stayed in his house for three days. [8]Publius' father was very sick with a fever and dysentery. But Paul went to him and prayed. Then he put his hands on the man and healed him. [9]After this, all the other sick people on the island came to Paul, and he healed them, too. [10-11]The people on the island gave us many honors. We stayed there three months. When we were ready to leave, they gave us the things we needed.

Today's Prayer

Holy Lord, I am thankful that you always keep your promises. Make my faith strong like Paul's, and help me tell others about your love. In Christ's name, amen.

Memory Verse
"With God's power working in us, God can do much, much more than anything we can ask or think of." Ephesians 3:20

Paul Reaches Rome

In the spring Paul's group found a ship on its way to Italy. After several stops, the ship reached Puteoli where Paul spent a week with the Christians there. Finally they reached Rome.

[15]The believers in Rome heard that we were there. They came out as far as the Market of Appius and the Three Inns to meet us. When Paul saw them, he was encouraged and thanked God. [16]Then we arrived at Rome. There, Paul was allowed to live alone. But a soldier stayed with him to guard him. [17]Three days later Paul sent for the

Jewish leaders there. When they came together, he said, "Brothers, I have done nothing against our people. I have done nothing against the customs of our fathers. But I was arrested in Jerusalem and given to the Romans. [18]The Romans asked me many qustions. But they could find no reason why I should be killed. They wanted to let me go free, [19]but the Jews there did not want that. So I had to ask to come to Rome to have my trial before Caesar. But I have no charge to bring against my own people. [20]That is why I wanted to see you and talk with you. I am bound with this chain because I believe in the hope of Israel."

[30]Paul stayed two full years in his own rented house. He welcomed all people who came and visited him. [31]He preached about the kingdom of God and taught about the Lord Jesus Christ. He was very bold, and no one tried to stop him from speaking.

Today's Prayer

Dear God, thank you for my Christian friends. I pray that you will watch over them and protect them. In Jesus' name, amen.

Memory Verse
"With God's power working in us, God can do much, much more than anything we can ask or think of." Ephesians 3:20

Being God's Friends

Paul often wrote letters to churches in different places. He used his letters to teach and encourage the believers. Here Paul says that we are God's friends.

5 We have been made right with God because of our faith. So we have peace with God through our Lord Jesus Christ. [2]Through our faith, Christ has brought us into that blessing of God's grace that we now enjoy. And we are happy because of the hope we have of sharing God's glory. [3]And we also have joy with our troubles because we know that these troubles produce patience. [4]And patience produces hope. [5]And this hope will never disappoint us, because God has poured out his love to fill our hearts. God gave us his love through the Holy Spirit, whom God has given to us. [6]Christ died for us while we were still weak. We were living against God, but at the right time, Christ died for us. [7]Very few people will die to save the life of someone else. Although perhaps for a good man someone might possibly die. [8]But Christ died for us while we were still sinners. In this way God shows his great love for us.

[9]We have been made right with God by the blood of Christ's death. So through Christ we will surely be saved from God's anger. [10]I mean that while we were God's enemies, God made friends with us through the death of his Son. Surely, now that we are God's friends, God will save us through his Son's life. [11]And not only that, but now we are also very happy in God through our Lord Jesus Christ. Through Jesus we are now God's friends again.

Today's Prayer

My Lord, thank you for making me your friend. Knowing you are my friend makes me happy. Thank you for loving us so much that you sent Jesus to die for us. I pray in his name, amen.

Memory Verse
"Be careful. Continue strong in the faith. Have courage, and be strong. Do everything in love."
1 Corinthians 16:13-14

A Winning Team

Paul was a winner. He was mistreated, put in prison and beaten, but he never gave up. Paul knew that nothing could keep God from loving and caring for him.

³¹So what should we say about this? If God is with us, then no one can defeat us. ³²God let even his own Son suffer for us. God gave his Son for us all. So with Jesus, God will surely give us all things.

³³Who can accuse the people that God has chosen? No one! God is the One who makes them right. ³⁴Who can say that God's people are guilty? No one! Christ Jesus died, but that is not all. He was also raised from death. And now he is on God's right side and is begging God for us.

³⁵Can anything separate us from the love Christ has for us? Can troubles or problems or sufferings? If we

have no food or clothes, if we are in danger, or even if death comes — can any of these things separate us from Christ's love? ³⁶As it is written in the Scriptures:

"For you we are in danger of death all the time.
People think we are worth no more than sheep to be killed."

³⁷But in all these things we have full victory through God who showed his love for us. ³⁸⁻³⁹Yes, I am sure that nothing can separate us from the love God has for us. Not death, not life, not angels, not ruling spirits, nothing now, nothing in the future, no powers, nothing above us, nothing below us, or anything else in the whole world will ever be able to separate us from the love of God that is in Christ Jesus our Lord.

Today's Prayer

Dear God, I am happy because I know nothing can defeat me as long as you are in me and with me. I am glad that Jesus is on my side and that he loves me. In his name, amen.

Memory Verse
"Be careful. Continue strong in the faith. Have courage, and be strong. Do everything in love."
1 Corinthians 16:13-14

Love Each Other

Paul told Christians how to treat others, even enemies and strangers.

⁹Your love must be real. Hate what is evil. Hold on to what is good. ¹⁰Love each other like brothers and sisters. Give your brothers and sisters more honor than you want for yourselves. ¹¹Do not be lazy but work hard. Serve the Lord with all your heart. ¹²Be joyful because you have hope. Be patient when trouble comes. Pray at all times. ¹³Share with God's people who need help. Bring strangers in need into your homes.

¹⁴Wish good for those who do bad things to you. Wish them well and do not curse them. ¹⁵Be happy with those who are happy. Be sad with those who are sad. ¹⁶Live together in peace

with each other. Do not be proud, but make friends with those who seem unimportant. Do not think how smart you are.

[17]If someone does wrong to you, do not pay him back by doing wrong to him. Try to do what everyone thinks is right. [18]Do your best to live in peace with everyone. [19]My friends, do not try to punish others when they wrong you. Wait for God to punish them with his anger. It is written: "I am the One who punishes; I will pay people back," says the Lord. [20]But you should do this:

"If your enemy is hungry, feed him;
    if your enemy is thirsty, give
        him a drink.
Doing this will be like pouring
        burning coals on his head."
[21]Do not let evil defeat you. Defeat evil by doing good.

Obey the Country's Laws

Without laws to protect us and keep order in the world, life would be difficult. Paul was a good Roman citizen. He used his rights under Roman law to protect himself and to preach God's word in Rome.

13 All of you must obey the government rulers. No one rules unless God has given him the power to rule. And no one rules now without that power from God. ²So if anyone is against the government, he is really against what God has commanded. And so he brings punishment on himself. ³Those who do right do not have to fear the rulers. But people who do wrong must fear them. Do you want to be unafraid of the rulers? Then do what is right, and the ruler will praise you. ⁴He is God's servant to help you. But if you do wrong, then be afraid. The ruler has the power to punish; he is God's servant to punish those who

do wrong. [5]So you must obey the government. You must obey not only because you might be punished, but because you know it is the right thing to do.

[6]And this is also why you pay taxes. Rulers are working for God and give their time to their work. [7]Pay everyone, then, what you owe him. If you owe any kind of tax, pay it. Show respect and honor to them all.

[8]Do not owe people anything. But you will always owe love to each other. The person who loves others has obeyed all the law. [9]The law says, "You must not be guilty of adultery. You must not murder anyone. You must not steal. You must not want to take your neighbor's things." All these commands and all others are really only one rule: "Love your neighbor as you love yourself." [10]Love never hurts a neighbor. So loving is obeying all the law.

Today's Prayer

Dear God, my Father, thank you for my country and for laws that protect me. Help me obey those laws. Please guide the leaders of our country to make wise decisions. In Jesus' name, amen.

Memory Verse

"Be careful. Continue strong in the faith. Have courage, and be strong. Do everything in love."
1 Corinthians 16:13-14

The Weak and the Strong

A really strong person will never mistreat or put down someone who is weak. When people try to show their strength by putting down others, they are showing weakness instead. The Christian's strength comes from God's power.

15We who are strong in faith should help those who are weak. We should help them with their weaknesses, and not please only ourselves. ²Let each of us please his neighbor for his good, to help him be stronger in faith. ³Even Christ did not live to please himself. It was as the

Scriptures said: "When people insult you, it hurts me."

[4]Everything that was written in the past was written to teach us, so that we could have hope. That hope comes from the patience and encouragement that the Scriptures give us. [5]Patience and encouragement come from God. And I pray that God will help you all agree with each other the way Christ Jesus wants. [6]Then you will all be joined together, and you will give glory to God the Father of our Lord Jesus Christ. [7]Christ accepted you, so you should accept each other. This will bring glory to God. [8]I tell you that Christ became a servant of the Jews. This was to show that God's promises to the Jewish ancestors are true. [9]And he also did this so that the non-Jews could give glory to God for the mercy he gives to them.

[13]I pray that the God who gives hope will fill you with much joy and peace while you trust in him. Then your hope will overflow by the power of the Holy Spirit.

Today's Prayer

Father, teach me to be kind and to help those who are weak. May I always use the power of faith and love to help others follow you. Hear my prayer in Jesus' name, amen.

Memory Verse
"Be careful. Continue strong in the faith. Have courage, and be strong. Do everything in love."
1 Corinthians 16:13-14

You Are God's Temple

In this letter to the church at Corinth, Paul says we are like a house that belongs to God. Our foundation is Christ. God lives in us as we follow him.

And you are a house that belongs to God. [10]Like an expert builder I built the foundation of that house. I used the gift that God gave me to do this. Others are building on that foundation. But everyone should be careful how he builds. [11]The foundation has already been built. No one can build any other foundation. The foundation that has already been laid is Jesus Christ. [12]Anyone can build on that foundation using gold, silver, jewels, wood, grass, or straw. [13]But the work that each person does will be clearly seen, because the Day will make it plain. That Day will appear with fire, and the fire will test every man's work. [14]If the building that a man puts on the foundation still stands, he will get his reward. [15]But if his building is burned up, he will suffer loss. The man will be saved, but it will be as if he escaped from a fire.

[16]You should know that you yourselves are God's temple. God's Spirit lives in you.

Today's Prayer

Dear God my Father, thank you for sending Jesus to be the foundation for my life. Give me wisdom to understand the teachings of Jesus and to share them with others. I pray in his name, amen.

Memory Verse
"Love is patient and kind. Love is not jealous, it does not brag, and it is not proud."
1 Corinthians 13:4

We Are One Body

The parts of our body work together for the good of the whole body. In the same way Christians should work together to help each other because we need each other. Each person is important to God.

[12]A person's body is only one thing, but it has many parts. Yes, there are many parts to a body, but all those parts make only one body. Christ is like that too. [13]Some of us are Jews, and some of us are Greeks. Some of us are slaves, and some of us are free. But we were all baptized into one body through one Spirit. And we were

all made to share in the one Spirit.

[14]And a person's body has more than one part. It has many parts. [15]The foot might say, "I am not a hand. So I am not part of the body." But saying this would not stop the foot from being a part of the body. [16]The ear might say, "I am not an eye. So I am not part of the body." But saying this would not make the ear stop being a part of the body. [17]If the whole body were an eye, the body would not be able to hear. If the whole body were an ear, the body would not be able to smell anything. [18-19]If each part of the body were the same part, there would be no body. But truly God put the parts in the body as he wanted them. He made a place for each one of them. [20]And so there are many parts, but only one body.

[27]All of you together are the body of Christ. Each one of you is a part of that body.

Today's Prayer

Dear Lord in heaven, thank you for all of the Christians who make up the body of Christ. Help me to do my part to make the body work together. May I serve with love. In Christ's name, amen.

Memory Verse

"Love is patient and kind. Love is not jealous, it does not brag, and it is not proud."
1 Corinthians 13:4

The Best Way of All

Saying "I love you" is not enough. Real love is shown by the way we treat others. I may be very smart and even give away all my money for the poor, but without love it means nothing. Paul tells us how loving people act toward others.

⁴Love is patient and kind. Love is not jealous, it does not brag, and it is not proud. ⁵Love is not rude, is not selfish, and does not become angry easily. Love does not remember wrongs done against it. ⁶Love is not happy with evil, but is happy with the truth. ⁷Love patiently accepts all things. It always trusts, always hopes,

and always continues strong.

[8]Love never ends. There are gifts of prophecy, but they will be ended. There are gifts of speaking in different languages, but those gifts will end. There is the gift of knowledge, but it will be ended. [9]These things will end, because this knowledge and these prophecies we have are not complete. [10]But when perfection comes, the things that are not complete will end. [11]When I was a child, I talked like a child; I thought like a child; I made plans like a child. When I became a man, I stopped those childish ways. [12]It is the same with us. Now we see as if we are looking into a dark mirror. But at that time, in the future, we shall see clearly. Now I know only a part. But at that time I will know fully, as God has known me. [13]So these three things continue forever: faith, hope and love. And the greatest of these is love.

Today's Prayer

Dear God, thank you for your great love which never ends. Help me to love as you have said and always be patient, kind, trusting, hopeful and forgiving. In Jesus' name, amen.

Memory Verse
"Love is patient and kind. Love is not jealous, it does not brag, and it is not proud."
1 Corinthians 13:4

What Will I Be Like?

People often wonder what we will be like when Jesus comes and brings everyone back from death. This question bothered some of the Christians at Corinth. Paul explains that we will be different then.

[35]But someone may ask, "How are the dead raised? What kind of body will they have?" [36]Those are stupid questions. When you plant something, it must die in the ground before it can live and grow. [37]And when you plant it, what you plant does not have the same "body" that it will have later. What you plant is only a seed, maybe wheat or something else. [38]But God gives it a body that he has planned for it.

And God gives each kind of seed its own body. [39]All things made of flesh are not the same kinds of flesh: People have one kind of flesh, animals have another kind, birds have another, and fish have another. [40]Also there are heavenly bodies and earthly bodies. But the beauty of the heavenly bodies is one kind. The beauty of the earthly bodies is another kind. [41]The sun has one kind of beauty. The moon has another beauty, and the stars have another. And each star is different in its beauty.

[42]It is the same with the dead who are raised to life. The body that is "planted" will ruin and decay. But that body is raised to a life that cannot be destroyed. [43]When the body is "planted," it is without honor. But it is raised in glory. When the body is "planted," it is weak. But when it is raised, it has power. [44]The body that is "planted" is a physical body. When it is raised, it is a spiritual body.

There is a physical body. And there is also a spiritual body.

Our Heavenly Home

Paul wrote a second letter to the Christians at Corinth. He told them not to worry if they had troubles or their bodies wore out. Paul then told them about the house God will give us in heaven.

5 We know that our body—the tent we live in here on earth—will be destroyed. But when that happens, God will have a house for us to live in. It will not be a house made by men. It will be a home in heaven that will last forever. ²But now we are tired of this body. We want God to give us our heavenly home. ³It will clothe us, and

we will not be naked. ⁴While we live in this body, we have burdens, and we complain. We do not want to be naked. We want to be clothed with our heavenly home. Then this body that dies will be fully covered with life. ⁵This is what God made us for. And he has given us the Spirit to be a guarantee for this new life.

⁶So we always have courage. We know that while we live in this body, we are away from the Lord. ⁷We live by what we believe, not by what we can see. ⁸So I say that we have courage. And we really want to be away from this body and be at home with the Lord. ⁹Our only goal is to please God. We want to please him whether we live here or there. ¹⁰For we must all stand before Christ to be judged. Each one will receive what he should get—good or bad—for the things he did when he lived in the earthly body.

Today's Prayer

Dear Lord, thank you for the promise of a wonderful home in heaven with you. Help me live each day as I should. In Jesus' name, amen.

Memory Verse
"Love is patient and kind. Love is not jealous, it does not brag, and it is not proud."
1 Corinthians 13:4

We Are Children of God

Paul wrote a letter to the churches of Galatia. He wanted them to understand that as Christians we are all the same. We become one people, the family of God. We are his children.

²⁶⁻²⁷ You were all baptized into Christ, and so you were all clothed with Christ. This shows that you are all children of God through faith in Christ Jesus. ²⁸Now, in Christ, there is no difference between Jew and Greek. There is no difference between slaves and free men. There is no difference between male and female. You are all the same in Christ Jesus. ²⁹You belong to Christ. So you are Abraham's descendants. You get all of God's blessings because of the promise that God made to Abraham.

4 I want to tell you this: While the one who will inherit his father's property is still a child, he is no dif-

ferent from a slave. It does not matter that the child owns everything. ²While he is a child, he must obey those who are chosen to care for him. But when the child reaches the age set by his father, he is free.

³It is the same for us. We were once like children. We were slaves to the useless rules of this world. ⁴But when the right time came, God sent his Son. His Son was born of a woman and lived under the law. ⁵God did this so that he could buy freedom for those who were under the law. His purpose was to make us his children.

⁶And you are God's children. That is why God sent the Spirit of his Son into your hearts. The Spirit cries out, "Father, dear Father." ⁷So now you are not a slave; you are God's child, and God will give you what he promised, because you are his child.

Today's Prayer

Dear God, thank you for being my heavenly Father. Thank you that I can be your child and become one of your family. Help me always to obey you. I pray in Christ, amen.

Memory Verse
"So you must stop telling lies. Tell each other the truth because we all belong to each other in the same body." Ephesians 4:25

Following the Spirit

Belief in Jesus changes people. A Christian becomes a new person inside because the Holy Spirit lives in him or her. Paul tells us how a Christian will behave.

[16]So I tell you: Live by following the Spirit. Then you will not do what your sinful selves want. [17]Our sinful selves want what is against the Spirit. The Spirit wants what is against our sinful selves. The two are against each other. So you must not do just what you please. [18]But if you let the Spirit lead you, you are not under the law.

[19]The wrong things the sinful self does are clear: being sexually unfaithful, not being pure, taking part in sexual sins, [20]worshiping false gods, doing witchcraft, hating, making trouble, being jealous, being angry, being selfish, making people angry with each other, causing divisions among people, [21]having envy, being drunk, having wild and wasteful parties, and doing other things like this. I warn you now as I warned you before: Those who do these things will not be in God's kingdom.

[22]But the Spirit gives love, joy, peace, patience, kindness, goodness, faithfulness, [23]gentleness, self-control. There is no law that says these things are wrong. [24]Those who belong to Christ Jesus have crucified their own sinful selves. They have given up their old selfish feelings and the evil things they wanted to do. [25]We get our new life from the Spirit. So we should follow the Spirit. [26]We must not be proud. We must not make trouble with each other. And we must not be jealous of each other.

Today's Prayer

Great Lord, thank you for sending us the Holy Spirit. Teach me to show love, joy, patience, kindness and gentleness. I pray in Christ, amen.

Memory Verse
"So you must stop telling lies. Tell each other the truth because we all belong to each other in the same body." Ephesians 4:25

God Gave Us New Life

Many of the Christians in Ephesus once worshiped idols. In this letter Paul reminds them of what it means to belong to Christ.

2 In the past your spiritual lives were dead because of your sins and the things you did wrong against God. ²Yes, in the past you lived the way the world lives. You followed the ruler of the evil powers that are above the earth. That same spirit is now working in those who refuse to obey God. ³In the past all of us lived like them. We lived trying to please our sinful selves. We did all the things our bodies and minds wanted. We should have suffered God's anger because of the way we were. We were the same as all other people.

⁴But God's mercy is great, and he loved us very much. ⁵We were spiritu-

ally dead because of the things we did wrong against God. But God gave us new life with Christ. You have been saved by God's grace. ^{6}And he raised us up with Christ and gave us a seat with him in the heavens. He did this for those of us who are in Christ Jesus. ^{7}He did this so that for all future time he could show the very great riches of his grace. He shows that grace by being kind to us in Christ Jesus.

^{8}I mean that you have been saved by grace because you believe. You did not save yourselves. It was a gift from God. ^{9}You cannot brag that you are saved by the work you have done. ^{10}God has made us what we are. In Christ Jesus, God made us new people so that we would do good works. God had planned in advance those good works for us. He had planned for us to live our lives doing them.

Today's Prayer

Holy Lord, I praise you for the new life I can have in Christ as a Christian. Help me live my new life doing the good works you have planned for me. In his name, amen.

Memory Verse
"So you must stop telling lies. Tell each other the truth because we all belong to each other in the same body." Ephesians 4:25

Be Like Christ

Paul encouraged the people of Ephesus to grow up to be like Christ. He told them how they should behave. His words are still true today.

[24]You were taught to become a new person. That new person is made to be like God—made to be truly good and holy.

[25]So you must stop telling lies. Tell each other the truth because we all belong to each other in the same body. [26]When you are angry, do not sin. And do not go on being angry all

day. ²⁷Do not give the devil a way to defeat you. ²⁸If a person is stealing, he must stop stealing and start working. He must use his hands for doing something good. Then he will have something to share with those who are poor.

²⁹When you talk, do not say harmful things. But say what people need— words that will help others become stronger. Then what you say will help those who listen to you. ³⁰And do not make the Holy Spirit sad. The Spirit is God's proof that you belong to him. God gave you the Spirit to show that God will make you free when the time comes. ³¹Do not be bitter or angry or mad. Never shout angrily or say things to hurt others. Never do anything evil. ³²Be kind and loving to each other. Forgive each other just as God forgave you in Christ.

Today's Prayer

I am growing up, dear God. Help me grow to be like Jesus. Keep me from being fooled by evil. Make me good and holy in your sight. In Jesus' name, amen.

Memory Verse
"So you must stop telling lies. Tell each other the truth because we all belong to each other in the same body." Ephesians 4:25

Wear the Armor of God

Ephesus was the capitol city of a Roman province, so many Roman soldiers were there. Paul uses a soldier's armor to tell how Christians can be strong in the Lord and can be prepared to serve him.

¹⁰Finally, be strong in the Lord and in his great power. ¹¹Wear the full armor of God. Wear God's armor so that you can fight against the devil's evil tricks. ¹²Our fight is not against people on earth. We are fighting against the rulers and authorities and the powers of this world's darkness. We are fighting against the spiritual pow-

ers of evil in the heavenly world. [13]That is why you need to get God's full armor. Then on the day of evil you will be able to stand strong. And when you have finished the whole fight, you will still be standing.

[14]So stand strong, with the belt of truth tied around your waist. And on your chest wear the protection of right living. [15]And on your feet wear the Good News of peace to help you stand strong. [16]And also use the shield of faith. With that you can stop all the burning arrows of the Evil One. [17]Accept God's salvation to be your helmet. And take the sword of the Spirit — that sword is the teaching of God.

[18]Pray in the Spirit at all times. Pray with all kinds of prayers, and ask for everything you need. To do this you must always be ready. Never give up. Always pray for all God's people.

Today's Prayer

Mighty God, teach me to be strong and ready to serve. Give me skill in using your teachings as a sword. Listen to my prayers, I ask in Christ's name, amen.

Memory Verse

"So you must stop telling lies. Tell each other the truth because we all belong to each other in the same body." Ephesians 4:25

Thanksgiving and Prayer

Philippians was a letter written to the church in Philippi. It is full of thankfulness and joy. Yet Paul wrote this book while he was in prison. He loved the Christians at Philippi, and his memory of them filled him with joy.

³I thank God every time I remember you. ⁴And I always pray for all of you with joy. ⁵I thank God for the help you gave me while I preached the Good News. You helped from the first day you believed until now. ⁶God began doing a good work in you. And he will continue it until it is finished when

Jesus Christ comes again. I am sure of that.

⁷And I know that I am right to think like this about all of you. I am sure because I have you in my heart. All of you share in God's grace with me. You share in God's grace with me while I am in prison, while I am defending the Good News, and while I am proving the truth of the Good News. ⁸God knows that I want to see you very much. I love all of you with the love of Christ Jesus.

⁹This is my prayer for you: that your love will grow more and more; that you will have knowledge and understanding with your love; ¹⁰that you will see the difference between good and bad and choose the good; that you will be pure and without wrong for the coming of Christ; ¹¹that you will do many good things with the help of Christ to bring glory and praise to God.

Today's Prayer

Dear Lord, thank you for letting me make choices. I need your help to know what is good and best for me and others. Please give me strength to choose the good. In Jesus' name, amen.

Memory Verse
"Be full of joy in the Lord always. I will say again, be full of joy." Philippians 4:4

On to the Goal

Paul was a faithful servant of Christ who had done great things. He had started many churches, but he wanted to be better. He had a goal—to be just like Jesus—and he always worked toward that goal.

¹⁰All I want is to know Christ and the power of his rising from death. I want to share in Christ's sufferings and become like him in his death. ¹¹If I have those things, then I have hope that I myself will be raised from death.

¹²I do not mean that I am already as God wants me to be. I have not yet reached that goal. But I continue trying to reach it and to make it mine. Christ wants me to do that. That is the reason Christ made me his. ¹³Brothers, I know that I have not yet reached that goal. But there is one thing I always do: I forget the things that are past. I try as hard as I can to reach the goal that is before me. ¹⁴I keep trying to reach the goal and get the prize. That prize is mine because God called me through Christ to the life above.

¹⁵All of us who have grown spiritually to be mature should think this way, too. And if there are things you do not agree with, God will make them clear to you. ¹⁶But we should continue following the truth we already have.

Today's Prayer

Dear precious Savior, even though I am human and make mistakes, forgive me and help me to keep trying. With each new day, help me strengthen my goal to serve my Jesus. In his service, amen.

Memory Verse

"Be full of joy in the Lord always. I will say again, be full of joy." Philippians 4:4

Joy in the Lord

How can you be happy in a prison? Paul knew the secret. In this letter, Paul told the Philippians how to be happy.

4 My dear brothers, I love you and want to see you. You bring me joy and make me proud of you. Continue following the Lord as I have told you.

⁴Be full of joy in the Lord always. I will say again, be full of joy.

⁵Let all men see that you are gentle and kind. The Lord is coming soon. ⁶Do not worry about anything. But pray and ask God for everything you need. And when you pray, always give thanks. ⁷And God's peace will keep your hearts and minds in Christ Jesus. The peace that God gives is so great that we cannot understand it.

⁸Brothers, continue to think about the things that are good and worthy of praise. Think about the things that are true and honorable and right and pure and beautiful and respected. ⁹And do what you learned and received from me. Do what I told you and what you saw me do. And the God who gives peace will be with you.

Today's Prayer

Wonderful Lord, there are times when everything seems to go wrong. When these times come, help me to remember all of the good things you have given me. I am thankful in Jesus, amen.

Memory Verse
"Be full of joy in the Lord always. I will say again, be full of joy." Philippians 4:4

Christ Is First

The Book of Colossians was written by Paul to the church in the city of Colosse. Paul wanted them to understand that there is nothing in the world more important than Christ. Through Christ, God gives us a new life and forgives our sins.

[15]No one has seen God, but Jesus is exactly like him. Christ ranks higher than all the things that have been made. [16]Through his power all things were made—things in heaven and on earth, things seen and unseen, all powers, authorities, lords, and rulers. All things were made through Christ and for Christ. [17]Christ was there be-

fore anything was made. And all things continue because of him. [18]He is the head of the body. (The body is the church.) Everything comes from him. And he is the first one who was raised from death. So in all things Jesus is most important.

[19]God was pleased for all of himself to live in Christ. [20]And through Christ, God decided to bring all things back to himself again—things on earth and things in heaven. God made peace by using the blood of Christ's death on the cross.

[21]At one time you were separated from God. You were God's enemies in your minds because the evil deeds you did were against God. [22]But now Christ has made you God's friends again. He did this by his death while he was in the body, that he might bring you into God's presence. He brings you before God as people who are holy, with no wrong in you, and with nothing that God can judge you guilty of.

Today's Prayer

Holy God, thank you for telling me that you are my friend and that you will never leave me. Take my life and make me a helper to share Jesus with my friends. In Jesus' name, amen.

Memory Verse
"Be full of joy in the Lord always. I will say again, be full of joy." Philippians 4:4

New Life

Paul tells the Christians that they cannot live as they did before they believed in Christ. He explains how to please God and how to bring peace and happiness to their lives.

[8]But now put these things out of your life: anger, bad temper, doing or saying things to hurt others, and using evil words when you talk. [9]Do not lie to each other. You have left your old sinful life and the things you did before. [10]You have begun to live the new life. In your new life you are being made new. You are becoming

like the One who made you. This new life brings you the true knowledge of God. ¹¹In the new life there is no difference between Greeks and Jews. There is no difference between those who are circumcised and those who are not circumcised, or people that are foreigners, or Scythians. There is no difference between slaves and free people. But Christ is in all believers. And Christ is all that is important.

¹²God has chosen you and made you his holy people. He loves you. So always do these things: Show mercy to others; be kind, humble, gentle, and patient. ¹³Do not be angry with each other but forgive each other. If someone does wrong to you, then forgive him. Forgive each other because the Lord forgave you. ¹⁴Do all these things; but most important, love each other. Love is what holds you all together in perfect unity. ¹⁵Let the peace that Christ gives control your thinking. You were all called together in one body to have peace. Always be thankful. ¹⁶Let the teaching of Christ live in you richly.

Today's Prayer

Heavenly Lord, thank you for giving us Jesus who has shown us how to have a better life. Teach me to be more like him each day. In him I pray, amen.

Memory Verse
"Be full of joy in the Lord always. I will say again, be full of joy." Philippians 4:4

How to Live

This book was written to the church in Thessalonica, a European city Paul visited. One of the things he tells them is to be ready for the time when Christ will come again. Then he ends with some rules to help them be prepared.

[12]Now, brothers, we ask you to respect those people who work hard with you, who lead you in the Lord and teach you. [13]Respect them with a very special love because of the work they do with you.

Live in peace with each other. [14]We ask you, brothers, to warn those who do not work. Encourage the people

who are afraid. Help those who are weak. Be patient with every person. ¹⁵Be sure that no one pays back wrong for wrong. But always try to do what is good for each other and for all people.

¹⁶Always be happy. ¹⁷Never stop praying. ¹⁸Give thanks whatever happens. That is what God wants for you in Christ Jesus.

¹⁹Do not stop the work of the Holy Spirit. ²⁰Do not treat prophecy as if it were not important. ²¹But test everything. Keep what is good. ²²And stay away from everything that is evil.

²³We pray that God himself, the God of peace, will make you pure, belonging only to him. We pray that your whole self—spirit, soul, and body—will be kept safe and be without wrong when our Lord Jesus Christ comes.

Today's Prayer

Dear Savior, when I see others who are shy and afraid, help me to encourage and comfort them. I know how much it hurts to have those feelings. Teach me how to get along with others. In Jesus' name, amen.

Memory Verse
"You are young, but do not let anyone treat you as if you were not important. Be an example to show the believers how they should live." 1 Timothy 4:12

Advice for Timothy

Paul had known Timothy for a long time, and he loved Timothy as if he were a son. While Timothy was still a young man, he began to preach. Paul wrote this letter giving him some advice.

2 Timothy, you are like a son to me. Be strong in the grace that we have in Christ Jesus. ²You and many others have heard what I have taught. You should teach the same thing to some people you can trust. Then they will be able to teach it to others. ³Share in the troubles that we have. Accept them like a true soldier of Christ

Jesus. ⁴A soldier wants to please his commanding officer, so he does not waste his time doing the things that most people do. ⁵If an athlete is running a race, he must obey all the rules in order to win.

²²Stay away from the evil things young people love to do. Try hard to live right and to have faith, love, and peace. Work for these things together with those who have pure hearts and who trust in the Lord. ²³Stay away from foolish and stupid arguments. You know that such arguments grow into bigger arguments. ²⁴And a servant of the Lord must not quarrel! He must be kind to everyone. He must be a good teacher. He must be patient. ²⁵The Lord's servant must gently teach those who do not agree with him. Maybe God will let them change their hearts so that they can accept the truth.

Today's Prayer

Great God in heaven, there are so many evil things all around me, I need your help to keep from becoming a part of them. Guide me to find friends who also want to follow you. In Jesus' name, amen.

Memory Verse
"You are young, but do not let anyone treat you as if you were not important. Be an example to show the believers how they should live." 1 Timothy 4:12

A Favor for a Slave

Philemon, a Christian, owned a slave named Onesimus. He had run away to Rome, taking some of his master's possessions. In Rome Onesimus met Paul and became a Christian. Paul then asked Philemon to forgive Onesimus and treat him as a brother, not a slave.

[10]I am asking you a favor for my son Onesimus. He became my son while I was in prison. [11]In the past he was useless to you. But now he has become useful for both you and me.

[12]I am sending him back to you, and with him I am sending my own heart. [13]I wanted to keep him with me to help me while I am in prison for the Good News. By helping me he would be serving you. [14]But I did not want to do anything without asking you first. Then any favor you do for me will be because you want to do it, not because I forced you to do it.

[15]Onesimus was separated from you for a short time. Maybe that hap-

pened so that you could have him back forever—[16]not to be a slave, but better than a slave, to be a loved brother. I love him very much. But you will love him even more. You will love him as a man and as a brother in the Lord.

[17]If you think of me as your friend, then accept Onesimus back. Welcome him as you would welcome me. [18]If Onesimus has done anything wrong to you, charge that to me. If he owes you anything, charge that to me. [19]I, Paul, am writing this with my own hand. I will pay back anything Onesimus owes. And I will say nothing about what you owe me for your own life. [20]So, my brother, I ask that you do this for me in the Lord. Comfort my heart in Christ. [21]I write this letter, knowing that you will do what I ask you and even more.

Today's Prayer

Dear Lord, I am sorry when I sin and hurt you, Jesus. Please forgive me. Help me to forgive others when they hurt me. In Jesus' name I pray, amen.

Memory Verse
"You are young, but do not let anyone treat you as if you were not important. Be an example to show the believers how they should live." 1 Timothy 4:12

Helping Others

Hebrews is a book written for Jewish Christians. As the writer ends the book, he gives advice for Christian living that is as important today as it was when it was first written.

13 Keep on loving each other as brothers in Christ. ²Remember to welcome strangers into your homes. Some people have done this and have welcomed angels without knowing it. ³Do not forget those who are in prison. Remember them as if you were in prison with them. Remember those who are suffering as if

you were suffering with them.

⁴Marriage should be honored by everyone. Husband and wife should keep their marriage pure. God will judge guilty those who take part in sexual sins. ⁵Keep your lives free from the love of money. And be satisfied with what you have. God has said,

"I will never leave you;
I will never forget you."

⁶So we can feel sure and say,

"I will not be afraid because the Lord is my helper.
People can't do anything to me."

¹⁴Here on earth we do not have a city that lasts forever. But we are looking for the city that we will have in the future. ¹⁵So through Jesus let us always offer our sacrifice to God. This sacrifice is our praise, coming from lips that speak his name. ¹⁶Do not forget to do good to others. And share with them what you have. These are the sacrifices that please God.

Today's Prayer

Precious Savior, thank you for your promise that you will never leave or forget me. Give me courage to help those around me who hurt and are in trouble. Through Jesus I pray, amen.

Memory Verse

"You are young, but do not let anyone treat you as if you were not important. Be an example to show the believers how they should live." 1 Timothy 4:12

True Worship

The Book of James tells us how to live as Christians. It is not enough to talk about belonging to Jesus. We must show it in our lives and treat others with love.

[19]My dear brothers, always be willing to listen and slow to speak. Do not become angry easily. [20]Anger will not help you live a good life as God wants. [21]So put out of your life every evil thing and every kind of wrong you do. Don't be proud but accept God's teaching that is planted in your

hearts. This teaching can save your souls.

²²Do what God's teaching says; do not just listen and do nothing. When you only sit and listen, you are fooling yourselves. ²³A person who hears God's teaching and does nothing is like a man looking in a mirror. ²⁴He sees his face, then goes away and quickly forgets what he looked like. ²⁵But the truly happy person is the one who carefully studies God's perfect law that makes people free. He continues to study it. He listens to God's teaching and does not forget what he heard. Then he obeys what God's teaching says. When he does this, it makes him happy.

²⁶A person might think he is religious. But if he says things he should not say, then he is just fooling himself. His "religion" is worth nothing. ²⁷Religion that God accepts is this: caring for orphans or widows who need help; and keeping yourself free from the world's evil influence. This is the kind of religion that God accepts as pure and good.

Today's Prayer

Heavenly Father, it is easy to become angry and to hurt others, but I know that is not your way. Teach me to accept your words and put love and good deeds to work in my life for Jesus. In his name, amen.

Memory Verse
"You are young, but do not let anyone treat you as if you were not important. Be an example to show the believers how they should live." 1 Timothy 4:12

Love All People

James teaches us that it is wrong to treat one person as more important than another. This was a problem for people long ago, and it is still a problem today.

2 My dear brothers, you are believers in our glorious Lord Jesus Christ. So never think that some people are more important than others. [2] Suppose someone comes into your church meeting wearing very nice clothes and a gold ring. At the same time a poor man comes in wearing old, dirty clothes. [3] You show special

attention to the one wearing nice clothes. You say, "Please, sit here in this good seat." But you say to the poor man, "Stand over there," or "Sit on the floor by my feet!" ⁴What are you doing? You are making some people more important than others. With evil thoughts you are deciding which person is better.

⁵Listen, my dear brothers! God chose the poor in the world to be rich with faith. He chose them to receive the kingdom God promised to people who love him. ⁶But you show no respect to the poor man. And you know that it is the rich who are always trying to control your lives. And they are the ones who take you to court. ⁷They are the ones who say bad things against Jesus, who owns you.

⁸One law rules over all other laws. This royal law is found in the Scriptures: "Love your neighbor as you love yourself." If you obey this law, then you are doing right. ⁹But if you are treating one person as if he were more important than another, then you are sinning.

Today's Prayer

Good Master, it is great to know that you love and accept each one of us just the way we are. Thank you that I do not have to be rich or popular to be special to you. In his name, amen.

Memory Verse
"Always give yourselves fully to the work of the Lord. You know that your work in the Lord is never wasted." 1 Corinthians 15:58

Tame Your Words

James knew that Christians do things that are wrong. No matter how hard we try, we are not perfect. That is why we pray to God for forgiveness. James tells us what is most difficult for us to control.

[2]We all make many mistakes. If there were a person who never said anything wrong, he would be perfect. He would be able to control his whole body, too. [3]We put bits into the mouths of horses to make them obey us. We can control their whole bodies. [4]It is the same with ships. A ship is very big, and it is pushed by strong winds. But a very small rudder controls that big ship. The man who controls the rudder decides where the ship will go. The ship goes where the man wants. [5]It is the same with the tongue. It is a small part of the body, but it brags about doing great things.

A big forest fire can be started with

only a little flame. ⁶And the tongue is like a fire. It is a whole world of evil among the parts of our bodies. The tongue spreads its evil through the whole body. It starts a fire that influences all of life. The tongue gets this fire from hell. ⁷People can tame every kind of wild animal, bird, reptile, and fish, and they have tamed them. ⁸But no one can tame the tongue. It is wild and evil. It is full of poison that can kill.

⁹We use our tongues to praise our Lord and Father, but then we curse people. And God made them like himself. ¹⁰Praises and curses come from the same mouth! My brothers, this should not happen. ¹¹Do good and bad water flow from the same spring? ¹²My brothers, can a fig tree make olives? Can a grapevine make figs? No! And a well full of salty water cannot give good water.

Today's Prayer

Dear God, when I say or think ugly, unkind things about people who hurt me, help me to remember Jesus. Help me do as he did—forgive and pray for others. In Jesus' name, amen.

Memory Verse

"Always give yourselves fully to the work of the Lord. You know that your work in the Lord is never wasted." 1 Corinthians 15:58

Do Right

Peter suffered as a Christian. He wrote this book to encourage Christians who were being hurt and mistreated. He tells us that sometimes we may suffer even when we do right.

[8]Finally, all of you should live together in peace. Try to understand each other. Love each other as brothers. Be kind and humble. [9]Do not do wrong to a person to pay him back for doing wrong to you. Or do not insult someone to pay him back for insulting you. But ask God to bless that person. Do this, because you yourselves were called to receive a blessing.

[10]The Scripture says,

"A person must do these things
to enjoy life and have many,
happy days.
He must not say evil things.
He must not tell lies.

¹¹He must stop doing evil and do
good.
He must look for peace and work
for it.
¹²The Lord sees the good people.
He listens to their prayers.
But the Lord is against
those who do evil."
¹³If you are always trying to do good,
no one can really hurt you. ¹⁴But you
may suffer for doing right. Even if that
happens, you are blessed.
"Don't be afraid of the things they
fear.
Do not dread those things.
¹⁵But respect Christ as the holy Lord
in your hearts."
Always be ready to answer everyone who asks you to explain about
the hope you have. ¹⁶But answer in a
gentle way and with respect. Always
feel that you are doing right. Then,
those who speak evil of your good life
in Christ will be made ashamed. ¹⁷It is
better to suffer for doing good than
for doing wrong. Yes, it is better, if
that is what God wants.

Today's Prayer

Eternal God, live in me so
much that even when
others insult and hurt me
I will not make unkind
remarks or hurt them in
return. Give me extra
strength when what they
say is untrue. Through Jesus
I pray, amen.

Memory Verse
"Always give yourselves fully to the work of the
Lord. You know that your work in the Lord is
never wasted." 1 Corinthians 15:58

God Is Love

Can you hate your neighbor and still love God? John tells us that is impossible. He explains where love comes from and why we must have it in our lives.

[7]Dear friends, we should love each other, because love comes from God. The person who loves has become God's child and knows God. [8]Whoever does not love does not know God, because God is love. [9]This is how God showed his love to us: He sent his only Son into the world to give us life through him. [10]True love is God's love for us, not our love for God. God sent his Son to be the way to take away our sins.

[11]That is how much God loved us, dear friends! So we also must love each other. [12]No one has ever seen God. But if we love each other, God lives in us. If we love each other,

God's love has reached its goal. It is made perfect in us.

¹³We know that we live in God and God lives in us. We know this because God gave us his Spirit. ¹⁴We have seen that the Father sent his Son to be the Savior of the world. That is what we teach. ¹⁵If someone says, "I believe that Jesus is the Son of God," then God lives in him. And he lives in God. ¹⁶And so we know the love that God has for us, and we trust that love.

God is love. Whoever lives in love lives in God, and God lives in him.

¹⁹We love because God first loved us. ²⁰If someone says, "I love God," but hates his brother, he is a liar. He can see his brother, but he hates him. So he cannot love God, whom he has never seen. ²¹And God gave us this command: Whoever loves God must also love his brother.

Today's Prayer

Wonderful Savior, you know that it is hard for me to love someone who is not kind and good to me. Teach me to love all others as I love my friends and as God loves me. In the love of Jesus, amen.

Memory Verse
"Always give yourselves fully to the work of the Lord. You know that your work in the Lord is never wasted." 1 Corinthians 15:58

A Look Ahead

In this section of Revelation, the writer John gives us a look at the wonderful things ahead for those who serve the Lord. He says those who obey God and Jesus, the Lamb, will be happy.

22 Then the angel showed me the river of the water of life. The river was shining like crystal. It flows from the throne of God and of the Lamb ²down the middle of the street of the city. The tree of life was on each side of the river. It produces fruit 12 times a year, once each month. The leaves of the tree are for

the healing of all people. ³Nothing that God judges guilty will be in that city. The throne of God and of the Lamb will be there. And God's servants will worship him. ⁴They will see his face, and his name will be written on their foreheads. ⁵There will never be night again. They will not need the light of a lamp or the light of the sun. The Lord God will give them light. And they will rule like kings forever and ever.

⁶The angel said to me, "These words are true and can be trusted. The Lord is the God of the spirits of the prophets. He sent his angel to show his servants the things that must happen soon."

⁷"Listen! I am coming soon! He who obeys the words of prophecy in this book will be happy."

²⁰Jesus is the One who says that these things are true. Now he says, "Yes, I am coming soon."

Amen. Come, Lord Jesus!

Today's Prayer

Amazing Lord, thank you for making a very beautiful place for me where there is no night, loneliness or suffering. In that place there is only good, and I can be with you forever. In Jesus, amen.

Memory Verse
"Always give yourselves fully to the work of the Lord. You know that your work in the Lord is never wasted." 1 Corinthians 15:58